THE PENGUIN CLASSICS

FOUNDER EDITOR (1944–64): E. V. RIEU

PRESENT EDITORS

Betty Radice and Robert Baldick

D0383751

PLAUTUS

THE POT OF GOLD
THE PRISONERS
THE BROTHERS MENAECHMUS
THE SWAGGERING SOLDIER
PSEUDOLUS

TRANSLATED BY
E. F. WATLING

PENGUIN BOOKS

Penguin Books Ltd, Harmondsworth, Middlesex, England
Penguin Books Inc., 7110 Ambassador Road, Baltimore, Maryland, 21207, U.S.A.
Penguin Books Australia Ltd, Ringwood, Victoria, Australia

—

This translation first published 1965
Reprinted 1968, 1970, 1972

—

Copyright © E. F. Watling, 1965

—

Made and Printed in Great Britain
by Hazell Watson & Viney Ltd
Aylesbury, Bucks
Set in Monotype Bembo

The terms for performance of these plays may be
obtained from the League of Dramatists,
84 Drayton Gardens, London SW10,
to whom any application for
permission should be made

CONTENTS

T. MACCIUS PLAUTUS (c. 254–184 B.C.) wrote comedies for the Roman stage, based on, and probably in part translated from, Greek comedies of the fourth and third centuries. His scenes and characters remain nominally Greek but reflect Roman manners and contemporary life and the influence of a popular taste for broad and lively rather than contemplative or romantic comedy.

A fuller discussion of the life and work of Plautus will be found in the Introduction to the first volume of this series of translations, *The Rope and Other Plays* (Penguin Classics).

THE POT OF GOLD
(AULULARIA)

INTRODUCTORY NOTE TO
THE POT OF GOLD

THE character of the miserly old man must have had an ancestry in the Greek Comedy which supplied Plautus with his models; among others, Smicrines in *The Arbitration* of Menander is a recognizable prototype of the Euclio of *Aulularia*, though Plautus's play as a whole bears no resemblance to any known Greek forerunner. A double clue to the dating, both of the original and the copy, has been detected in the references to women's extravagance and the office of 'censor of female conduct': placing the Greek comedy in the decade 317-07 B.C., when this topic engaged the attention of Demetrius of Phalerum, governor of Athens under Macedonian rule, and the Roman comedy near to 195 B.C., when relief was obtained from the restraints of the 'Oppian Law'. Neither of these ascriptions has conclusive validity.

Of the numerous successors of Euclio, the Harpagon of Molière's *L'Avare* is the best known and most complete reincarnation; yet the comparison between the two plays shows a world of difference in the authors' treatment of the subject and the character. Euclio's avarice – or rather his unexpected acquisition of unearned wealth – brings only gentle ridicule upon his head and involves him in a train of inconveniences, from which he eventually escapes with his honour and good nature unimpaired. Harpagon remains a miser and a curmudgeon to the end.

The end of *Aulularia* is, in fact, only known to us in outline from the 'arguments' (those metrical summaries of the plot, usually in two alternative versions, added to the plays by later Roman editors). These inform us that Euclio recovered his gold and made a present of it to his daughter and son-in-law; and note may also be taken of the one significant line among a few unplaceable fragments surviving from the missing last act: *nec noctu nec diu quietus unquam eram; nunc dormiam* ('I have never had a moment's peace by day or night; now I am going to sleep'). From these clues I have ventured to construct a final scene, to indicate the probable denouement and to restore the completeness of this peculiarly enjoyable and genial comedy. Here

9

Plautus, as nowhere else in his work, concentrates his attention on a single and simple topic, building the play around its central personage, with the minimum of digression or adventitious by-play; indeed there is not a single incident that does not connect neatly and necessarily with the progress of the plot.

There is one curious piece of confusion in the texts, with regard to the names of the slaves. The received texts assign the speech at line 363 to a slave named Pythodicus, who makes no other appearance. On the other hand, the slave of Lyconides, who appears at line 587, has been labelled 'Strobilus', on the doubtful evidence of lines 697 and 804, where this name appears to have been given to him, although it is also the name of the head steward in Megadorus's house. It is very unlikely, and dramatically unsuitable, that these two Strobiluses should be one and the same person; one is a responsible factotum in Megadorus's employ, the other a mischievous youth and the property of Lyconides. It seems an obvious solution (as indicated in Lindsay's text) to eliminate Pythodicus, whose one speech is entirely appropriate and indeed necessary to Strobilus, and to leave the younger slave anonymous.

CHARACTERS

LAR FAMILIARIS	*a Household God, as Prologue*
EUCLIO	*a miserly old man*
STAPHYLA	*his housekeeper*
MEGADORUS	*his neighbour, an elderly bachelor*
EUNOMIA	*sister of Megadorus*
LYCONIDES	*a young man, son of Eunomia*
STROBILUS	*steward to Megadorus*
CONGRIO	*a cook hired by Megadorus*
ANTHRAX	*another cook*
A SLAVE	*of Lyconides*
PHAEDRIA (*unseen*)	*daughter of Euclio*

Slaves, Cooks, and Flute-girls

*

*The scene is at Athens, outside the houses of Euclio and Megadorus.
The houses are at some distance apart, and between them a shrine
of Fides (Good Faith), a small structure which can be entered by a
door.*

THE POT OF GOLD

[LAR *appears, as Prologue, from the house of* EUCLIO; *he addresses the audience.*]

LAR: In case you don't know who I am, let me briefly introduce myself. I am LAR FAMILIARIS, the guardian spirit of this house – *that* house from which I have just come. I have been in charge of this house now for a great many years; I have looked after it for the present owner, and his father, and his grandfather. It was the grandfather who put into my care, a long time ago, with great secrecy, and with many sacred oaths, a large sum of money. He had buried it under the hearth of the central hall, and he charged me on my honour to keep it safe for him. On his deathbed, miser that he was, he never said a word about the money to his son; he would rather leave his own son a pauper than let him know about this secret hoard. All he left him was a little bit of land from which he could scrape a living by sweat and toil.

So he died – the old man who entrusted me with the money – and I began to take notice of how the son would treat me, whether he would be more, or less, dutiful than his father. He was far less dutiful, as it turned out; and far less respectful to me. Likewise, I did as little as possible for him; and he likewise died, having issue, to wit the son who now owns the property. He is a man of similar character to his father and grandfather. But he has a daughter; she is very kind to me – brings me daily offerings of incense or wine or something; flowers too. So, as a return for these attentions, I have arranged that Euclio – that's her father – shall find this treasure and thus be in a position to give her in marriage, if he so wishes.

As a matter of fact, a certain young man of good family has already been to bed with her. He knows quite well who she is, but she doesn't know who he is; and the father doesn't know anything about it at all; he thinks she is still a virgin.

What I am going to do is to get the old gentleman who lives next door to ask for her in marriage; that will make it easier for the young man – the one who has slept with her – to pop the question. This old gentleman is an uncle of the young man – uncle, you understand, of the boy who seduced her that night; it was Harvest Eve.

[*Noises are heard in Euclio's house.*]

There's the master, shouting as usual. He's turning his old house-keeper out of the house, so that she shan't know what he's up to. I expect he wants to have a look at his money, to make sure it hasn't been stolen.

[EUCLIO *appears at his door, pushing the old dame* STAPHYLA *out into the street.*]

EUCLIO: Get out, I say; go along with you! Get the hell out of here, you snooping swivel-eyed old busybody!

STAPHYLA: What have I done, I'd like to know? Why must you beat a poor long-suffering woman?

EUCLIO: To give you something to be long-suffering about. And to make you suffer as much trouble as you cause.

STAPHYLA: But why do you have to turn me out of the house?

EUCLIO: Why, why? Do I have to give you reasons? My word, you're just asking for a crop of bruises. Go on, get away from the door. Walk! . . . [*She shuffles a few steps away.*] . . . Just look at her; that's what she calls walking . . . I'll tell you something, woman; if I can get my hand on a club or a goad, I'll quicken up that tortoise pace of yours.

STAPHYLA: Let the gods goad me to a gallows if I'll put up with this sort of slavery any longer.

EUCLIO: What's the wicked old hag muttering to herself? . . . I've a good mind to poke your two eyes out, you damned old witch, so that you won't have one to keep on my business. Go on now . . . shoo! . . . farther off . . . farther [*She marches to the other side of the stage.*] . . . That'll do. Stop there. Now, by the head of Hercules, if you move from that spot the breadth of a finger or the width of a nail, before I tell you to, I'll send you to school with the hang-man, by Hercules I will . . . She's the wickedest old beldame I've ever seen, I'm sure she is. I go in daily terror of her getting the better of me by some sly trick or other, or sniffing out that hidden gold. She's got eyes in the back of her head, blast her! . . . Now I must go and take a look at my gold, and make sure it's where I

put it. The damned stuff is driving me off my head with worry.
[*He goes back into the house.*]

STAPHYLA: God save me if I know what's troubling the master –
whether he's off his head or what. I've known him turn me out of
the house like this ten times in one day. I don't know what's come
over him, indeed I don't. Sometimes he'll stay awake all night, and
then spend the whole day sitting indoors like a crippled cobbler.
And his poor daughter, with a baby coming – how I'm going to
save her from disgrace I don't know: it'll have to be hushed up
somehow, but goodness knows how. There's nothing for it, it
seems to me, but to find a rope and make myself into a capital I.
[*She puts herself into the posture of a hanging corpse.*]

[*EUCLIO comes back, reassured.*]

EUCLIO: All's safe. I feel better with that load off my mind. [*To
Staphyla*] All right, you; you can get back in; and keep an eye on
things in there.

STAPHYLA: Keep an eye on things? What for? Is somebody going to
steal the house? There's nothing inside it worth stealing, I'm sure;
nothing in the house at all but cobwebs.

EUCLIO: You'd like Jupiter to make me as rich as King Philip or
Darius, wouldn't you, poison-mouth? I'll keep my cobwebs, thank
you, and I want them kept safe. I'm a poor man; yes, a poor man
and content to be poor. I take what the gods give. Get inside, and
lock the door. I shall be back in a few minutes. And mind you don't
let any strangers into the house. Somebody may come asking for a
light; put the fire out, then they can't ask for a light. Do you hear?
If every fire is not out when I come back – I'll put you out. And if
anyone wants water, say the well has gone dry. Knives, axes,
pestles, mortars – any utensil that neighbours are always borrowing
– say they've all been stolen by burglars. I don't want any single
soul let into my house while I'm away. Mind what I say now; if
Dame Fortune herself should call, don't let her in.

STAPHYLA: I'm sure she's the last person to want to come in. She's
never been anywhere near this house yet.

EUCLIO: Hold your tongue, and get inside.

STAPHYLA: I'll get inside; and I'll hold my tongue. [*She goes in.*]

EUCLIO: And bolt the door! Both bolts! I'll be back in a minute . . .
[*To the audience*] I wish I hadn't got to leave the house at all; God

knows I wouldn't if I could help it. But I have an urgent reason; the chairman of our ward has a donation to distribute, and if I don't turn up to claim my share everybody will suspect that I've got some cash hidden away at home; they're bound to; it wouldn't look natural for a poor man to miss the chance of a free gift however small. It's a funny thing, though; now that I take every precaution to prevent people knowing my secret, everybody seems to know it! They all treat me with far more respect than they ever did before. Folks come up to me, stand and talk to me, shake me by the hand, hope I'm quite well, ask me what I'm doing, how things are going with me. Well, I must be on my way; and get back home as soon as I possibly can. [*He hurries off along the street.*]

[*From the house next door also, someone is being extruded into the street, though less peremptorily. It is the owner,* MEGADORUS, *a genial and complaisant old gentleman, being ushered out by his sister* EUNOMIA *for a private conference, or lecture.*]

EUNOMIA: I hope you understand that I am only speaking to you as a sister has a right to speak, in your own interest and as my conscience bids me. Oh, I know no man loves a sister; we talk too much, they say; they're right, we do; there was never a woman born, in this age or any other, who could keep her thoughts to herself. But I *am* your nearest relative, don't forget, and you're mine. It's only natural that we should discuss things together and give each other what advice seems best; not keep each other in the dark, or be afraid to speak frankly. I want to have no secrets from you, and I hope you have none from me. That's why I've brought you out here away from your household, to give you a little private talk about your affairs.

MEGADORUS [*with a whimsically gallant gesture*]: I kiss your hand, good madam.

EUNOMIA [*thinking he sees someone behind her*]: Who's that? Who's your good madam? Who are you talking to?

MEGADORUS: You, of course. You're the best woman I know.

EUNOMIA: Me? Really? [*Flatly, not flattered*] You don't mean it.

MEGADORUS [*with a shrug*]: Just as you like.

EUNOMIA: You shouldn't tell such fibs, my dear brother. No woman can be the *best* woman you know. Each one is worse than another in some way.

MEGADORUS: I quite agree, my dear sister. You're perfectly right.

EUNOMIA: Well, give me your attention for a moment, please.

MEGADORUS: You have it. Say and command as you will.

EUNOMIA: I have been thinking about what you ought to do, in your own best interest, and that is what I have come to advise you about.

MEGADORUS: You are very kind – as always – dear sister.

EUNOMIA: And I want you to do as I say.

MEGADORUS: What is it?

EUNOMIA: For your own advantage, in this world and the next, and in the hope of your fathering a family –

MEGADORUS: Please God, no.

EUNOMIA: – I should like to see you married.

MEGADORUS [wincing as if struck]: Murder! Help!

EUNOMIA: Whatever is the matter with you?

MEGADORUS: Talk of marriage and you might as well beat my brains out with a stone.

EUNOMIA: Nonsense. Just do as your sister tells you.

MEGADORUS: If it were anything pleasant.

EUNOMIA: It's for your own good.

MEGADORUS: Oh ye gods, I'd rather die than get married. But all right ... if I must I must ... anyone you like. But on one condition: she comes into my house tomorrow – she's carried out feet first the day after. On these terms, who is it to be? Hand her over, and order the wedding feast.

EUNOMIA: I can find you a girl with a rich dowry ... woman rather ... middle-aged. If you like, I'll make the proposal for you.
     [But after considering this for a moment, MEGADORUS has a trump card of his own to play.]

MEGADORUS: May I ask you a question?

EUNOMIA: Certainly you may.

MEGADORUS: Suppose an elderly man marries an elderly woman; and suppose this elderly man, by some stroke of luck, gets this elderly woman with child; don't you think that's practically condemning the child to the name of Postumus – to grow up parentless? I do. However, as it happens, I think I can save you the trouble of finding me a wife. Thanks to the gods and my forebears, I am as comfortably off as I have any need to be. As for those high and mighty ladies with fat dowries, loud voices, and imperious manners, with their ivory chariots, their fine purple raiment – no thank you; that sort of wife only drags a husband into the slavery of extravagance.

EUNOMIA: Well, who is the woman you want to marry?

MEGADORUS: I'll tell you. Do you know this man Euclio who lives next door? Quite a poor man.

EUNOMIA: Yes, I know him. A very decent person, I believe.

MEGADORUS: He has a virgin daughter. She is the girl I want to marry. Now don't jump down my throat. I know what you are going to say. She's a pauper. I know she is; and pauper or not, she pleases me.

EUNOMIA: May the gods be good to you.

MEGADORUS: That's what I say.

EUNOMIA: If that's all, then . . . you've nothing more to say to me?

MEGADORUS: Good day to you, sister.

EUNOMIA: And to you, brother. [*She goes.*]

MEGADORUS: I'll go and see Euclio now, if he's at home . . . Why, here he comes . . . I wonder where he's been.

[EUCLIO *comes along the street, in no good temper and muttering to himself.*]

EUCLIO: I had a feeling I was going on a wild goose chase. I never wanted to leave the house. I went against my better judgement. Nobody turned up; none of my fellow wardmen, and no chairman with money to distribute. Now I must get home again, double quick. I'm out here, but my mind is in there all the time! . . .

MEGADORUS: Ah, Euclio; I hope you're well and happy and ever will be.

EUCLIO: Thanks, Megadorus. May the gods be with you. [*Trying to hurry into his house.*]

MEGADORUS: How are you keeping? In the best of health, I hope?

EUCLIO [*aside*]: A rich man doesn't pay compliments to a poor man for nothing. He knows I've got money; that's why he's so smarmy.

MEGADORUS: You *are* well, I trust?

EUCLIO: Not as well off as I should like to be.

MEGADORUS: Ah, but contentment is the thing. As long as you have that, you're a happy man and have all you need for a good life.

EUCLIO [*aside*]: The old woman has told him about the money, I know she has, it's as plain as a pikestaff. By God, I'll cut her tongue out; I'll scratch her eyes out, the minute I get into the house.

MEGADORUS: Talking to yourself, eh? What about?

EUCLIO: Just grumbling about my poverty. I've got a daughter, you know, unmarried; can't give her a dowry; can't get anyone to take her off my hands.

MEGADORUS: Oh, don't say that, Euclio. We'll find someone for her. I'll help you. Anything I can do, just let me know and I'll do it, I promise.

EUCLIO [aside]: Just asking, that's all his promising is. He's got his mouth wide open, waiting to swallow down that gold. Bread in one hand and a stone in the other. A rich man toadying to a poor man – I wouldn't trust him an inch. Holding out the hand of friendship and ready to smite you with it. I know 'em – barnacles that cling on to anything they touch. [He makes to go into his house.]

MEGADORUS: Please give me your attention a minute, Euclio, if it's worth your attention to listen to something I have to say that concerns us both.

EUCLIO: Oh my god, he's got his hooks into that gold. He wants to do a deal with me, I know he does. I must pop inside and see if everything's all right . . .

MEGADORUS: Where are you off to?

EUCLIO: I'll be back in a minute. I must see to something in the house. [He disappears into the house.]

MEGADORUS: Oh dear, I'm afraid he'll think I'm pulling his leg if I mention his daughter and ask for her hand. He's certainly more thrifty with his poverty than any man I ever saw.

[EUCLIO returns, relieved again.]

EUCLIO [aside]: All's well, thank the gods. As long as it's there, it's all right. I'm getting too jumpy; I was out of my mind with worry before I went in . . . Now then, Megadorus, here I am; what was it you wanted to say? I am at your service.

MEGADORUS: I am obliged to you. I want to ask you something, and please don't hesitate to say exactly what you think of it.

EUCLIO: As long as it isn't something about which I'd rather *not* say what I think!

MEGADORUS: What kind of family do you think I come from?

EUCLIO: A very good family, I'm sure.

MEGADORUS: What do you know of my character?

EUCLIO: An excellent character.

MEGADORUS: And my record?

EUCLIO: Nothing against it.

MEGADORUS: You know my age?

EUCLIO: A pretty good age, I believe ... and a pretty good bank balance.

MEGADORUS: May I say I have always regarded you, and still do, as a most worthy and honest citizen?

EUCLIO [aside]: He's on the scent of that gold ... Well, what is it? What can I do for you?

MEGADORUS: Since we know all about each other, I hope it will turn out an advantageous proposition both for me and for you, and for your daughter, if I ask for her hand in marriage. Please say you agree.

[EUCLIO is about to give a short answer to this, but on second thoughts he switches his tactics.]

EUCLIO: Now, now, Megadorus, that won't do. That's not worthy of you; to make fun of a poor innocent man who never did you or yours any harm. I'm sure I've never said or done anything to deserve that sort of treatment.

MEGADORUS: But goodness gracious, I had no intention of making fun of you, and I mean nothing of the sort. I wouldn't dream of doing such a thing.

EUCLIO: What's the idea, then, in asking for my daughter?

MEGADORUS: It occurred to me that you might benefit by an association with me, as I shall by an association with you and your family.

EUCLIO: The first thing that occurs to me, Megadorus, is that you are a rich man, a man of influence, and I'm a poor man, poorest of the poor. And the second thing that occurs to me is that for me to make you my son-in-law would be like yoking an ox with an ass; you'd be the ox and I'd be the ass. Unable to pull my share of the load, I, the ass, would be left sprawling in the mud, and you, the ox, would take no more notice of me than if I had never been born. I should be out of your class, and my class would disown me; if there were a question of divorce or anything like that, my footing in either stable would be very – unstable. The asses would

20

be at me with their teeth, and the bulls with their horns. It's asking for trouble for an ass to promote himself to the bull-pen.

MEGADORUS: Nonsense; an alliance with an honourable family can do you nothing but good. Take my advice; accept my offer and let me marry your daughter.

EUCLIO: I shan't have a penny of dowry to give her.

MEGADORUS: Don't give her a halfpenny. Let her bring me her virtue and good name; that's dowry enough.

EUCLIO: I only mentioned it lest you might be under the impression that I had found some hidden treasure somewhere.

MEGADORUS: Say no more; I know all about you. You'll give her to me, then?

EUCLIO: As you will. [*Suddenly startled*] Jupiter Almighty! What's that? I'm ruined!

MEGADORUS: What's the matter?

EUCLIO: I'm sure I heard a spade – [*He dashes back into the house.*]

MEGADORUS: I've got a man digging up my garden ... Where the devil has he gone to now? Dashed off without a word of explanation. He's taken a dislike to me now for seeming to seek his friendship. It's the way of the world. Let a rich man make overtures to a poor man, and the poor man immediately shies off, becomes suspicious, takes offence. Then, when he's lost his chance, he comes back, cap in hand, too late.

[EUCLIO *comes back, shouting at Staphyla within.*]

EUCLIO: By the head of Hercules, if I don't have your tongue torn out by the roots I give you leave and orders to have me gelded by anyone you choose!

[*He slams the door and returns to Megadorus.*]

MEGADORUS: My goodness, Euclio, are you playing a game with me? You seem to take me for an old dotard – which is far from being the case, I assure you.

EUCLIO: No indeed, Megadorus, excuse me. I don't play games with anyone – can't afford it.

MEGADORUS: Well, what do you say? Will you give me your daughter?

EUCLIO: I will, on the terms I mentioned, as regards the dowry.

MEGADORUS: You promise then?

EUCLIO: I promise.

[*This is a formal exchange of agreement; they shake hands on it.*]

MEGADORUS: May the gods prosper it.

EUCLIO: I pray they will. You won't forget that point, will you? It is agreed that my daughter brings you no dowry?

MEGADORUS: I won't forget.

EUCLIO: Maybe not; but I know how you gentlemen can get an agreement tangled up; what was agreed turns out to be not agreed, or vice versa, just as it suits you.

MEGADORUS: I am sure there will be no disagreement between you and me. How about the ceremony? Is there any reason why it shouldn't take place today?

EUCLIO: None at all. Excellent.

MEGADORUS: I'll go and make preparations, then. If you will excuse me –

EUCLIO: Certainly. Good day to you.

MEGADORUS [*calling to his steward, as he goes into his house*]: Hey there, Strobilus, I want you to come with me to market right away ...

EUCLIO: That's got rid of him. Gods above, what money can do! I bet he's heard that I've got a hoard hidden away at home. That's what he's after; that's why he's so set on this marriage.

[*He goes to his house and calls to Staphyla.*]

Hey you, where are you, you blatherer who's been telling all the neighbours I've got a dowry to give my daughter? Staphyla! I'm calling you; are you deaf?

[STAPHYLA *hurries out.*]

Hurry and get all the crockery cleaned up. I'm getting my daughter married today; she's going to marry Megadorus.

STAPHYLA: The gods prosper it. But she can't get married all of a sudden, like this, for goodness' sake!

EUCLIO: Shut up, and go away. See that everything is ready when I get back from market. And lock up the house. I shan't be gone long. [*He goes off.*]

STAPHYLA: Oh my goodness, what ever shall I do now? It'll be the death of me, and the young mistress. It'll all come to light now, her disgrace, and the baby. There's no chance of keeping it a secret any longer. I must go and do as the master said, and get things ready before he comes back. Oh deary me, I've mixed myself a nice cup of trouble and sorrow this time! [*She goes in.*]

*

[*An hour later. At the house of Megadorus the steward* STROBILUS *has returned from market with provisions for the wedding feast. These include a large supply of victuals, two live sheep, and a crew of hired cooks and flute-girls.*]

STROBILUS: Now then – all this stuff that my master's bought in the market, and you cooks and flute-girls he's hired – he wants me to split the whole lot into two parts.

ANTHRAX [*a young cook*]: No one's going to split me into two parts, by Hercules! Just tell me where I'm to go and I'll go, all in one piece.

CONGRIO [*a rude cook*]: One piece of tart! I shouldn't have thought you'd object to anyone taking a slice off you if he wanted it.

[ANTHRAX *about to retort, but* STROBILUS *intervenes.*]

STROBILUS: That was not my meaning, Anthrax; and [*to Congrio*] there's no need for your insinuations either. Now listen; my master is getting married today.

ANTHRAX: Whose daughter is he marrying?

STROBILUS: His next-door neighbour's, Euclio's daughter. That's why he wants me to let him have half this stuff, with one of the cooks and one of the flute-girls.

ANTHRAX: What, half of us to go in there, and half to your place?

STROBILUS: You've got it right exactly.

ANTHRAX: Couldn't the old man afford a wedding dinner for his own daughter?

STROBILUS: Hah!

ANTHRAX: What do you mean, hah?

STROBILUS: What do I mean? Why, you'd get more out of squeezing a pumice stone than you could out of that old beggar.

ANTHRAX: Go on!

CONGRIO: You're telling me.

STROBILUS: I am telling you; if he loses so much as a grain of salt he thinks he's being robbed. He raises heaven and hell if he sees a puff of smoke escaping from his roof. Do you know, when he goes to sleep, he ties a balloon on his mouth?

ANTHRAX: What does he do that for?

STROBILUS: So as not to lose his wind, while sleeping.

ANTHRAX: Does he stuff up the other end too? He might lose some wind that way.

STROBILUS: You believe my story, boy, and I'll believe yours.

ANTHRAX: Oh, I believe it.

STROBILUS: And I'll tell you something else. It makes him weep to see the water pouring away when he washes himself.

[*They enjoy a few loud guffaws at these tales.*]

ANTHRAX: Do you think we could get him to give us the price of our freedom?

STROBILUS: Don't make me laugh. He wouldn't *lend* you the price of a day's starvation. I'll tell you another one: the other day he had the barber trim his toenails; so what does he do, he collects all the clippings and takes them home!

[*This goes down well too.*]

ANTHRAX: He must be a measly mean old creature.

STROBILUS: Can you imagine anyone so miserly? The other day [*they all gather to listen eagerly again*] a hawk stole his dinner; so he goes off to the magistrate to lodge a complaint and spins a long tale of woe, asking to be allowed to bring an action against the hawk! Oh, there are hundreds of tales I could tell you if I had the time . . . Now then, to work. Which of you is the quicker worker, tell me that?

ANTHRAX: I'm sharper than he is.

STROBILUS: I dare say you are. It's a cook I want, not a crook.

ANTHRAX: I mean at cooking.

STROBILUS [*to Congrio*]: What do you say?

CONGRIO: Take me as you find me.

ANTHRAX: He's a fair cook, he is; he can only get a job on fair-days.

CONGRIO: That's enough from you, you . . . three-letter word . . . nip!

ANTHRAX: And nip to you, you three-times-throttled thief!

STROBILUS: Stow it now, and take one of those lambs – whichever is the fatter - into our house.

ANTHRAX: Very good, sir. [*He selects a lamb and takes it in.*]

24

STROBILUS: You, Congrio, take the other in there. You [*to some of the slaves*] go with him; the rest of you, come with me.

CONGRIO: That's not a fair division. They've got the fatter lamb.

STROBILUS: All right, you shall have the fatter flute-girl. Go with him, Phrygia darling. Eleusium, you come with me.

CONGRIO: It's a dirty trick, Strobilus, making me go and work for that mean old devil. Anything I need, I can ask for till my throat's sore before I'll get it.

STROBILUS: You're a fool, Congrio. I get no thanks for doing you a good turn, it seems.

CONGRIO: A good turn? What do you mean?

STROBILUS: Don't you see? Well, look; in that house you'll have nobody getting in your way – it's practically empty. Anything you need to use you'll have to take with you; it'll be no use asking. In our house on the other hand, there's crowd and bustle everywhere; utensils, gold and silver plate, cloths and all that; consequence is, if anything's missed – which won't happen in your case, since there's nothing there to tempt you – with us it's 'those cooks have stolen it, catch them, bind them, beat them, chuck 'em in the dungeon'. You won't have to fear anything of that sort, in a place where there's nothing to steal. Come along, I'll show you.

CONGRIO [*reluctantly*]: All right.

[*They go up to Euclio's house;* STROBILUS *knocks.*]

STROBILUS: Hey, Staphyla! Come and open this door.

STAPHYLA [*within*]: Who's there?

STROBILUS: Me, Strobilus.

[STAPHYLA *comes out.*]

STAPHYLA: And what do you want?

STROBILUS: I've brought you some cooks, and a flute-girl, and some provisions for the wedding. With Megadorus's compliments to Euclio.

STAPHYLA [*looking over the provisions*]: Is it going to be a dry wedding, then?

STROBILUS: Why?

STAPHYLA: I don't see any wine.

STROBILUS: That'll be coming, when the boss gets back from market.

STAPHYLA: We haven't any wood.

CONGRIO: Have you got any rafters?

STAPHYLA: Of course we have.

CONGRIO: Then you've got wood, without sending out for it.

STAPHYLA: Wretch, what do you mean? You may be a fire-worshipper, but do you expect us to burn our house down to cook a dinner or to give you employment?

CONGRIO: I expect nothing, madam.

STROBILUS: Show them the way, please.

STAPHYLA: Come with me.

[*She takes the party indoors.*]

STROBILUS [*as they go in*]: Mind your manners now! ... I must go and keep an eye on my cooks. I shall have my hands full looking after that lot. It would save trouble if I put 'em in the dungeon first and made them cook there – and pull up the cooked dinner in baskets! Only they might pull it *down* and eat it all *up*; then there'd be a dinner for the powers below and none for the powers above! ... But I mustn't stand here talking, as if I'd nothing to do, with all these *rapscullions* in the house. [*He goes into Megadorus's house.*]

[*EUCLIO comes along the street from the town.*]

EUCLIO: It's no use. I meant to bring myself up to scratch, and make a decent show for my daughter's marriage; but I couldn't do it. I went to the market and asked for some fish; they showed me some, far too expensive. Lamb, a terrible price; same with beef, veal, pork, tunny fish – all far too dear. Too dear for me anyway; I simply hadn't the money on me. So I came away in a bad temper, finding nothing I could buy. Serve the thieving rascals right too! Thinking it over on my way back, I said to myself: if you throw your money away on a special occasion, you'll find yourself starving on ordinary days unless you've got something put by. And having comforted my conscience, and my belly, with that reflection, I made up my mind to give my daughter a wedding at the least possible expense. So I've bought her this little packet of incense and a few flowers; we'll put them on our house-god's altar and pray for his blessing on the nuptials. [*He moves towards his house.*] But what's this? The door open ... and all that noise inside? I'm being robbed, am I?

CONGRIO [*inside*]: I tell you you'll have to get a bigger pot from somewhere; this little one won't hold it all.

EUCLIO: Oh! I'm ruined! He's got the gold, he's asking for another

pot. Oh my goodness, I'm done for if I don't get into the house
as quick as quick. Apollo, come to my aid; help me, I implore
you; slay with your arrows these treasury-robbers as you have in
time past helped others in like case. But I can't stop now; I must
run or I shall be ruined utterly. [*He rushes into the house.*]

[*At the same moment* ANTHRAX *comes out of the other house,
turning to give orders to the cooks within.*]

ANTHRAX: Get those fish skinned, Dromo. You, Machaerio, bone
the conger eel and the murena as well as you can. I must go and
borrow a baking dish from Congrio next door. And you, boy, get
that cock plucked; mind, I want it shaved as smooth as a ballet-
dancer ... But what's all that noise next door? Those cooks are
cooking up something hot, I reckon. I'd better get back, in case
there's trouble of that sort at our place. [*He goes back to the house.*]

[CONGRIO *erupts from Euclio's house, uttering the customary howls
for help to the audience. His assistants follow in quick succession.*]

CONGRIO: Help, help, help! People all, great and small, townsmen,
boundsmen, and all-arounds-men – don't stop me, let me get
away, clear the streets and let me run. Why? It's a madhouse in
there – first time I ever came to cook for a Bacchic orgy. Me
and my mates have been beaten to rags; the old man has used me
as a punchball until I'm sore all over and practically dead ... Oh!!
here he comes, the madhouse is open again, he's after me, I'm a
dead man for certain ... But I'll get even with him, by his own
methods. They've got some good wood in there, I will say – best
I've ever seen; he's cudgelled us out of the house with his
timber.

[EUCLIO *emerges from the house, battling with the last of his victims.*
CONGRIO *is retreating down among the audience.*]

EUCLIO: Come back, you! Where are you off to? Stop him, somebody.

CONGRIO: What do you want with me, you old idiot?

EUCLIO: I want to report you to the magistrates.

CONGRIO: Do you? Why?

EUCLIO: For carrying a knife.

CONGRIO: Can't a cook carry a knife?

EUCLIO: And threatening me with it.

CONGRIO: I was wrong there. I ought to have stuck it in your guts.

EUCLIO: You're the most infernal villain alive. I don't know anyone to whom I would do more deliberate harm with less compunction.

CONGRIO [*rubbing his head*]: You don't need to tell me that. Facts speak for themselves. I've been beaten to a jelly. What did you have to set on us for, you stingy old skinflint?

EUCLIO: As if you didn't know. Or are you complaining of getting less than you'd earned?

CONGRIO: Anyway, you'll be sorry for it, I swear you will, if this head knows anything.

EUCLIO: It knows something now, at all events; as to the future, I can't say. What business had you in my house at all, without my orders, behind my back? Just tell me that.

CONGRIO: Come off it. We came to cook for your wedding.

EUCLIO: And what the devil has it got to do with you whether I eat my food cooked or raw – you're not my keeper, are you?

CONGRIO: All I want to know is, are we or are we not to cook this dinner for you?

EUCLIO: All *I* want to know is, will my property be safe while you're in the house?

CONGRIO: If I get *my* property back safe, what I brought with me, that's all I ask. I've no wish to pinch any of yours.

EUCLIO: I know – you needn't tell me – I know all about you.

CONGRIO: I can't see why you don't want us to cook for you. What have we said or done to offend you?

EUCLIO: What have you done, rascal? Making a thoroughfare of every room and passage in my house? If you'd stayed where you belonged, in the kitchen, you wouldn't have a broken head to take home. You deserved all you got. This is my last word and verdict: if you come anywhere near this door again without my leave, you'll wish you had never been born. That is my last word and verdict. [*He goes back into the house.*]

CONGRIO: Hey, where are you going? Come back. By the Goddess of Thieves, you let me have my pots back or I'll stay here and scream your house down with curses . . . Now what am I going to do? My luck was out when I landed this job. Instead of earning a day's pay it'll cost me more than that to see a doctor.

[*He and his crew linger in the street, uncertain of the next move, until* EUCLIO *comes out again with the pot of gold muffled up under his arm.*]

EUCLIO [*aside*]: Here it is, thank God, and I'll keep it on me wherever I go. I'll carry it round everywhere, that's what I'll do. I'm not going to leave it in there any longer – much too dangerous. [*To the cooks*] Get inside, all of you, cooks and flautists. [*To Congrio*] Hey you, take as many greedy rascals as you like and get on with your cooking or whatever you're doing; you can get to work now as fast as you please.

CONGRIO: About time too . . . after breaking all our heads.

EUCLIO: Get along in; you were hired to work, not to talk.

CONGRIO: If it comes to that, old cock, I shall want to be paid compensation for being beaten. I was hired as a cook, not a chopping-block.

EUCLIO: You can sue me for damages, then. Don't bother me any more. Go and cook the dinner, or go to hell and hang yourself.

CONGRIO: And the same to you . . . Come on. [*He takes his gang indoors.*]

EUCLIO: Thank goodness he's gone. Oh ye gods, it's asking for trouble for a poor man to have any dealings with a rich man. Here's this Megadorus landing me in all sorts of trouble, pretending to send me these cooks as a compliment, when all he really wants is to give them a chance of stealing *this*. And as if that wasn't enough, even the old woman's pet rooster very nearly ruined me, when he went scratching around near the very place where this pot was buried. That got me riled, naturally; so I upped with a stick and knocked his head off – a thief caught in the act. I wouldn't be surprised if the cooks had offered him a reward for finding something. Anyway I nipped that little scheme in the bud. And that started the cock-fighting! . . . Hullo, here comes my future son-in-law, back from town. Now what? I can't very well go by without speaking to him.

[*But* MEGADORUS *is in the mind for a long soliloquy;* EUCLIO *stands aside and listens, fascinated.*]

MEGADORUS: I have been telling all my friends about my marriage prospects. Everybody speaks highly of the girl. 'Well done,' they say, 'an excellent idea.' I quite agree. Indeed I think it would be an excellent thing if more rich men married poor men's daughters, without dowries. It would make for harmony in the community, and there would be much less friction in the home. The wives would learn obedience, and the husbands wouldn't have to spend so much money. The mass of the people would welcome such a reform; the only opposition would come from the greedy minority, whose avarice and cupidity are beyond the power of law or leather to restrain. If you ask me then 'Whom are the rich heiresses to marry, if the poor are to be so privileged?' I say let them marry as they please, but not with dowry for company. On those terms, they'll perhaps improve their morals, and bring good characters with them instead of the dowries which they now contribute to the home. Under my law, I'd warrant that mules, which now cost more than horses, would become cheaper than Gallic geldings.

EUCLIO: It's really a pleasure to hear him sticking up for thrift.

MEGADORUS: No, I never want to hear a wife say 'I brought you more in dowry than your whole property was worth, so I have a right to expect you to give me purple and gold, mules, servants, stablemen, footmen, page-boys, and carriages to ride in.'

EUCLIO: He knows wives all right, doesn't he? I'd like to see him made censor of women's morals.

MEGADORUS: Nowadays, wherever you look, you see more vehicles outside the town houses than you ever see when you're on holiday in the country. And that's nothing to what you have to put up with when the creditors are at the door. Here come the cloth-fuller, the embroiderer, the goldsmith, the wool-weaver; the designers of fringes, makers of underwear, inventors of veils, dyers in purple and saffron, sleeve-stitchers, linen-weavers, perfumiers; shoe-makers and slipper-makers, sandal-fitters and leather-stainers, all waiting to be paid; repairers, corset-makers, girdle-experts. And when these have been got rid of – in come another three hundred with their bills; the hall full of needlewomen, cabinet-makers, bag-makers ... Is that the lot? No; more dyers, more ... any damned pest with a pocket to fill.

EUCLIO: I'd interrupt him, only I don't want to stop his discoursing on the ways of women. I'll let him go on.

MEGADORUS: And when all these tradesmen in trash have been satisfied, here comes a poor soldier, asking for his pay. Oh dear, the banker must be consulted, the accounts looked into; the soldier meanwhile standing there hungry, waiting for his money. When the figures have been totted up with the banker, it turns out the account is overdrawn! The soldier must wait till another day ... These are only a few of the plaguey and iniquitous extravagances that follow from large dowries. A wife without a dowry is under her husband's thumb; with one, she can condemn him to misery and bankruptcy ... Oh, here is my dear father-in-law. What are you doing now, Euclio?

EUCLIO: Digesting your very palatable lecture.

MEGADORUS: Oh, did you hear it?

EUCLIO: From start to finish.

MEGADORUS: H'm ... [looking Euclio over] All the same, my dear fellow, I don't think it would be a bad idea if you were to spruce yourself up a bit for your daughter's wedding.

EUCLIO: No, sir. People who dress up for an occasion, or put on a show to match their possessions, are only reminding themselves of their own rank. I tell you, Megadorus, we poor men don't keep up a state above our station.

MEGADORUS: Enough is enough, I agree; and may the gods make it so for you. May they ever preserve for you that which you now hold.

EUCLIO [aside]: That which I now hold! I don't like the sound of that. He knows what I've got as well as I do myself. The old woman has blabbed, I knew she would.

MEGADORUS [seeing him abstracted]: You seem to have withdrawn from the debate?

EUCLIO: I have. I was meditating how I could bring an action against you, as you well deserve.

MEGADORUS: What ever for?

EUCLIO: What for? For filling every hole and corner of my house with thieves, curse you! For sending me five hundred cooks, each with six hands like a tribe of Geryons. Argus with all his eyes – the fellow whom Juno set to watch Io – would have his work cut out to keep an eye on that crew. Not to mention a flute-girl who, once the wine starts flowing, is likely to cost me a Pirenian spring of drink. And the food –

MEGADORUS: I'm sure there's enough food for an army. I sent you a whole sheep, didn't I?

EUCLIO: Sheep! A more careworn animal I never saw.

MEGADORUS: How can a sheep be careworn, pray?

31

EUCLIO: This one was. It was nothing but skin and bone. It must have been worried to death. You could inspect its entrails by simply holding it up to the daylight; it was as transparent as a parchment lantern.

MEGADORUS: I paid to have it slaughtered for us.

EUCLIO: Then you'd better pay for its funeral; I expect it's dead by now.

MEGADORUS [laughing this off]: Well, well . . . you and I must have a drink together today, Euclio.

EUCLIO: I'm not drinking, thanks.

MEGADORUS: But I'm having a cask of old wine sent over to you.

EUCLIO: No, thank you. I'm drinking nothing but water.

MEGADORUS: Rubbish – I'll see you under the table tonight, as I live. Water indeed!

EUCLIO [aside]: I see his little game. What he's after is to get me dead drunk and then take my property for a walk. I'll forestall him there, by putting it somewhere out of the house. Then he'll have wasted his time, and wasted his wine as well.

MEGADORUS: Well, if you'll excuse me, I'll go and wash before paying my vows. [He goes into his house.]

EUCLIO: Oh dear, oh dear; my precious pot, you and the gold in your care have many enemies. But don't worry; I've decided to take you to the shrine of Good Faith here. You'll be safe and sound there. [He goes up to the shrine.]

Good Faith, you know me, as I know you. Promise me you will not belie your name if I entrust this treasure to you. I put all my faith in you, Good Faith. [He takes the pot into the shrine.]

[A young SLAVE comes along the street; he is the personal servant of Lyconides, Megadorus's nephew. He makes a cautious reconnaissance around Euclio's house, and then turns to introduce himself to the audience.]

SLAVE: I'm a good slave, I am. I think a good slave should do as I've always tried to do – serve his master without hesitation or complaint. Any slave that wants to please his master should put his master's good first and his own last. He should never forget he's a slave – not even when he's asleep. For instance, if his master is in love, as my young master is, and if he sees that love is getting him

32

down, it's his duty, in my opinion, to rescue him from danger, not push him over the brink. It's like when boys are learning to swim – they tie themselves to wicker floats; that gives them confidence and makes it easier for them to strike out with their arms and swim. So I think a slave ought to be a kind of life-preserver to his master, to buoy him up so that he doesn't sink like a lead weight. And another thing: a slave has to anticipate his master's orders – use his eyes to read his master's mind; and then carry out his wishes as quick as a racing chariot. That way he'll save himself a dose of the strap ... and won't find himself putting a polish on a nice pair of fetters! ... Now my young master, you see, is in love with the daughter of this poor man Euclio; and he's just heard that she is going to be married to Megadorus. So he's sent me to see what's going on, so that whatever is going on he can be in on it! ... I think I'll sit down quietly by this shrine here, where no one will take any notice of me; then I can keep an eye on things in both directions.

[*He sits at a corner of the shrine, and presently* EUCLIO *comes out at the opposite side, not noticing the Slave.*]

EUCLIO: There you are, Good Faith; mind you don't tell anybody about my gold. It's well hidden; there's no fear of anyone finding it by accident. By God, anybody that did find it would have a tidy haul – a pot full of gold! But don't let that happen, Good Faith, I beseech you ... Now I must go and wash before making my vows, and not keep my friend waiting. I want him to take my daughter home with him as soon as he comes ... Once again, Good Faith, be sure and have that pot safe for me when I come back for it. I trust you with it; it's in your ground and sanctuary. [*He returns to his house.*]

SLAVE: Gods above, what have I overheard! The old man has hidden a pot full of gold in this shrine! The shrine of Good Faith. Well, Good Faith, I hope you're not going to be more faithful to him than to me ... He's the father, I suppose, of my master's girl ... I'm going to search the shrine and see if I can find this gold while the old man is out of the way. If I find it, Good Faith, I'll give you a quart of good faithful wine; I'll do that much for you, I promise; and I'll buy one for myself, if this job comes off! [*He sneaks into the shrine.*]

33

[*A few moments later,* EUCLIO *comes back in a panic.*]

EUCLIO: I'm sure something's wrong. A raven croaked on my left; scratched on the ground with its claws too, and then let out a croak. My heart began doing a dance and jumped up into my throat. I must get in there quick.

[*He darts into the shrine. Sounds of altercation are heard and* EUCLIO *returns dragging the Slave out.*]

EUCLIO: Come out of it, you worm, you reptile! You must have just crawled out of the ground; you were not in sight a minute ago; now you've come to light just in time to be exterminated. What are you, a magician? I'll show you a trick or two before I've finished with you.

SLAVE: What the hell's the matter with you? What do you want with me, you old idiot? What have I done to be dragged around and beaten by you?

EUCLIO: Beating is all you're fit for, [*whacking him three times*] thief . . . thief . . . and thief!

SLAVE: What have I stolen?

EUCLIO: Give it back, will you.

SLAVE: Give what back?

EUCLIO: As if you didn't know.

SLAVE: I haven't stolen anything of yours.

EUCLIO: Then give me back whatever you have stolen. Are you going to?

SLAVE: Am I going to what?

EUCLIO: You're not going to get away with it.

SLAVE: What the hell are you talking about?

EUCLIO: You know quite well what I want.

SLAVE: I know what I think you want, old daddy.

EUCLIO: Then give it me, and stop arguing; I've no time to waste.

SLAVE: What is it you want, then? Can't you give it a name, whatever it is? I swear I haven't taken or touched a thing.

EUCLIO: Show me your hands.

SLAVE: Here they are; look at them.

EUCLIO: I see. [*He looks first at one hand, then at the other.*] Is that all the hands you've got?

SLAVE: The old fool's stark staring raving mad . . . You've done me wrong, haven't you?

EUCLIO: I've done you grievous wrong in not hanging you on the spot. I will, though, if you don't confess.

SLAVE: Confess what?

EUCLIO: What have you stolen from this shrine?

SLAVE: God strike me dead if I've taken anything of yours or ever wanted to.

EUCLIO: Shake out your cloak.

SLAVE: All right. [*He does so.*]

EUCLIO: Anything under your shirt?

SLAVE: Feel, wherever you fancy.

EUCLIO: Artful young devil ... think you can take me in with those innocent airs ... I know your game. Come, show me your hands again. The right hand.

SLAVE: There it is.

EUCLIO: Now the left.

SLAVE: Both at once if you like; there! ...

EUCLIO: Oh well, it's no use searching you any more. Give it back.

SLAVE: What am I to give back?

EUCLIO: Don't waste any more time. I know you've got it.

SLAVE: Have I? Got what?

EUCLIO: You'd like me to tell you, but I'm not going to. Give me back whatever you've got that is mine.

SLAVE: You're crazy. You've searched me from head to foot and haven't found anything of yours on me.

EUCLIO: Stop! Who's in there? Who else was in there with you? Help! There's someone rummaging about in there, and this one [*the Slave he has caught*] will get away if I let him. But then I've searched this one all over, and he hasn't anything ... [*to the Slave*] All right, you can go.

SLAVE: Jupiter and all the gods destroy you.

EUCLIO: There's gratitude for you. I'm going in here to strangle the life out of your accomplice. Get out of my sight, will you! Are you going?

SLAVE: I'm going.

EUCLIO: And don't let me catch you here again. [*He goes into the shrine.*]

SLAVE: I'd rather die a horrible death than lose the chance of doing this old chap down. Now he'll never dare leave the gold hidden in here again. He'll bring it out and put it somewhere else, I expect ... St! ... the door's opening ... here he comes, and he's got the gold with him. I'll wait behind the door here.

[EUCLIO *comes out with the pot.*]

EUCLIO: I thought Good Faith could be trusted if anyone could, and there she's very nearly done me in the eye. If it hadn't been for that raven, I'd have been finished. I'd very much like to meet that informative bird again and give him something ... I'd give him my compliments, anyway ... can't afford to waste food on him. Now I shall have to find some other safe place to hide this in. I know; there's a lonely grove of Silvanus outside the walls, all overgrown with willows. That's where I'll put it. I'd rather trust Silvanus than Good Faith any day. [*He goes off with the pot.*]

SLAVE: Whoopee! The gods are looking after me! I'll nip along there before the old man and climb a tree and watch where he hides the gold. My master did tell me to wait for him here ... but ... well, I'd rather get a pasting as long as I can get my hands on this gold first. [*He dashes off.*]

*

[*A little later,* LYCONIDES, *the lover of Euclio's daughter, comes along the street with his mother* EUNOMIA.]

LYCONIDES: Now, mother, I have told you everything, haven't I? You know all that I know about Euclio's daughter. Please, please, do what I've begged you to do, and speak to my uncle.

EUNOMIA: You know I want everything to be exactly as you want, my dear boy; and I'm sure I can persuade my brother to help us. You've got a very good reason on your side – if it is true, as you tell me, that you seduced the girl after you had been drinking.

LYCONIDES: It is perfectly true; do you think I would tell you a lie, mother?

[*Inside the house of Euclio, the girl* (PHAEDRIA) *is heard groaning in travail.*]

PHAEDRIA: Nurse, nurse! I'm in pain! Oh, Juno Lucina, help me!

LYCONIDES: You hear that, mother? There is an even more pressing reason. The poor girl is crying out in labour.

EUNOMIA: Come in with me and see your uncle. I am sure I can get what you want out of him.

LYCONIDES: I'll follow you, mother. [EUNOMIA *goes in.*] I wonder where my slave has got to. I told him to wait for me here ... Ah well, I suppose if he's about my business I can't be angry with him. I'll go in here, where my fate is being decided by the court. [*He follows his mother into Megadorus's house.*]

[*The* SLAVE *returns in high glee, with the pot of gold in his possession.*]

SLAVE: Look at me! I'm richer than the Griffins who live in the Golden Mountains! I'm richer than – but I can't mention all those other kings, mere paupers anyway. I'm richer than King Philip himself. Oh glorious day! ... I went from here, as you saw, and got to the place well before the old man, and had plenty of time to get up into a tree, and from there I watched while he buried the gold. When he had gone I jumped down from the tree and dug up the pot crammed full of gold! Then I nipped out of the way, just in time to see him go back to the place a second time. But he didn't see me; and I kept off the road on the way back ... Look out! Here he comes now ... I'm going to put this away safe at home. [*He hurries off.*]

[EUCLIO *arrives, in a state of utmost misery and rage.*]

EUCLIO: Oh! ... I'm dead, finished, and done for! I don't know which way to turn ... Stop thief! Stop him! ... Stop whom? Who is he? I don't know, I can't see, I'm as helpless as a blind man, I can't tell where I'm going or where I am, I'm not even certain who I am ... Help me, please, good people; help me; I beg and beseech you; show me the man who has taken it ... What do you say, sir? I'll believe you, I can see you've an honest face ... What's that? You're laughing at me, are you? I know you; I know this place is full of thieves – all sitting there looking so respectable in your nice clean clothes ... Has nobody here got it? I'm done for, then. Eh? What's that? Who's got it, then? You don't know? ... Oh misery me, I'm a dead man, I'm ruined, I'm utterly destitute. This is my day of doom, disaster, and damnation; I am reduced to starvation and beggary. No man on earth has had more to suffer. What has life left for me, now I have lost the treasure which I guarded with such loving care? I have denied myself all the pleasure and joy of life, and others are now making

37

merry over my loss and ruin. Oh, I can't bear it! . . . I cannot bear it! . . .

[LYCONIDES *appears from the neighbouring house.*]

LYCONIDES: Who ever can that be, howling and moaning outside our house? . . . Why, I do believe it's Euclio. Oh dear, this looks bad for me. I expect he knows his daughter is having a baby. Oh dear, what ever shall I do? Shall I stay here or run away? Shall I go up to him or keep out of his way? I don't know what to do . . .

EUCLIO: Who is that?

LYCONIDES: A very unhappy man, sir.

EUCLIO: Are you? So am I, utterly ruined, the victim of every misery and misfortune.

LYCONIDES: You can take comfort, though.

EUCLIO: How the devil can I take comfort?

LYCONIDES: Because the wicked deed that causes you all this distress was my doing; I confess it.

EUCLIO [*stunned*]: What's that you say?

LYCONIDES: Only the truth.

EUCLIO: My dear young man, how can I have deserved such treatment from you? That you should do this terrible thing; that you should want to ruin me and all my family –

LYCONIDES: It was some divine power that drove me to it, that tempted me to take what was not mine.

EUCLIO: How could you?

LYCONIDES: I know I am to blame, I confess my sin; and now I come to beg you to forgive me with an open heart.

EUCLIO: How could you dare to lay hands on what was not yours?

LYCONIDES: What can I say? It's done, and cannot be undone. I believe it was the will of the gods; I am sure it could not have happened otherwise.

EUCLIO: I believe it is the will of the gods that I should hang you like a criminal in my own house.

LYCONIDES: No, don't say that.

EUCLIO: What induced you to touch my property without my leave?

LYCONIDES: Love – and drink.

EUCLIO: Impudent rascal! You have the face to come to me with that kind of story! If that is what you call an excuse, we might as well all go around in broad daylight robbing women of their jewels, and if we're caught say we did it for love, and drink. Damn love and drink, I say, if a drunken lover is to do as he pleases with impunity.

LYCONIDES: But I have come of my own free will to beg your pardon for my foolishness.

EUCLIO: I've no use for people who when they've done wrong come whining with apologies. You knew you were taking what you had no right to take; you should have kept your hands off.

LYCONIDES: But having touched, my only plea is that I may possess entirely.

EUCLIO: What!! Do you think you're going to keep something that is mine, with my leave or without it?

LYCONIDES: Not without your leave. But I think you ought to give me leave. I am sure you will find that you ought.

EUCLIO: If you don't give me back –

LYCONIDES: Give you *back*?

EUCLIO: – give me back my property that you've stolen, by Hercules, I'll drag you off to court and sue you, prosecute you.

LYCONIDES: I – stolen something of yours? Where from? What have I stolen?

EUCLIO: God be good to you! If you don't know –

LYCONIDES: If you won't tell me what you've lost –

EUCLIO: The pot of gold! That's what I'm talking about, that's what I'm asking for – the pot of gold which you confess you've stolen.

LYCONIDES: Gods above, I never did. I never said I stole it.

EUCLIO: You deny it now?

LYCONIDES: Of course I absolutely deny it. I know nothing whatever about your gold or your pot.

EUCLIO: The one you stole from the grove of Silvanus – hand it over. Come on . . . [*Gradually changing his tone*] Come on . . . I'll give you half, if you like . . . you've robbed me, but I won't be hard on you . . . Come on . . . give it up.

LYCONIDES: You're out of your senses – calling me a thief. Look, Euclio, I thought it was something quite different you had found out about me. It happens to be a matter of some importance which I'd like to discuss with you quietly, if you're not too busy.

EUCLIO: Tell me, on your honour – you didn't steal that gold?

LYCONIDES: On my honour, I didn't.

EUCLIO: And you don't know who did?

LYCONIDES: I do not, on my honour.

EUCLIO: If you should find out who did it, you'll tell me?

LYCONIDES: I'll tell you.

EUCLIO: You won't grab a share for yourself and let the thief go free?

LYCONIDES: I won't.

EUCLIO: If you do –

LYCONIDES: If I do, let great Jupiter punish me as he will.

EUCLIO: Good enough. Now what is it you wanted to say?

LYCONIDES: In case you don't know all about me and my family –
I am the nephew of your neighbour Megadorus. My name is
Lyconides, my father was Antiochus, my mother is Eunomia.

EUCLIO: I know the family. Well, what do you want?

LYCONIDES: You have a daughter.

EUCLIO: Certainly I have. She's at home just now.

LYCONIDES: I believe you have promised her to my uncle.

EUCLIO: You're perfectly right.

LYCONIDES: Well, now he has asked me to tell you he has changed
his mind.

EUCLIO: Changed his mind! With the wedding arranged and everything ready! May all the gods and goddesses damn him to perdi-
tion! It was owing to him that I lost all that gold today, wretch
that I am.

LYCONIDES: But please don't be upset, Euclio. Save your curses. It
may all be for the best for you and your daughter. Say 'May the
gods prosper it'.

EUCLIO [*helplessly*]: May the gods prosper it.

LYCONIDES: And so say I. Now listen. A man who has committed
a fault cannot be so mean-hearted as not to repent and make
amends. I beg you, Euclio, if I have rashly committed a wrong
against you or your daughter, to pardon me and to give her to me
in lawful wedlock. I confess I did your daughter wrong ... last
Harvest Eve ... in a moment of ... intoxication ... and youthful
ardour.

EUCLIO: Oh my gracious goodness! You confess to such an abomin-
able sin? You –

LYCONIDES: There is no need to be angry. Thanks to me, you will be able to attend your daughter's wedding as a grandfather. Her child is born; it is ten moons now, if you work it out. That's why my uncle has changed his mind. Go in and see whether I am telling the truth.

EUCLIO: This is the end. Calamities swarm one upon another to my undoing. I will go in, and find out how much of this is true. [*He goes into his house.*]

LYCONIDES: I will be with you directly . . . I think we're nearly safe home; but where in the world that boy has got to, I cannot imagine. I shall have to wait here for him a little longer. Then I'll join the old man. I'll give him a few minutes to get the whole story from his daughter's old nurse and duenna; she knows everything.

[*His* SLAVE *returns, at the opposite side of the stage.*]

SLAVE: Oh gods and goddesses, you have made me a happy man today! A four-pound jar full of gold! I'm the richest man on earth! Is there any man in Athens for whom the gods have done more good than what they have done for me?

LYCONIDES: I think I hear somebody.

SLAVE: Do I see my master over there?

LYCONIDES: Isn't that my slave?

SLAVE: It *is* him.

LYCONIDES: So it is.

SLAVE: I'd better go and speak to him.

LYCONIDES: I'll go and meet him. I expect he has been talking to the old woman, the girl's nurse, as I told him to.

SLAVE: Shall I tell him about this prize I've found? . . . Shall I tell him all about it? . . . I think I will. Then I can ask him to free me . . . Yes, I'll go and tell him. [*He goes up to his master.*] Sir, I've found something.

LYCONIDES: Have you? What have you found?

SLAVE: Not what the little boy found, the kernel in the nut; something more important than that.

LYCONIDES: I suppose you're pulling my leg as usual. [*Going*] I haven't time –

SLAVE: No, sir, wait; listen, I'll tell you.

LYCONIDES: Tell me then.

SLAVE: Today, sir . . . I've found, sir . . . a huge sum of money.

LYCONIDES: Where in the world did you find that?

SLAVE: In a jar – a four-pound jar, I tell you, full of gold.

LYCONIDES: What villainy have you been up to now?

SLAVE [grinning]: I pinched it from old Euclio.

LYCONIDES: Where is it now?

SLAVE: In a chest at home. Now I'd like to have my freedom, please.

LYCONIDES: Freedom! Do you think I'm going to free you, quintessence of iniquity!

SLAVE: Go on, boss. [Grinning, as if his story was all a joke.] I know what you were thinking. I can read your mind like a book. You were meaning to get it off me. What would you have done if I really had found it?

LYCONIDES [irritated]: I can't listen to any more of your silly stories. But if you have got the gold, give it back.

SLAVE: Give it back?

LYCONIDES: Go and get it, and give it to me, so that I can return it to the old man.

SLAVE: Where am I to get it from?

LYCONIDES: From the chest, of course, where you just said it was.

SLAVE: Oh, I only tell silly stories. It's the way I talk.

LYCONIDES: You give it back, or –

SLAVE: Kill me, if you like; by Hercules, you'll never get that gold away from me, not if you were to –

[LYCONIDES makes a grab at him, but the SLAVE escapes and disappears.]

*

[Here the text ends; the conclusion is reconstructed as follows]*

LYCONIDES: The wicked young devil! I'm pretty sure he has stolen the gold, but he's so artful it's difficult to tell when he's lying and when he's telling the truth. And if he has got it, how am I going to force him to give it up? He's a useful boy, and I should be sorry to have to inflict dire penalties upon him for this escapade. What is

* See Introductory Note, p. 9

most important, however, is that I should be able to return the gold to Euclio; perhaps he would then think better of me ... Here comes my uncle. I must see if he can give me any good advice.

[MEGADORUS *comes out of his house, speaking to his sister within.*]

MEGADORUS: All right, all right ... I don't need any more of your tutoring at the moment, thank you ... Really, that sister of mine can be an intolerable nuisance. I might be a child of six, the way she tries to guide and instruct me in every single thing I do. This morning she was on the point of forcing me to accept the wife she had been kind enough to select for me; and now when I had countered that scheme by agreeing to marry the girl of *my* choice, she comes up with this story that my nephew is the girl's lover and earnestly desires to marry her. Well, let him. I dare say it will be all for the best, and I shall be well out of it. If I let my sister have her way for her son, perhaps she will let me go my own way without interference in the future. ... Hullo, Lyconides my boy, what are you doing here? You don't look as happy as I should expect. Have you seen Euclio yet? Have you made your peace with the old man and obtained his consent to this marriage you've set your heart on?

LYCONIDES: The old man, I am sorry to say, is more obstinate than ever.

MEGADORUS: Did you confess your peccadillo?

LYCONIDES: I did.

MEGADORUS: And he refuses to forgive you? He is still angry with you?

LYCONIDES: He's angry with me for what I did, and he's angry with you for going back on your word.

MEGADORUS: I am surprised at that, since he didn't seem any too willing for me to marry his daughter in the first place.

LYCONIDES: But most of all he is angry and distracted almost to madness by the loss of a potful of gold which it seems has been stolen from him today.

MEGADORUS: Ah, that would account for his ill temper, I've no doubt. But how did he come to have a potful of gold in his possession? This morning he was moaning to me about not being able to afford a dowry for his daughter. The old miser – he must have had money hidden away all the time. Well, serve him right if he has lost it. Who do you think can have taken it?

LYCONIDES: I know who has taken it. At least I think I do.

MEGADORUS: You do? Who?

LYCONIDES: My own slave, according to his own account – unless he's playing some silly trick on me.

MEGADORUS: Well, then, you know what to do. Punish him, strap him, torture him until he confesses the truth, and if he has got the money, make him give it up, then you can give it back to Euclio, and I don't mind betting he'll then be perfectly willing to give you his daughter in exchange.

LYCONIDES: Yes, I believe he would. But the question is, whether I can get hold of the money. That young slave of mine is a decent lad; I have never been a hard master, and he has always served me honestly and willingly. It would distress me terribly to have to use extreme measures against him.

MEGADORUS: Do you think he's anxious to obtain his freedom?

LYCONIDES: What slave isn't?

MEGADORUS: Exactly. So what I suggest is that you talk to your boy quietly; pretend you don't know, or don't care, whether he came by the money honestly or not, and give him the chance of purchasing his freedom for the price of that windfall that he has picked up. Don't you think he would agree?

LYCONIDES: I'm pretty sure he would. Yes, uncle, that's a brilliant idea; that's what I'll do. But one thing troubles me: are you sure that it would be honest for me to connive at a theft, if theft it was, and allow my slave to reap the reward of freedom for his dishonest act?

MEGADORUS: My boy, your scruples do you credit. But if you take my advice, you will trouble your head less, at this moment, about the niceties of strict morality, and more about what is to the best interests of all concerned. After all, what is money, apart from what it can buy? And when was money more harmlessly employed than when used to purchase the happiness and contentment of at least three people at once? This money, wherever it came from – and we have no means of knowing whether or not it was honestly earned in the first place – will now, if you play your cards correctly, be the means of securing for you the bride of your choice, for your slave his freedom, and for Euclio the restoration of his peace of mind and recovery of his beloved treasure; not to mention for me, I hope, a quiet life and a providential escape from a step which I might well have lived to regret. If a paltry pot of gold can achieve all these desirable ends, we are surely entitled to put it to work for us without inquiring too closely into its past history.

LYCONIDES: I can find no fault with your reasoning, uncle, and I will do as you advise. I will go and find my slave, then, and make him a fair offer of his freedom in exchange for the gold.

MEGADORUS: Be back here as soon as you can. Euclio's marriage feast must be pretty nearly cooked, if not spoiling, by now; we don't want to waste a good dinner for lack of a bridegroom.

LYCONIDES: I'll be back in no time. [*He goes off.*]

MEGADORUS: I think we are in sight of a happy solution of our problems. If I could just have a word with Euclio now, I dare say I could put him into a more amenable frame of mind and prepare him for a welcome surprise . . . Hullo, what's going on there?

[EUCLIO *is emerging from his house, shouting orders to the inmates.*]

EUCLIO: . . . and you can tell those cooks to pack up their traps and clear out, and take all that food back to where it came from; there's not going to be any dinner, there's not going to be any wedding . . .

MEGADORUS: Why, Euclio, whatever is the matter? Has some misfortune occurred?

EUCLIO: The misfortune occurred when I ran into you this morning. You and your family have made this day the blackest day of the whole of my life.

MEGADORUS: You are not angry with me, I hope, for having waived my claim to your daughter's hand in favour of my nephew, who, it appears, has a prior right to it.

EUCLIO: I'll see my daughter dead before I enter into any association whatever with you or your nephew or anyone of your kin.

MEGADORUS: But he has made, I understand, a full confession and apology for his sins; you surely cannot be so inhuman as to deny your daughter the consolation of lawful marriage and her child the right of home life and parental care?

EUCLIO: There are ways and means of disposing of the child. More-over, as I told you this morning, I can't afford to give my daughter the dowry that she ought to have. Since this morning, let me tell you, thanks to your interference and the invasion of my house by a gang of thieves sent there by you in the guise of cooks and caterers, I have been robbed of all my life's savings, all that I had put by to protect me from starvation in my declining years.

MEGADORUS: Yes, I have heard about that; and I am sorry indeed to have heard of it.

EUCLIO: You have heard about it? Then you know who stole it? It *was* one of your employees, was it? I thought as much. I'm going down to town this minute to lodge an accusation against you, and by Hercules I'll –

MEGADORUS: Not so fast, Euclio, please. I don't know who stole your money, if stolen it was, and it was certainly not done with any connivance from me. But would you be interested if I told you that I think there is a good chance of your getting your property back again very soon?

EUCLIO: I don't know what to think. If you don't know who stole it, you evidently know where it is now.

MEGADORUS: I can't exactly say that I know that much. But wait, and I think you will very soon hear something to your advantage.

EUCLIO: Well ... I've heard nothing but bad news all this blessed day; it can't do me much more harm to await a final blow.

[CONGRIO, *the cook, comes out of the house.*]

CONGRIO: Now, sir, we've done as you ordered, raked out the fires and taken off the pots and packed up the food, and we're ready to be off.

EUCLIO: Good; you can go as soon as you please.

CONGRIO: That'll be when we've got our pay.

EUCLIO: Pay? I'm not paying anybody for turning my house upside down, prying into my private business – and wasting my firewood. There's the man who hired you; ask him for your pay.

MEGADORUS: You'll get your pay all right, Congrio; but not before you've completed your day's work. We may need your services after all; you had better go back into the house and have everything in readiness for a wedding dinner.

CONGRIO: Go away – stay here – cook the dinner – don't cook the dinner – whose orders am I to obey, I should like to know?

MEGADORUS: Mine. I hired you, and I shall pay you, and with

Euclio's permission, I want you to take charge of his kitchen until further orders.

CONGRIO: I said it was a madhouse I'd been engaged to cook for ... [*He goes in, grumbling.*]

EUCLIO: Well, I don't know whether I'm on my head or my heels. I'm not allowed to give orders in my own house now, it seems –

MEGADORUS: Cheer up, Euclio. We shall soon have some good news for you, I think. Here comes my nephew.

[LYCONIDES *arrives, carrying the pot under his cloak, the* SLAVE *following him.*]

EUCLIO: That impudent and shameless boy! He's the last person I wish to see.

LYCONIDES: I can quite understand that, sir. But though you may be unwilling to look at me, perhaps you can bring yourself to look at what I have with me.

EUCLIO [*his face averted*]: I don't wish to look at you or anything you have with you.

LYCONIDES: Then I must leave it to my uncle to persuade you.

[*He hands the pot to* MEGADORUS *who approaches Euclio.*]

MEGADORUS: I think we have something of yours here, Euclio.

EUCLIO [*turning, unwillingly*]: What ... what? ... what have you ... why, that's my pot of gold! Jupiter almighty! Has it come back to me? Where did you get it? Who found it?

MEGADORUS: My nephew is the person who can tell you that.

EUCLIO [*to Lyconides*]: You – is it you I have to thank for recovering my precious treasure? My dear boy, let me bless you –

LYCONIDES: You may thank me for restoring it to you; but for having found it, and having honestly desired me to return it to its owner, the credit is due to this young slave of mine – whom I have already rewarded by the gift of freedom.

EUCLIO: Your slave? You don't say so? Well done, my boy – come here and let me thank you and congratulate you on your freedom; you are well rewarded for an action that should be an example to all young men. Come here, boy.

[*The* SLAVE *comes sheepishly forward;* EUCLIO *only now recognizes him.*]

Why, surely I have seen you before somewhere? Yes, wasn't it you I caught hanging around this shrine?

SLAVE: Yes, sir, it was.

EUCLIO: And I thought you'd stolen the pot from where I left it?

SLAVE: Yes, sir, you did.

EUCLIO: But you had never touched it?

SLAVE: No, sir, I hadn't.

EUCLIO: And then later on you found it, by chance, somewhere else?

SLAVE: Yes, sir, I . . . found it . . . by chance.

EUCLIO: And, thinking it might be mine, you told your master about it?

SLAVE: Yes, sir, I told my master.

EUCLIO: And asked him to return it to me?

SLAVE: No, sir, he – [LYCONIDES *gives a warning cough*] yes, sir, I asked him to return it to you.

EUCLIO: My goodness, Megadorus, if we all had slaves as honest as this lad, how easy life would be. I've a good mind to . . . here, my boy . . . this is for you [*He picks a small coin out of the pot and gives it to the slave.*]

SLAVE: Thank you, sir.

LYCONIDES [*aside to Megadorus*]: Now, uncle, this is the time to press him again about my marriage.

MEGADORUS: Yes, yes, I will . . . Well, Euclio, we all rejoice at this happy conclusion of the affair. May we now return to the question of your daughter's marriage to my nephew, in the hope that your objections are now withdrawn?

EUCLIO [*vaguely*]: Eh? What? . . . Oh yes, by all means, let 'em get married, let 'em get married . . .

LYCONIDES: Oh, thank you, sir; your generosity is more than I could ever –

EUCLIO: But first I must see this treasure safely put away . . . I'm just wondering what is the best thing I can do with it . . . Here, you take it.

LYCONIDES: I take it?

EUCLIO: Yes, take it, keep it, spend it on my daughter, let her have it as her dowry. It's no use to me.

MEGADORUS: My dear friend, that is most magnanimous of you.

EUCLIO: It's nothing of the sort. If that money can go where it will do some good, I shall be the happiest man in the world, instead of the most miserable, which is what I have been ever since it came into my possession. Day or night, I've not had a moment's peace with that treasure on my mind. Every hour I have thought of some thief nosing round my house, some accident exposing the whereabouts of the hidden hoard. A dozen times a day I have tried to find new hiding places for it, dug pits in my garden, pulled up the hearth-stones, looked for secret crannies in the rafters. A dozen times a night I have waked to hear a spade scratch or a lock turned. Now at last – I'm going to sleep.

MEGADORUS: There speaks a wise man. Contentment, peace of mind, and sound sleep at night, are worth more than a dozen pots of gold. Shall we go in, then, and celebrate the happiness of our two young people?

EUCLIO: Yes, yes, come in.

[*They move towards the house.*]

LYCONIDES: Wait, uncle; aren't you forgetting something?

MEGADORUS: What? . . . Oh yes, [*to the audience*] to all our friends here, we would gladly extend an invitation to join us; but, though enough is as good as a feast, what is enough for six would be poor fare for six hundred; so let us wish you good feasting at home, and ask, in return, your thanks.

EXEUNT

THE PRISONERS
(CAPTIVI)

INTRODUCTORY NOTE TO
THE PRISONERS

EVER since the eighteenth century, criticism of this play has been somewhat overawed by the enthusiastic opinion of the German poet and philosopher Lessing, who pronounced it the most perfect comedy ever to appear on any stage. It is true that it is exceptional among the works of Plautus for its high moral tone – as emphatically advertised in its own Prologue and Epilogue; for its central theme of unselfish heroism, the mutual trust and affection between a master and his slave; and for its complete avoidance of the topic of sexual attraction, whether in a romantic or frivolous context. Commended thus for its suitability for scholastic use, it must often have been the first, and still more often the only Latin play to come to the notice of the young student.

No Greek original can be identified; but wherever Plautus found the story, that he found it a congenial one is proved by his handling of the relationship of Tyndarus and Philocrates, in their 'swapped' characters of master and slave, which he has depicted with a sincerity and sensitivity unapproached anywhere else in his work. The father, Hegio, is also a subtle and convincing creation, in all his changeable moods of geniality, gullibility, and even his impulsive cruelty. Yet beside these merits the play's patent defects can only stand out all the more conspicuously. Its construction abounds in rough edges and loose ends, arbitrary coincidences and inexplicable short cuts. The question, for example – when exactly did the captive master and slave decide to exchange identities? – cannot be satisfactorily answered. It must have been before they met Hegio, and yet after they had heard of his plan to ransom his son; and in any case, when would they have had an opportunity to disguise themselves? Again, the problem of the time required for the double journey between Aetolia and Elis – even granting a mythical topography – admits of no reasonable solution. Not only did the stage convention require the action of the play to be confined to one day, but the activities of Ergasilus draw special attention to this time-limit. Only a little, but not much, approach to verisimilitude is gained by supposing the action to begin in the early morning and end late in the evening of a single day.

The best that can be said of these and other discrepancies is that they are of the kind which, in actual performance, can be rendered invisible under the magic influence known as *optique du théâtre*, and only occur to the critic in retrospect. It is less easy to justify the uneven balance of the play as a whole; too much time is given to preparatory explanation, repeated in the Prologue and in Ergasilus's first monologue, and again in the early scenes up to the departure of Philocrates; while, at the other end of the play, the return of Philocrates and the recognition of Tyndarus, not to mention the very unlikely and unexplained discovery of Stalagmus, are crammed into a hurried finale.

While the plot delays and stagnates, the time is filled up, rather too incongruously for our taste, with the comic relief which is almost entirely the province of that particularly tiresome character, the 'parasite'. This character, a kind of professional diner-out and jester, seems, both as a social institution and as a stage type, to have been a source of inexhaustible amusement to the Roman public. But his translation into English is an unsatisfactory business; the word *parasite*, for us either a biological term or an insult, is no longer applicable, even if there were any contemporary type of person to whom it could be applied. 'Table-companion' is the nearest literal equivalent to the original word and may perhaps stand as an approximation. Whatever we call him, his jests are, of course, mainly based on Roman manners and local topics, regardless of relevance to the Greek scene and action of the play. More unfortunately, a tinge of conventional comicality blurs the portrait of Tyndarus; it is quite out of character for this excellent man, the faithful companion and conscientious guardian of his young master, to utter the comic patter of panic and despair when caught in a tight place. But he is a slave, and that is the sort of language expected of a slave in Plautine comedy. Like any other, this play must be judged by the standards and conventions of its age and kind; it is, in fact, a particularly good example of Plautus's 'impressionistic' method, wherein extreme contrasts of tone are permissible, and any type of speech, joke, or situation is exploited for its own momentary effect, irrespective of strict relevance or consistency.

CHARACTERS

HEGIO   *a wealthy Aetolian gentleman*
PHILOCRATES   *an Elian prisoner of war*
TYNDARUS   *his slave and companion, also a prisoner*
PHILOPOLEMUS   *Hegio's son, taken prisoner in Elis*
ARISTOPHONTES   *another prisoner from Elis*
ERGASILUS   *a 'parasite', dependent on Philopolemus*
STALAGMUS   *a former slave of Hegio*
A BOY   *in Hegio's house*
Slave-warders in Hegio's employment

*

*The scene is in a town of Aetolia, outside the house of Hegio.
A Prologue is spoken by an unnamed character.*

THE PRISONERS

[*Outside the house of Hegio two prisoners are standing, shackled together with heavy chains and secured to a ring in the wall. They are young men of about the same age, but* TYNDARUS *will appear to be the stronger and more serious in demeanour,* PHILOCRATES *more youthful and light-hearted. Though both are prisoners, Tyndarus is still fairly smartly attired as an officer, his companion being apparently his slave or personal servant.*

The speaker of the PROLOGUE *enters, looks the prisoners over, and addresses the audience.*]

PROLOGUE:

    Friends – the two prisoners you see standing there
    Are standing there . . . because . . . well, standing there
    Because they can't sit down . . . as you'll agree!
    This house [*showing the scene*] . . . belongs to Hegio; and he
    Is father of *this* prisoner [*showing Tyndarus*]. But how,
    You well may ask . . . and I shall tell you now . . .
    If you will kindly listen and behave . . .
    How comes this man to be his father's slave?
    There were *two* sons; this one, when four years old,
    Was stolen by a wicked slave and sold,
    In Elis; and the man he sold him to
    Was *this* man's [*showing Philocrates*] father . . . [*He breaks off.*]
Have you got all that? . . . Good . . . What? Oh dear, a man at the back says he can't hear me . . . Come nearer, then! . . . No seat for you? Then go and take a walk outside! . . . Do you want to make a poor actor lose his job? I'm not going to rupture myself to suit you, don't think it. [*To the front stalls*] I'll tell the rest of my tale to you gentlemen of property . . . I'll pay my debts to you . . . I don't like not paying my debts. As I was saying . . .
    The child was stolen by an absconding slave
    And sold to *this* man's father; who then gave

The child – having bought him – to his little son
As personal servant and companion;
Their ages were about the same, you see.
Now, after many years, we find that *he* [*showing Tyndarus*]
(See how the gods make playthings of us men!)
The missing son, at last comes home again
Unknown to his own father Hegio,
To be his slave and prisoner. Now you know
How this one son was lost. But furthermore,
Aetolia and Elis being at war,
An elder son was taken prisoner too
And sold, in Elis, to be servant to
A doctor named Menarchus. Hegio, then,
Hoping to get that lost son back again
(Not knowing the other is here) has now begun
To buy up Elian prisoners, seeking one
Fit to be offered for his son's return.
And yesterday he had the luck to learn
That here, a prisoner, there was one young man,
A knight, of an exalted Elian clan.
To save his son, no price could be too high;
This was the way to get him home – to buy
Two Elian prisoners from the auctioneer,
The young knight, and his slave – whom you see here.

Meanwhile these two, the master and the man,
Have been devising an ingenious plan;
The slave intends to let his master go
As envoy to his father's home; and so
They interchange their names and clothes; and thus
Philocrates [*touching him*] . . . is now called Tyndarus;
And Tyndarus [*touching him*] . . . is called Philocrates . . .
Complete exchange of personalities!
So now the slave – that's Tyndarus – will contrive
To let his master get back home alive,
And, by the same stroke, set his brother free
And bring him back to home and liberty
And father, all unknowing. Such is chance –

More good is often done in ignorance
Than by design. As you will see, these two
Have plotted more astutely than they knew;
The scheme devised by their inventive brains
Will now ensure that Tyndarus remains
In his own father's house, a slave, unknown,
Unknowing, unrecognized among his own.
Man is a thing of nought, you well may say,
As we perform, and you attend, our play.

[*He appears to have ended his formal prologue, but adds the following afterthoughts:*]

There's one other point I'd like to add for your information. You will find this play worth your close attention; it is something quite new – not a rehash of old ideas; and it contains no smutty lines that you would be ashamed to repeat. There is no double-crossing pimp in this play – nor loose woman – nor bragging soldier. Yes, I did mention that Aetolia and Elis are at war; but don't let that frighten you; the battles all take place off stage. Well, it would be practically cheating, wouldn't it, for a comedy company to present you with a tragedy without warning? So if anyone wants a battle, he had better go and pick his own quarrel somewhere else . . . and woe betide him if he picks on an opponent stronger than himself . . . that's the last he'll want to see of battle scenes!

Well, that's all. Good health to you – judges as incorruptible in the field of peace as you are invincible fighters in the field of war. [*Exit.*]

*

[ERGASILUS, *the 'parasite', enters from the town.*]
ERGASILUS: My name – that is, the nickname given to me by our young people – is The Harlot. Why? Because at their tables I am *employed*, not *invited*. I know some superior people think this a rather far-fetched joke; but I see the point. When a lover throws the dice after dinner, he employs the name of his harlot to bring him luck; so you can say she is employed. And the term certainly applies to us professional table-companions; nobody ever *invites* us – nor, for that matter, do they call upon us to bring them luck!

No, we're like mice, always nibbling at other people's food. When the vacation comes, and everybody goes off to the country, then our teeth have to take a vacation too. Like snails in the hot season, hiding in their shells, living on their own juice for lack of dew – so we poor table-companions, in holiday time, have to creep into our holes and live off our own juice, while the people we batten on enjoy their *fêtes champêtres*. In the off season we are as lean as grey-hounds; when business reopens, we are house-dogs, fat and fed and a devil of a nuisance. And by God, in this town people of our sort have to put up with having their ears boxed and pots broken on their heads; if they don't like that, they can always go and earn a living as baggage-porters outside the Triple Gate. And that is where, by the look of things, I am very likely to find myself before long. Now that my lord and master has fallen into the enemy's hands ... in this war between Aetolia and Elis ... *this* is Aetolia, where we are now, and Philopolemus, my patron, is a prisoner over there in Elis ... and he's the son of old Hegio, who lives in this house here – now a house of misery as far as I'm concerned; I can't look at it without weeping. Anyway, this old gentleman, out of concern for his son's welfare, has got himself involved in a rather undignified business, quite out of keeping with his own character. He is buying up prisoners of war, in the hope of finding one of suitable rank to be offered as an exchange for his captured son. And don't I jolly well hope he succeeds! If he doesn't recover his son, there's no hope of recovery for me. The young men of today are no use at all – far too self-centred. Hegio's boy was one of the old type; I could get anything out of him by just stroking his cheek. Fortunately his father is of the same decent sort. So now I am going to pay a call on him ... [*He approaches the house*] How many times have I stepped out of this door well wined and dined! ... [*He listens at the keyhole, and hears a movement*] ... and here's someone coming out now ... [*He retires to a corner.*]

[*A* GUARD *comes out of the house to inspect the prisoners; he is followed shortly by* HEGIO, *who calls the Guard to him.*]

HEGIO: Come here, you. Listen: those two prisoners I bought yesterday out of the spoils of war are to be given separate handcuffs, not chained together with heavy irons as they are now; take them off. And let them walk about as they wish, in the house or outside.

But see that they are carefully watched, of course. A prisoner given partial liberty is like a wild bird; the first chance of escape, he's off, and you'll never catch him again.

GUARD: I'm sure we'd all rather be free than slaves.

HEGIO: But not you, it seems.

GUARD: As I haven't got the money to give you for my freedom, what do you expect me to give you – the slip?

HEGIO [amiably]: Just you try it, and I shall have something to give you.

GUARD: I might turn myself into a wild bird, as you were saying.

HEGIO: Yes, you might; if you do, I shall have to put you in a cage. But that's enough of that – just do what I told you, and then you can go. I am going round to my brother's, to have a look at my other prisoners, in case there has been any trouble in the night. I'll be back very soon.

[The GUARD removes the prisoners into the house.]

ERGASILUS: Poor old man, it really is a shame to see him become a dealer in prisoners, all because of the sad loss of his son. However, if it will help to get the boy back, I'd be content to see him cut their throats with his own hand.

HEGIO [stopping on his way out]: Did I hear someone speak?

ERGASILUS: It's me – what's left of me, for I'm pining and starving and wasting and fading away with grief and sympathy for you. I'm worn to a shadow, nothing but skin and bone. I can't seem to enjoy anything I eat at home, though every mouthful I take elsewhere does me a power of good.

HEGIO: Well, good morning to you, Ergasilus.

ERGASILUS [with exaggerated sympathy]: May the gods be kind to you, Hegio.

HEGIO: Cheer up; there's nothing to weep about.

ERGASILUS: Nothing to weep about? Can I help weeping for the fate of your dear boy, such a fine fellow as he was?

HEGIO: Of course I have always known what a good friend you were to him; and he to you, I believe.

ERGASILUS: Ah yes; a man never knows the value of what he possesses, until he has lost it. Only since your son fell into enemy hands have I realized what he meant to me, and now I miss him terribly.

HEGIO: And how do you think a father feels, at losing his only son, if his loss can so affect a stranger?

ERGASILUS: A stranger? I a stranger to him? Oh, Hegio, don't say that; don't think that; as he is your only son, so he was my only – my more than only – friend.

HEGIO: It is good of you indeed to feel your friend's misfortune as your own. But come, don't give way to grief.

ERGASILUS: Oh, but it hurts me so ... [*clutching his stomach*] this is where it hurts. All my eating equipment has been put out of commission.

HEGIO [*joining pleasantly in the joke*]: Haven't you been able to find anyone in the meantime to recommission it for you?

ERGASILUS: What do you think? Since dear Philopolemus was taken prisoner, the commission he held is going begging; not a soul will touch it.

HEGIO: I am not surprised that no one will undertake his commission. You need such an enormous army to keep you going; you need a bakery corps, and that includes breadmakers and pastry cooks; you need a flying squad, to catch your game and poultry; and marines to look after the fishing.

ERGASILUS [*delighted with the old man's wit*]: What genius lurks in unsuspected places! Here's a born commander unemployed.

HEGIO: But don't be downhearted, my dear fellow. I am confident that I shall have him back home in a few days. As you see, I've got a young Elian prisoner here, a son of a very rich and aristocratic family. I count on being able to exchange him –

ERGASILUS: I hope you will, with the help of heaven. But now, sir, are you invited out anywhere for dinner today?

HEGIO: Not so far as I know. Why do you ask?

ERGASILUS: Because this is my birthday; and it would give me great pleasure to ... be invited to dinner with you.

HEGIO: Ha, ha! That was sharp of you. Well, all right, if you can put up with simple fare.

ERGASILUS: Not too simple, I hope; I get plenty of that at home. Right, then – going, going, gone ... 'subject to the purchase price being satisfactory to the vendor and his associates' ... I'm for sale, you see, like a plot of land.

HEGIO: A plot of land? More like a yawning pit, I should say. But if you're coming, come in time.

ERGASILUS: I'm ready now.

HEGIO: You'd do better to go and catch your hare; at present you've only got a hedgehog. It's stony ground I live on.

ERGASILUS: Ah, no, you can't put me off like that, Hegio. I shall come with my teeth well shod.

HEGIO: They'll have rough work to do.

ERGASILUS: Why, do you eat brambles?

HEGIO: No, but I live off the soil.

ERGASILUS: Pork, then? That lives off the soil.

HEGIO: I use a lot of herbs.

ERGASILUS: You ought to be a doctor. Well ... I'll see you, then?

HEGIO: Don't be late.

ERGASILUS: As if I needed telling! [*He goes away.*]

HEGIO: I must go and look at my accounts, and see how much money I've got in the bank. After that I shall be going to my brother's, as I said. [*He goes into the house.*]

> [*The* GUARD *now comes out again, with one or more assistants, parading several prisoners of war; among them are* TYNDARUS *and* PHILOCRATES, *now not linked together, but more lightly chained.*]

GUARD: Now, you men ... if it's God's will that you have to be the unlucky ones, the best thing you can do is to take it patiently; that way, it won't seem so hard. You were free men at home, I dare say; now you're slaves, and if you're wise you'll accept that, and accept your master's orders, and use your commonsense to make your position as comfortable as possible. What your master orders is right, even if it seems to you wrong.

> [*The prisoners weep and groan.*]

And there's no need to weep and groan. We can see you're unhappy without that. When in trouble, keep your pecker up; that's the best way.

TYNDARUS: We can't help feeling sorry for ourselves, chained up like this.

GUARD: The master would feel sorry for himself, wouldn't he, if he let you off your chains, let you go loose after paying good money for you?

TYNDARUS: What is he afraid of? We know our duty, and would respect it, if he let us go unchained.

GUARD: Ho, would you? I know what you're up to; you're planning an escape.

PHILOCRATES: We escape? Where should we escape to?

GUARD: Back to where you live, I expect.

PHILOCRATES: Oh rubbish; we're not the sort of men to behave like runaways.

GUARD: Well, I wouldn't be the one to discourage you – *if* you got the chance.

TYNDARUS [*approaching the Guard confidentially*]: Just do us one favour, will you?

GUARD: What's that?

TYNDARUS: Let me and my friend have a word together where you and these others can't hear us.

GUARD: Certainly. [*To the other prisoners*] Move away, you men. [*To his assistants*] We'll go over here . . . But make it short.

TYNDARUS: That's what I meant to do. [*To Philocrates*] Come this way.

GUARD [*to some prisoners still remaining*]: Clear off, you; leave them alone.

TYNDARUS: Thank you; we are both very grateful to you for giving us this opportunity to . . . do what we want to do.

PHILOCRATES [*quietly to Tyndarus*]: I think we had better go farther off, don't you? We don't want any of them overhearing our talk, or the whole scheme will be out.

[*They remove themselves as far as possible from the rest.*]

A clever trick is no trick at all unless it's neatly executed; it's sheer murder if the secret gets out. Now, you are pretending to be my master, and I am pretending to be your slave; all right; but we've still got to keep our eyes open and go carefully, if we want to bring this off coolly, without a hitch, and without giving the game away. We've taken on a big thing; we can't afford to go to sleep on it.

TYNDARUS: I won't disappoint you, sir.

PHILOCRATES: I hope you won't.

TYNDARUS: And I don't need to tell you that to save your dear life I'm offering to sell my own dear life for a song.

PHILOCRATES: I know it.

TYNDARUS: You won't forget it, I hope, when you've got what you want. It's a way most men have, to be on their best behaviour when they're asking for something they want, and as soon as they've got

it turn as nasty and deceitful as a man can be. So I hope *you* won't
disappoint *me*. And what I say to you, I'd say to my own father.

PHILOCRATES: I could almost call *you* my own father, if I dared.
You have always been a second father to me.

TYNDARUS: Yes, I have.

PHILOCRATES: That is why I can't remind you too often of our new
roles; I am not your master any longer; I am your slave. This is the
one important thing; I must beg and implore you – since the gods
have seen fit to make me, your former master, now your fellow-
slave, so that instead of ordering you as I had a right to do before,
I must now beseech you – remember our dangerous position,
remember that we are both slaves here, as a result of the fortune of
war, remember my father's kindness to you, remember your duty
to me now as well as when you were my slave; and above all,
while remembering who you were, remember who you are
now.

TYNDARUS: I've got all that clear, sir; for the present I am you and
you are me.

PHILOCRATES: Good; as long as you never forget that, there is hope
of success for our scheme.

[HEGIO *comes out again.*]

HEGIO [*to someone within*]: I'll be back in a minute; I want to ask
these men something ... But where are they?

[*The other prisoners have by now been removed from the scene,*
TYNDARUS *and* PHILOCRATES *remaining in a secluded corner, with
one guard keeping an eye on them.*]

Where are the men I had brought out here?

PHILOCRATES [*coming forward*]: You're taking good care we don't
get far away, master, chained as we are and watched on every side.

HEGIO [*in a cheerful humour*]: No care is too much care for a man who
is taking care not to be duped; as often as not, a man who thinks
he has taken care enough, with all his caution finds himself caught
out. Don't you think I have good reason to have you carefully
watched, eh? ... after paying an enormous price for you in ready
cash?

PHILOCRATES: Oh certainly, sir, we have no right to think ill of you
for looking after us – nor you of us, if we should happen to escape,
given the chance.

HEGIO: As you are under guard here, so is my son at this moment under guard in your country.

PHILOCRATES: He is a prisoner?

HEGIO: Exactly.

PHILOCRATES: So we were not the only cowards.

HEGIO: Come over here, my boy. [*He separates him from Tyndarus.*] I want to ask you a few questions. And I don't want you to tell me any lies.

PHILOCRATES: What I know I will tell you truthfully; what I don't know, I'll tell you truthfully that I don't know.

TYNDARUS [*aside*]: Now for it! The boy has got the old man in the chair and the scissors at his neck – and not even offered him a towel to keep his clothes clean! It remains to be seen whether he'll give him a close crop or only a trim; if he's any good at his business he'll scrape the skin off him.

HEGIO: Tell me, my boy, would you rather be a slave or a free man?

PHILOCRATES: Whichever offers the greatest advantage and the least disadvantage, that is what I would prefer. I can't say that being a slave was ever much trouble to me; I was treated just like one of the family.

TYNDARUS: Bravo! What price Thales of Miletus now? He couldn't hold a candle to this boy for subtlety; he puts on the slave's manner to the life.

HEGIO: And your master Philocrates – what kind of family does he come from?

PHILOCRATES: Polyplusius is the family name; and it's the most influential and respected family in the country.

HEGIO: And he himself – how does he stand?

PHILOCRATES: At the top; respected by all the best people.

HEGIO: I see. And if he's as highly thought of in your country as you say, he's well off, I suppose? Got plenty of money, eh?

PHILOCRATES: His old man is rolling in it.

HEGIO [*still more pleased*]: His father is alive, then?

PHILOCRATES: He was when we left him; whether he's now alive or dead, only the gods below can tell you.

TYNDARUS: We're safe! The lad can talk philosophy as well as he tells lies.

HEGIO: What was the father's name?

PHILOCRATES [*inventing*]: Thesaurochrysonicochrysides.

HEGIO: Oh yes ... I see ... a name given to him on account of his wealth?

PHILOCRATES: No, on account of his iniquitous avarice. His original name was Theodoromides.

HEGIO: You mean he's a close-fisted man, your master's father?

PHILOCRATES: Iron-fisted. I'll give you an example: whenever he makes a sacrifice to his divine protector, all the utensils he uses for the ceremony have to be of the cheapest pottery, lest the holy god himself should steal them. You can imagine how much trust he puts in anyone else.

HEGIO: Well now, come over here with me. I'm going to put the same questions to your master. [*He goes over to Tyndarus;* PHILOCRATES *halts at a respectful distance, listening carefully*.] Now, Philocrates – your man has been behaving in a very sensible and honest manner; I know all about your family; he has told me everything. If you are willing to be equally frank with me, it will be to your advantage; in any case I have all the facts from him.

TYNDARUS: He did no more than his duty in telling you the truth, although I admit I was hoping to keep you in ignorance of my rank, my family name, and my wealth; and of course, now that I have lost my liberty and my home, I cannot expect him to fear my displeasure more than yours. The fortune of war has made us equals. I remember the time when he wouldn't have dared speak a rash word in my presence; now he is at liberty to raise his hand against me. You see how it is; luck makes what she will of a man, shapes him in any way she pleases. She has turned me from a free man into a slave, brought me from the top to the bottom. I was always used to command; now I am subject to another man's orders. But this I will say: if I can find as good a master as I was to my own servants, I shall have no fear of being harshly or unjustly treated. I would give you one piece of advice, sir, if I might be so bold.

HEGIO: Speak as freely as you like.

TYNDARUS: Till now I was a free man like your son; like him, I was deprived of my freedom by enemy hands; as I am a slave here in your country, so he is a slave in mine. There is surely a God above, who sees and hears all we do; how he will care for your son over there will depend on your treatment of me here; he will reward kindness with kindness, I am sure; and unkindness with its like. You long to see your son again; so does my father long to see me.

HEGIO: I do not forget that. Now do you confirm what your servant has told me?

TYNDARUS: I confirm that my father is a wealthy man in our country, and that our family is one of the highest. But I must beg you, sir, not to let my wealth tempt you into fantastic expectations; although I am his only son, my father might see fit to leave me here, well fed and clothed at your expense, rather than reduce himself to poverty at home, where he would have to bear the brunt of the disgrace.

HEGIO: Oh, as to that, I am as well off as I need to be, thanks to the gods and my forebears. Nor do I consider every bit of profit an unmixed blessing to a man. I am quite sure that many a man has been corrupted by profit; there are even times when a loss can be more beneficial than a gain. I have no good word for gold; it has too often tempted too many people into wrongdoing. Just you listen to me, then we shall both know what I have in mind. My son is a prisoner and a slave in your land of Elis; you get him back for me, and you needn't give me a penny of ransom more than that; I shall let you and your servant go free on those terms – but on no others.

TYNDARUS: That is a most fair and honourable proposition, sir; it is the offer of a gentleman. Can you tell me whether your son is a slave in private ownership or in the public service?

HEGIO: He is the property of a doctor named Menarchus.

PHILOCRATES [breaking in impulsively]: Well! He is one of my master's clients! [To Tyndarus] Sir, this'll be as easy as falling off a log!
[TYNDARUS gives him a stern look, and he moves away again.]

HEGIO: Then you can use your influence to get my son ransomed.

TYNDARUS: I'll do that, sir. But there is one thing –

HEGIO: What? I'll do anything to help you, provided it is not against my own interests.

TYNDARUS: I'll explain, sir. I don't, of course, expect you to let me go before your son arrives back here. But I would like you to let me send my servant, on bail, to my father, so that he can arrange for your son's ransom.

HEGIO: No . . . I think I would rather send one of my own men, as soon as we have an armistice, who could get in touch with your father and be relied on to carry out your instructions exactly.

TYNDARUS: I'm afraid it will be useless to send a stranger to my father; you would only be wasting your time. Why not send my man, sir? He'll settle the whole business, once he gets there. I assure you, no man you could send would be more reliable or more likely to be trusted by my father; there isn't a slave in the world he thinks more highly of, or to whom he would more readily entrust his own son. To set your mind at rest, sir, I'll answer with my life for his fidelity; I know I can depend on him, because he knows I am his good friend.

HEGIO: Very well . . . if that is what you wish, I will send him, on bail, and on your recognizance.

TYNDARUS: It is what I wish; and I wish it to be done as soon as possible.

HEGIO: And if he doesn't come back – would you agree to paying me a forfeit of, say, two thousand drachmas?

TYNDARUS: Fair enough.

HEGIO [to a Guard]: Release this man at once – in fact release both of them. [Their chains are removed, Tyndarus's first.]

TYNDARUS: May the gods give you every blessing, sir, for treating me so honourably, and for letting me off the chain. [Aside] I feel better already, with that collar off my collarbone.

HEGIO: It does a good man good to do a good turn to another good man. Now, if you're going to send your lad home, you had better have a word with him, give him his instructions and tell him what you want him to say to your father. Shall I send him to you?

TYNDARUS: Please do.

[PHILOCRATES has been having his chains removed; HEGIO goes over to him.]

HEGIO: Now, young man; in an enterprise which we hope will be to the benefit of myself, my son, and you two men, I order you, as your new master, to pay careful attention to the instructions of your former master. I have put you at his disposal, on a bail of two thousand drachmas, and he proposes to send you on an errand to his father, with the object of ransoming my son from his captivity in your country, and so effecting a mutual exchange of sons between us.

PHILOCRATES: I am your willing servant, sir, and his; use me as your wheel; I will spin this way or that, as you require.

HEGIO: I am glad to see that you accept your servitude in the proper spirit; and you will find that your willingness will be to your own advantage as much as anyone else's. Come this way. [*To Tyndarus*] He's yours.

TYNDARUS: Thank you, sir; it is good of you to grant my request and let me send this man back to my parents; he will be able to give my father a full account of what I am doing here and what I want him to do for me there. [*To Philocrates*] Listen ... Tyndarus; the gentleman and I have agreed that I am to send you home to my father, on bail; if you fail to return, I am to pay a forfeit of two thousand drachmas.

PHILOCRATES: I think that's an excellent arrangement, sir. Your father will be expecting to hear from us, either by me or some other messenger.

TYNDARUS: Yes; well now, listen carefully to the message I want you to take home to my father, a message from us here to my father at home.

PHILOCRATES: Sir ... Philocrates ... you can depend on me to do my very best to promote your interests, as I have always done, wherever we have been, in the past; to that end I shall strive with all my heart and mind and attention.

TYNDARUS: That is what I should expect of you. Listen to this then: in the first place, give my greetings to mother and father, and our family, and any other kind friends you may meet; say that I am in good health here, and that the master whom I serve is one of the best and is treating me – has always treated me – with the utmost consideration.

PHILOCRATES: No need to remind me of that, sir; I shall never forget it.

TYNDARUS: Well, it's true. Except for having a guard at hand, I feel just like a free man. Then tell my father about the agreement this gentleman and I have come to about the exchange of his son.

PHILOCRATES: You needn't repeat that either, sir. I shall remember.

TYNDARUS: He is to ransom Hegio's son and send him back here in exchange for us two.

PHILOCRATES: I know.

HEGIO: But it must be soon; at the earliest possible moment; that is what we should both desire.

PHILOCRATES: You may be sure, sir, he is as anxious to see his son again as you are.

HEGIO: Of course, I love my son, as every father does.

PHILOCRATES: Are there any other messages for your father, sir?

TYNDARUS: Only ... that I am quite well; and ... don't be afraid to speak up for yourself, Tyndarus ... say that you and I have always hit it off well together, that you have never misbehaved yourself, nor had I any occasion to be hard with you; that you have been a good servant to me in all that we have been through ... a slave who has never failed his master, in act or thought, in any danger or adversity. I am sure, Tyndarus, when my father hears this – when he hears of your devotion to his son and to himself – even his hard heart will not be able to deny you the free gift of your freedom; in any case, if I get safely back from here, I shall use all my efforts to make him agree to give it to you. It is thanks to your efforts, your kindness, your courage – yes, and your cleverness, in revealing to our master the truth about my family and my wealth – that I now have this chance to return to my parents; your cleverness, in fact, has delivered your master from his bonds.

PHILOCRATES: It was, as you say, sir, my doing; and I am glad you do not forget it. But I have done no more than you deserve. Oh ... Philocrates ... if I were to speak again of all your many kindnesses to me, night would end the day before I had finished; you could not have done more for me if you had been my slave.

HEGIO: God bless me, what fine young men they are, and so devoted to each other; it brings tears to my eyes ... to hear a slave speak so highly of his master.

PHILOCRATES [*perhaps inadvertently forgetting which is the slave*]: The compliments he has paid me, sir, are not a hundredth part of what he himself deserves.

HEGIO [*not noticing the lapse, if it was one*]: Anyway, my man, now is your chance to crown your good record with this supreme benefaction, if you perform your errand faithfully.

PHILOCRATES: My wish to see it done, sir, will be equalled by my zeal in doing it. To assure you – I swear, as Jove Almighty is my witness, that I will never forget my duty to Philocrates.

HEGIO: Spoken like a man.

PHILOCRATES: And that there is nothing I would not do for him as I would do it for myself.

TYNDARUS: All I ask is that you confirm those words in act and deed. But there is one thing more that I would wish to say – and I hope you will not take it ill ... Tyndarus. In case I have not sufficiently impressed upon you what I expect of you ... remember this above all: you are being allowed to go home, on bail, on my responsibility; I remain here, staking my life on your return. You will not forget me, I hope, as soon as you are out of my sight ... you will not forget me, left here to slave it out for your sake ... while you count yourself a free man, breaking your bond, and never giving another thought to your task of saving me by bringing this man's son home. There is a price of two thousand drachmas on your head, remember. Be true to one who has always been true to you; let nothing shake you from your duty. I am sure my father will do what is right by us; it is for you to make me your friend for ever, and gain a new friend in our friend here [*indicating Hegio*]. So then ... your hand in mine ... I ask you again, be as true to me as I have been to you ... Now off you go; all my life and hope goes with you; from now on you are my master, my protector ... my father.

PHILOCRATES: I understand all you say, sir. Will it do if I come back with all your wishes accomplished?

TYNDARUS: That'll do.

PHILOCRATES: I shall come back with a prize that will satisfy you, and (*to Hegio*) you, sir. Is that all, then?

TYNDARUS: Only come back as soon as you can.

PHILOCRATES: Of course.

HEGIO: Come with me to my banker's, and I will give you money for your journey; at the same time we'll get you a passport from the praetor.

TYNDARUS: A passport?

HEGIO: He'll have to show it to the army authorities, in order to obtain permission to leave the country. You can go in, Philocrates

TYNDARUS: Good luck – Tyndarus!

PHILOCRATES: Goodbye – Philocrates!

[TYNDARUS *goes into the house.*]

HEGIO: Well, I certainly did the right thing for myself when I bought those two prisoners of war. Now, God willing, I have rescued my son from captivity. And yet for some time I was in two minds whether to buy them or not. [*To the Guards*] You men, kindly keep a careful watch on that man inside; he is not to be allowed out anywhere without a guard. I shall be back very soon; I'm only going to have a look at my other prisoners at my brother's house. I might inquire at the same time whether there is anyone there who knows this man I've got. [*To Philocrates*] But the first thing to be done is to see you safely off. Come along, my boy. [*They go.*]

*

[*An hour later.* ERGASILUS *comes from the town, tired and dejected.*]

ERGASILUS: Pity the man who has to go looking for food for himself and has a hard job finding it. And pity still more the man who has a hard job looking for it and doesn't find it! There's nothing worse than having an empty stomach and nothing to put in it. Curse this day! I'd like to give it a bash in the eye . . . it's given everybody an extra allowance of uncharitableness towards me . . . I've never seen a more extravagantly stingy day . . . a more bloatedly barren day . . . a more hopelessly unsuccessful and disappointed day. My throat and stomach have been celebrating a festival of starvation. So much for the parasitical profession – to hell with it! Young people nowadays turn their backs on the hungry humorist; they have no use for us hardy Spartans, the long-suffering bottom-benchers, traditional knock-takers, who have no money in the bank and no food in our larders – nothing but our witty conversation to live on. They only want the guests who are ready to return hospitality in their own homes. The young men even do their own shopping nowadays – which always used to be our job. And on the way back from town, they'll call in to bargain with a pimp, bold as you please and as straight-faced as a juryman pronouncing a verdict of guilty. No, they don't give tuppence for us jokers – they're far too fond of themselves.

I'll tell you – just after I left you, I went up to some young fellows in the forum. 'Good morning, fellows', I said, 'where are we lunching?' Dead silence. 'Any takers? Do I hear someone say "With me"?' All dumb as mutes; not even a smile. 'What about dinner, then?' The gentlemen shake their heads. So I told them a funny story, one of my best, one I could have dined out on for a month in the old days. Nobody laughed. Of course it was a conspiracy – I could see that at once. Laugh? – not one of them could bring himself to show his teeth and grin like a dog. So I left them, seeing that I was being made a laughing-stock of. I went on to another group, then another, then another; same story; all in a plot, like the oil-merchants in the Velabrum. Well, I had enough of being made a fool of down there, so I came away. There were some other poor devils like me prowling about in the forum too, wasting their time. I'll get my own back, though; I'll prosecute them, that's what I'll do, under the law they have in certain foreign countries – I shall bring an action against persons who have conspired to deprive us of life and maintenance, and I shall demand damages – ten dinners each, to be given at the time chosen by me; that'll be when provisions are most expensive. That'll settle them. Now I'll go and try the harbour; that's my only remaining dinner-prospect. If there's nothing doing there, I shall be back here to partake of the old gentleman's hard tack. [*He goes off.*]

[*From the direction of the town,* HEGIO *now returns, in very good humour; he is followed, at a little distance, by a new prisoner,* ARISTOPHONTES, *with guards keeping an eye on him, though the prisoner himself is unchained.*]

HEGIO: I must say it makes a man feel pleased with himself, to have done a good stroke of business and contributed to the common good at the same time. That is what I did yesterday when I bought those prisoners. I can't move a yard without someone coming up to congratulate me. But oh dear, it's a fatiguing business being stopped and buttonholed at every turn; I've barely escaped with my life from the ovation. However, I managed to reach the praetor's office and, as soon as I could recover my breath, asked for the passport. They gave it to me without demur; and I gave it to Tyndarus; and he's now on his way home. That done, I made tracks for home too; but first I looked in at my brother's, where

my other prisoners are. I asked if there was anyone among them
who knew Philocrates of Elis; and eventually this man spoke up
and said he knew him very well. 'I've got him at my house,' I
said; whereupon the fellow begged and besought me to let him
see his friend. I immediately ordered his release, and here he is.
[*He summons Aristophontes*] Now, young man, if you'll come with
me, you shall have your wish and meet your friend.

[*A moment earlier,* TYNDARUS *has peeped out of the house and seen
what is happening. By concealing himself in some corner, he manages
to escape notice while* HEGIO *takes* ARISTOPHONTES *into the
house, and is now alone outside.*]

TYNDARUS: Oh my goodness, now I'd much rather be dead than
alive! Now all hope and help and support are lost and gone for
ever. It's goodbye to life for me today – exit, and no way out of the
exit! Not a chance to cheer me up. Not a shred of hope to cover
the nakedness of my subtle scheme of deception, or mask the
fraudulence of my pretensions; no excuse for my duplicity, no
escape for my sins, no asylum for my audacity, no shelter for my
shrewdness. The secret is out, the plot uncovered, the cat out of
the bag. Nothing is left for me now but to meet ignominious
death, taking upon myself my master's doom – and my own. And
the cause of my destruction is that man who has just gone in
there – Aristophontes, he knows me; he's a friend of Philocrates,
and related to him. So now Salvation herself could not save me if
she wanted to. There is nothing to be done, unless my brain can
invent some further ingenuity. But what? Damn it, what ingenuity? Can I think of anything? Not a thing; it's hopeless; I
haven't a chance.

[HEGIO *and* ARISTOPHONTES *come out again.*]

HEGIO: Where in the world has that fellow got to? He must have just
bolted out of the house.

TYNDARUS: Your hour has come, Tyndarus; the enemy are upon
you. Is there anything I can say – any story I can tell? Anything I
can confess or deny? It's touch and go ... but what's my luck
worth? If only the gods could have removed Aristophontes from
the world before he was removed from his country ... instead of
letting him come and upset everything I had set up. If I can't
think of one more stupendous lie, this is the end.

75

[HEGIO *has been searching around, in and out of the house, and now discovers Tyndarus.*]

HEGIO: Why, here he is. [*To Aristophontes*] Come along, here's your friend; go and speak to him.

TYNDARUS: Who'd be in my shoes now? [*He attempts to avoid Aristophontes.*]

ARISTOPHONTES: Well, Tyndarus! What's all this? Why are you trying to avoid my sight, turning your back on me as if I were a stranger – as if you'd never seen me before? I know we're both slaves now; but I was a free man at home, while you have been a slave in Elis ever since you were a boy.

HEGIO: Tyndarus? I'm not surprised he doesn't want to meet you, or look at you, or have anything to do with you, if you call him Tyndarus when his name is really Philocrates.

TYNDARUS [*in a flash of desperate inspiration*]: Please, sir, don't take any notice of his ramblings; he was known to be a lunatic in Elis. He once attacked his father and mother with a spear, in their own house; and from time to time he suffers from epileptic fits. You had better come farther away from him.

HEGIO [*in alarm*]: Keep that man away from me! [*The guards restrain Aristophontes.*]

ARISTOPHONTES [*to Tyndarus*]: What do you mean, damn you? I a lunatic . . . attacked my parents with a spear . . . had epileptic fits?

HEGIO: It's nothing to be alarmed about, my good man; it's a disease many people suffer from, and they have usually been helped, even cured, by being spat on.

ARISTOPHONTES: Do you mean to say you believe him too?

HEGIO: Believe him?

ARISTOPHONTES: Believe that I am mad?

TYNDARUS: Take care, sir; he looks very dangerous. You had better leave us, sir. As I said, there's a fit coming on; be careful.

HEGIO: Of course I could tell he was insane, the moment he called you Tyndarus.

TYNDARUS: Oh yes, he sometimes forgets his own name – doesn't know who he is.

HEGIO: But he did say that you were a friend of his.

TYNDARUS: It's the first I've heard of it! Unless Alcmaeon and Orestes and Lycurgus are friends of mine too!

ARISTOPHONTES: You miserable cur! How dare you speak like that of me! Not know you indeed!

HEGIO: It's perfectly obvious you don't know him, when you call him Tyndarus instead of Philocrates. You are speaking of a man who isn't here; the man who is here is someone you don't know.

ARISTOPHONTES: On the contrary, he is pretending to be someone else and denying that he's the person he is.

TYNDARUS: You seem to be setting up your word against that of your friend Philocrates?

ARISTOPHONTES: As I see it, you are setting up plain falsehood against the simple truth. *Look* at me, for God's sake.

TYNDARUS: Well?

ARISTOPHONTES: Now then – do you deny that your name is Tyndarus?

TYNDARUS: I do.

ARISTOPHONTES: And you say your name is Philocrates?

TYNDARUS: I do.

ARISTOPHONTES [*to Hegio*]: Do you believe him?

HEGIO: I'd rather believe him than you. Indeed I couldn't believe myself more – for the man you take him for has this very morning left for Elis, to visit this man's father.

ARISTOPHONTES: This man's father? But this man is a slave.

TYNDARUS [*still hoping Aristophontes will understand*]: So are you a slave – now – though you were a freeman at home; and a freeman is what I hope to be again, if I succeed in bringing this man's son home to freedom.

ARISTOPHONTES: You scoundrel! Are you now claiming that you are a freeman by birth?

TYNDARUS: No! I am a Philocrates by birth!

ARISTOPHONTES: You see, Hegio, the rascal is just playing with us. He's a slave right enough; and if he ever *had* a slave it was himself!

TYNDARUS: Just because you have been reduced to poverty in your own country and haven't a penny to live on, you want to make out that everyone is in the same case. It doesn't surprise me; beggars are always spiteful and envious of respectable people.

ARISTOPHONTES: Hegio, I warn you not to go on putting your blind trust in this man. It's clear to me, he's scored a hit against you

77

already. That story of his hoping to ransom your son – I don't like it at all.

TYNDARUS: I know you don't like it; but I shall do it, God willing. [*Trying to get it across to Aristophontes*] I shall get this man's son back, and then *he* will return me to my father in Elis. That is why I have sent *Tyndarus* with a message to *my* father.

ARISTOPHONTES: But *you* are Tyndarus; there's certainly no other slave of that name in Elis.

TYNDARUS: Must you go on taunting me with being a slave, when I have only become one as a result of war?

ARISTOPHONTES: Oh! . . . I shall burst!

TYNDARUS: Hear him, sir! Fly for your life. Have him arrested or he'll be attacking us with stones.

ARISTOPHONTES: It's unbearable!

TYNDARUS: Look how his eyes flash! This is it, Hegio. Look at those livid blotches all over his body. He's suffering from black bile.

ARISTOPHONTES: If this gentleman had any sense, you'd be suffering under black pitch at the stake and your head a flaming torch.

TYNDARUS: Delirious. He's possessed of a devil.

HEGIO: Do you think I should have him put under restraint?

TYNDARUS: It would be much the wisest thing.

ARISTOPHONTES: Oh! Why haven't I got a stone to bash the villain's brains out with, before he drives me raving mad with his nonsense!

TYNDARUS: You hear that? A stone.

ARISTOPHONTES: Hegio, please let me have a word with you alone.

HEGIO: Say what you want from over there. I'm listening.

TYNDARUS: That's right. If you go too near him he may bite your nose off.

ARISTOPHONTES: For pity's sake, Hegio, don't believe I am mad, or ever have been, or have ever had the sickness as he alleges. Look – you can have me chained up, if you're afraid of me; I have no objection, provided he is chained up too.

TYNDARUS: There you are, Hegio, chain him up, if he has no objection – but not me.

ARISTOPHONTES: Shut up, you. I'll find some way of proving that you're really Tyndarus, though you call yourself Philocrates . . . What are you glowering at me for?

TYNDARUS: Am I glowering?

ARISTOPHONTES [*to Hegio*]: I don't know what he'd be doing if you weren't here.

HEGIO [*to Tyndarus*]: Don't you think I had better go and talk to the madman?

TYNDARUS: What's the use? He'll only bluff you with a lot of nonsense you can't make head or tail of. Dress him up in the proper costume and he'd be mad Ajax to the life.

HEGIO: I don't care; I'm going to talk to him. [*He goes over to Aristophontes.*]

TYNDARUS [*aside*]: Now I'm done for. I'm between the axe and the altar now. I don't know what more I can do.

HEGIO: Well, Aristophontes, I'm listening. What is it you want to say?

ARISTOPHONTES: What I want to tell you is the truth, which you persist in disbelieving. But in the first place, I want to put you right about me; I am *not* insane, and there's nothing wrong with me – except that I'm a prisoner. And I swear – as I pray Almighty God to restore me to my native land – that man is no more Philocrates than you or I.

HEGIO: Good gracious! Who is he, then?

ARISTOPHONTES: I've been telling you ever since I came here who he is. If I'm wrong, I am willing to forfeit home and liberty and stay here as your prisoner for ever.

HEGIO [*to Tyndarus*]: And what have you to say for yourself?

TYNDARUS: I say that I am your servant and you are my master.

HEGIO: That's not the question. Were you once a free man?

TYNDARUS: I was.

ARISTOPHONTES: Rubbish! He never was.

TYNDARUS: What do you know about it? How can you be so sure – you weren't my mother's midwife, were you?

ARISTOPHONTES: We met as children.

TYNDARUS: And now we meet as adults – that's my answer to that. And I'd be glad if you would stop meddling with my business; I'm not meddling with yours, am I?

HEGIO [*to Aristophontes*]: Was his father Thesaurochrysonicochrysides?

ARISTOPHONTES: No, he wasn't; and I've never heard of such a name before. But Philocrates's father was Theodoromides.

[HEGIO *remembers this, and is nearly convinced.*]

79

TYNDARUS [*aside*]: My hour has come. Stop beating, my heart . . . or go to the devil and be damned . . . if you're going to jump up and down like this, while I can hardly stand still for fear.

HEGIO: Then this man was a slave in Elis, and he is not Philocrates at all? Can I take that as proved?

ARISTOPHONTES: Proved beyond all possible doubt. But where, then, is Philocrates?

HEGIO: Where he most wants to be, and where I wish he wasn't! And in that case I've been made a fool of, had my tail twisted by this scheming villain; he only wanted to mislead me, and he's done it. But . . . are you sure . . .?

ARISTOPHONTES: I've told you what I know and I am absolutely sure of my facts.

HEGIO: Beyond all doubt?

ARISTOPHONTES: Beyond all possible shadow of doubt. Philocrates and I have been friends since childhood.

HEGIO: What does your friend Philocrates look like? Describe him.

ARISTOPHONTES: Narrow face, sharp nose, light complexion, dark eyes, crisp curly hair, of a reddish tint.

HEGIO: That's the man.

TYNDARUS [*aside*]: And this is the man who's put his foot in it! Woe betide those birch-rods that are going to perish on my back today! . . .

HEGIO: I've been done!

TYNDARUS: Come on, chains . . . run and wrap yourselves round my legs and I'll look after you . . .

HEGIO: Yes, they've done me nicely, haven't they – those two damned prisoners? This one pretending to be the master and the other the slave! They've done me . . . cleaned out the nut and left me with the shell for a memento. Made a fool of me . . . flung the whole paint-pot in my face. But by God, this one is not going to have the last laugh. [*He rushes to his door*] Colaphus! Cordalio! Corax! Come out here, and bring straps with you!

[*Slaves come out.*]

A SLAVE: What's up, sir? You want some wood fetched?

HEGIO: Tie up this criminal.

[*The slaves deal with Tyndarus.*]

TYNDARUS: What's this for? What have I done?

HEGIO: You well may ask – when you're the man who has sowed and hoed, yes and reaped, all this crop of mischief.

TYNDARUS: Haven't you forgotten 'harrowed'? Harrowing always comes before hoeing on the best farms.

HEGIO: Look at him! Still standing up to me, as bold as brass.

TYNDARUS: Why shouldn't a poor innocent and harmless slave stand up for himself, particularly in his master's presence?

HEGIO: Tie up his hands, for goodness' sake – as tightly as you can.

TYNDARUS: Have them cut off, if you like; I'm your property. But I'd like to know what the trouble is, and why you're so angry with me.

HEGIO: Because you . . . have taken it upon yourself . . . with your wicked, deceitful, lying imposture . . . to blow me and my project to smithereens, smash up all my hopes, bring all my plans and calculations to nothing. That's what you've done; you've used a trick to get Philocrates out of my hands. You made me believe he was the slave and you the master – didn't you – you said it was so, and exchanged your names for the purpose?

TYNDARUS: Yes . . . you are quite right . . . I confess it all. We tricked you into letting Philocrates go. I was the inventor and moving spirit of the plot. But still I ask, in all seriousness, can you be angry with me for it?

HEGIO: You did it, and you shall pay for it with the direst penalties.

TYNDARUS: I shall not complain – so long as I am not sent to my death as a criminal. Die I must, if my master does not honour his promise to return; but then what I have done will be remembered to my credit after I am dead – how I saved my master, when a prisoner, out of his captivity and out of the hands of his enemies, and sent him back to freedom, to his country and his father – how I chose to imperil my own life rather than let him die.

HEGIO: I hope you enjoy the credit of it in the next world.

TYNDARUS: To die in an act of courage is not to suffer everlasting death.

HEGIO: Death or everlasting death, I shan't mind what it's called, after I've treated you to the direst tortures and sent you to the stake. Once you're dead, they can say you're still alive, for all I care.

TYNDARUS: You do any such thing to me, and I swear you'll suffer for it, if my master comes back, as I am sure he will.

ARISTOPHONTES [*aside*]: Gods above! The whole thing is clear to me now. My friend Philocrates is free, and at home with his father. Well, I'm glad he is; I don't know anyone to whom I would wish better luck. But I am sorry to have done this poor fellow a bad turn; it's owing to me and my information that he is now in handcuffs.

HEGIO [*to Tyndarus*]: I warned you, didn't I, not to tell me anything but the truth?

TYNDARUS: You did, sir.

HEGIO: Then why did you dare to lie to me?

TYNDARUS: Because the truth would have harmed the man I was trying to help. As it is, my lies have helped to save him.

HEGIO: And will harm you instead.

TYNDARUS: As they should. At all events, I have saved, and am happy to have saved, the young master whom my elder master had put into my care. You think that a crime?

HEGIO: An atrocious crime.

TYNDARUS: Then I must beg to differ from you. I say it was right. Don't you think you would be grateful to any slave of yours who would do the same for your son? Would you not feel like giving that slave his freedom? Would you not call him the best slave you ever had? . . . Would you or wouldn't you?

HEGIO: I dare say I would.

TYNDARUS: Then why are you angry with me?

HEGIO: I am angry that you should have put your duty to him above your duty to me.

TYNDARUS: And I only yesterday taken prisoner, the most recent recruit to your service! Did you expect to be able to train me in twenty-four hours to be a better servant to you than to the man I have spent my life with?

HEGIO: I hope he'll be grateful to you for it. [*To the slaves*] Take him away, and fit him with the stoutest and heaviest chains you can find. [*To Tyndarus*] Then it's the stone-quarries for you; where, to every other man's eight blocks a day, you will produce half as much again, or your number will be Six Hundred . . . whiplashes.

ARISTOPHONTES: Hegio, by god and man, let me entreat you not to send him to his death.

HEGIO: Oh, they'll look after him all right. At night he'll be safely under lock and key, and by day he'll be hewing stone underground. I want him to suffer as long as possible; you don't think I'll let him off with one day?

ARISTOPHONTES: Is that sentence irrevocable?

HEGIO: Irrevocable as death. Off with him! Take him straight to Hippolytus the blacksmith and get a stout pair of fetters clapped on to his legs. Then have him escorted outside the town and handed over to my freedman Cordalus, for the quarries. And say I want him to be given no less consideration . . . than the lowest class of prisoner.

TYNDARUS: Well, I will not plead for my life against your fixed resolve. What risk I stand under now is your risk too. If I die, I shall have no evil to fear in death; if I live, even to a great age, it is only a short time in which to endure the punishment you are putting upon me. Farewell, and be happy, little though you deserve it. And farewell, Aristophontes – as well as you have earned of me; it was you that brought me to this.

HEGIO: Take him away.

TYNDARUS: One last request, Hegio: if Philocrates does come back – please let me see him.

HEGIO: Take him out of my sight this minute, or you are all dead men!

[TYNDARUS *is roughly hustled away.*]

TYNDARUS: Help! Assault! Must I be dragged and pushed . . .

HEGIO: So off to prison with him, where he belongs. It'll be a lesson to those other prisoners not to try any such tricks. If it hadn't been for this young man who put me wise to the situation, they'd have gone on leading me by the nose with their cunning. By heaven, I'll never trust a living soul again; once is enough . . . But the pity of it is, I thought I had bought my son out of captivity; now that hope has vanished. One son I lost long ago, stolen by a slave at four years old, and never a trace of son or slave have I seen since; and now his elder brother is a prisoner of war. Why should I be so cursed? Have I begotten sons only to be left childless in my old age? . . . [*He turns to Aristophontes*] Come this way. You're going back to where you came from [*He hands him over to the guards.*] No one is going to get any of my pity, since there is none anywhere for me. [*He goes into his house.*]

ARISTOPHONTES: I thought that fate was offering me a chance of freedom; now it seems that re-imprisonment is to be my fate. [*He is led away.*]

*

[*It is late afternoon when* ERGASILUS *returns from his promenade, but he returns a changed man.*]

ERGASILUS: Jupiter Almighty be praised! I am saved! I am a made man! Jupiter has blessed me, Jupiter is offering me gain and glory, joy and jollity, feasting and fun and fullness and fatness, food and drink to my belly's content, and happiness ever after. Never again need I go begging to any man. Now I am free to be good to my friends and be a pest to my enemies, for this blessed beautiful day has beatified me with its beatitude. I have become the beneficiary of a stupendous legacy – with no strings to it. And now I'm legging it as fast as I can to old Hegio . . . I've got something for him . . . I'm going to make him a present of everything he could possibly ask from heaven, and more. How shall I do it? . . . I know . . . I'll come on like the slave in a comedy, with my cloak bundled round my neck like this . . . running like blazes to be the first to bring him the news. [*He prepares to re-enter as described, giving an imitation of an excited messenger.*]

[HEGIO *comes out of his house.*]

HEGIO: The more I think about this unhappy affair, the more wretched I feel. That I should have been treated with such impertinence – and couldn't see through the imposture. I shall be the laughing-stock of the town, when it gets about. I shan't be able to go near the market-place without everyone saying: 'There goes that clever old gentleman who allowed himself to be made a mug of.' . . . Who's that over there? Is it Ergasilus? What is he doing with his cloak tucked up like that? . . .

[ERGASILUS *comes bustling in, acting like a person of importance who must not be delayed.*]

ERGASILUS: Hurry up, Ergasilus, hurry up, this is important . . . Make way, there, make way, in the name of the law, out of my way – anyone that's not tired of living! Anybody who stops me will find his head in the dust. [*He pantomimes with fists and elbows.*]

HEGIO [*aside in a corner*]: Here's someone looking for a fight.

ERGASILUS: I mean what I say ... everybody keep to his own side of the street ... no loitering here to talk business. This fist is a cannon-ball, this elbow's a catapult, this shoulder a battering-ram, and a knock with this knee will lay a man flat. Anybody I bump into will be left picking his teeth ... up.

HEGIO: Why all this pugnacity? Extraordinary thing!

ERGASILUS: He won't forget this day or place, or person, for the rest of his life. Anyone stops me – I'll see that he stops living.

HEGIO: He must have got some big idea in his head, with all this bluster; I wonder what it is.

ERGASILUS [*now with the air of a constable controlling the market-place*]: And I don't want anyone getting into trouble unnecessarily, through his own fault; I give you fair warning – stay at home, keep out of my way or I might hurt you.

HEGIO: A full stomach is the only thing that can have given him such a conceit of himself. I'm sorry for the man who had to provide the meal that has made him so cocky.

ERGASILUS [*strutting about, appears to fancy himself as an inspector of nuisances*]: Yes, keep out of my way ... keep out of my way, you pig-farming millers who feed bran to your swine, making such a stink that nobody dare go near your mill; if I catch sight of one of those pigs on the public highway, I'll make bran mash of its owner.

HEGIO: Giving orders like an emperor! He's had a good tuck-in somewhere – a bellyful of assurance.

ERGASILUS: And any fishmonger ... jogging to town on a bone-shaking nag to offer rotten fish for sale and drive everybody out of the market-hall into the street by the smell of it – I'll wipe his face with his own fish-basket, to show him what other people have to put up with. And what about the butcher ... who robs the poor ewes of their little darlings, and then, after pretending to have a young lamb freshly killed for a customer, palms him off with mutton, at twice the price ... and what they call mutton is usually a tough old ram. Let me catch sight of old father ram on the high-road – he and his master will be sorry for themselves!

HEGIO: Issuing magistrates' bye-laws now, if you please! He must have been appointed market-inspector for Aetolia.

ERGASILUS [*returning to his normal character and manner*]: You see, I'm no longer anybody's paid table-companion, but a regular royal king! My ship has come in – with a gigantic cargo of comestibles for my consumption! ... But I must waste no time in carrying the load of good news to Hegio. He's the lucky man now – the luckiest man on earth.

HEGIO: A load of good news for me? What can that be, I wonder? [*Still without observing Hegio,* ERGASILUS *goes to knock at his door.*]

ERGASILUS: Where are you? Anyone there? Will someone open this door!

HEGIO: So now he has come to me for his supper, I suppose.

ERGASILUS: Open this door – both doors – before I batter them to bits.

HEGIO: I shall have to speak to him ... [*Still from a distance, and perhaps partly concealed*] Ergasilus!

ERGASILUS: Who calls me?

HEGIO: Look my way.

ERGASILUS [*cautious, not looking*]: That'll be more than Good Luck ever does, or will do. Who are you?

HEGIO: Look, it's me – Hegio.

ERGASILUS: Well! This is a pleasure ... best of my best friends ... I'm delighted to see you.

HEGIO [*suspecting his effusiveness*]: You didn't seem to want to see me; you've been down to the harbour and found someone else to give you a supper, eh?

ERGASILUS: Shake hands!

HEGIO: Shake hands?

ERGASILUS: Give me your hand – at once – please.

HEGIO [*does so*]: All right.

ERGASILUS: And smile.

HEGIO: Why should I smile?

ERGASILUS: Because I tell you to. Smile and be happy.

HEGIO: Happy! I've more cause for sorrow than happiness.

ERGASILUS: Never mind; I shall soon wipe every spot of sorrow off you. Be of good cheer and rejoice!

HEGIO: Very well, I rejoice; but I don't know what I have to rejoice about.

ERGASILUS: That's better. Now, go and give the orders –

HEGIO: What orders?

ERGASILUS: First, for a big blazing fire –

HEGIO: A blazing fire?

ERGASILUS: That's what I said – a *huge* fire.

HEGIO: Oh indeed, you carnivorous creature! You think I'm going to set my house on fire to suit your pleasure?

ERGASILUS: Now, now, don't be offended. Surely you could oblige me by telling your staff to get the pots on the hob, and all the dishes washed out ... and some bacon on to boil, and ... a feast of good things frizzling on the fire. And send someone out shopping for fish.

HEGIO: The man must be day-dreaming!

ERGASILUS: And another for pork, and lamb, and poultry ...

HEGIO: You know what's good for you – when you can get it!

ERGASILUS: And mussel, and lamprey, and pickled mackerel, and stingray, and tunny ... and cream cheese.

HEGIO: Easier said than ... eaten, in my house, Ergasilus.

ERGASILUS: But you don't think I'm asking all this for *myself*, do you?

HEGIO: At my table you won't starve, I promise you, but you'll get no more than enough; so you had better bring no more than a normal appetite.

ERGASILUS: Ah, go on; I can make you so eager to make a spread, there'll be no holding you.

HEGIO: I, make a spread?

ERGASILUS: You.

HEGIO: My master, are you?

ERGASILUS: No, your benefactor. Will you let me make your happiness complete?

HEGIO: I'd prefer it to complete misery.

ERGASILUS: Give me your hand!

HEGIO [*resigned*]: There it is ...

ERGASILUS: The gods are with you!

HEGIO: I can't say I've noticed it.

ERGASILUS: You would – if you were a *wood*man – ha, ha! But do please tell your people to get the holy vessels ready for the service ... immediately ... and order a prime fat lamb.

HEGIO: What for?

ERGASILUS: For the sacrifice.

HEGIO: To what god, forsooth?

ERGASILUS: To me, bless your heart, to me! I am now your Jupiter
Almighty, your Salvation, your Fortune, your Light, your Glad-
ness, your Felicity; I am one in all, and all in one. Here is the god
whom you must propitiate with fatness.

HEGIO: You're looking for a meal, I take it?

ERGASILUS: That's right, but *I* take it.

HEGIO: Oh well, have your way. I'll consent to anything.

ERGASILUS: Your habit from boyhood, I believe.

HEGIO: And damn your insults.

ERGASILUS: You should be damned . . . damned grateful to me for
the news I have for you. I've just come from the harbour, man . . .
with a load of luck for you. That's why I want to be your guest.

HEGIO [*tired of him*]: Oh go away, you idiot. You've lost your chance;
you're too late.

ERGASILUS: You'd have had more reason to say that if I had come
earlier. As it is, I come to bring you joy; listen – I have seen, a
few minutes ago, at the harbour, your son Philopolemus – seen
him, I tell you, alive, safe and well, in the state launch; and with
him that young Elian prisoner, and your slave Stalagmus, the one
who ran away from you, taking your four-year-old son with him.

HEGIO: The devil damn you! You're making a fool of me.

ERGASILUS: No, Hegio! By Saint Abundance, and may she bestow
her name upon me for ever, I swear, I saw him.

HEGIO: You saw my son?

ERGASILUS: I saw your son – my divine protector.

HEGIO: And that Elian prisoner?

ERGASILUS: Ay, by Apollo.

HEGIO: And that wretched slave Stalagmus who stole my child?

ERGASILUS: Ay, by Cora.

HEGIO: Is it possible?

ERGASILUS: Ay, by Praeneste.

HEGIO: After all this time?

ERGASILUS: Ay, by Signia.

HEGIO: You're positive?

ERGASILUS: Ay, by Frusino.

HEGIO: Please –

ERGASILUS: Ay, by Alatrium. [*He has been invoking the names of*

*towns in the neighbourhood of Rome, supposedly harsh to his native
Greek tongue – and perhaps to be varied, ad lib, at different performances.*]

HEGIO: Why do you take oaths by those outlandish places?

ERGASILUS: Because they are jaw-breakers, like your meals.

HEGIO: Plagues on your head!

ERGASILUS: On yours, if you won't believe the solemn truth I'm
telling you. This Stalagmus – what nationality was he of, when you
last saw him?

HEGIO: Sicilian.

ERGASILUS: Well, he's now a Slav – with a slave's collar to wear . . .
married to a ball and chain, I reckon . . . so he can get children of
his own . . .

HEGIO: For heaven's sake, tell me, on your word of honour, is all
this true?

ERGASILUS: On my word of honour.

HEGIO: Gods above! This is new life for me – if it *is* true.

ERGASILUS: Do you mean to say you still have doubts, when I
have sworn on my solemn oath? All right, then, if an oath isn't
good enough for you, go down to the harbour and see for yourself.

HEGIO: I certainly will. You go and see to things in the house.
Take anything you want, ask for anything, help yourself out of
the store room. I make you my butler.

ERGASILUS: So heaven help me, if my prophecy doesn't come true,
you can trounce me with a truncheon.

HEGIO: And if it does . . . you shall have free maintenance for life.

ERGASILUS: Who will supply that?

HEGIO: I and my son.

ERGASILUS: Promise?

HEGIO: Promise.

ERGASILUS: And I promise you your son has come back.

HEGIO: Get us a good dinner ready! [*He hurries off.*]

ERGASILUS: Have a good walk – and a happy return! . . . So there
he goes . . . and leaves me in supreme control of the victuals! Oho,
gods in heaven! Watch me decapitating carcases! Ho, for the
slaughter among the swine, the pestilence upon the pork! Let
tripes tremble and crackling crumble, butchers and bacon-curers
faint with fatigue! Let . . . no, let us not waste time enumerating all
that may contribute to the stomach's sustenance. I go – to sit in

judgement on the bacon, and put out of their misery the poor hams hanging in the balance. [*He goes into the house.*]

[*A brief interval, punctuated by sounds of commotion within, indicates turmoil in the kitchen, until a* BOY *escapes from the fray.*]

BOY: May all the gods damn that Ergasilus and his greedy guts; and damn all the tribe of cadgers and all who support them from now on. It's chaos, ruin, and riot in that house. The man is like a ravenous wolf; I was afraid he would attack me too. One look at his hungry jaws and gnashing teeth, and I had to run for my life. In he comes and tears down the meat-rack and everything on it; grabs a weapon and chops the collops off three carcases; smashes up pots and dishes, all except the biggest ones. I heard him asking the cook if the brine vats couldn't be used for boiling! Then he goes through all the pantries, breaking down doors and opening cupboards. [*He calls through the door*] Watch him, lads! I'm going to look for the old man and tell him he'd better lay in fresh supplies if he wants any for himself; at the rate this fellow's laying on, everything must be about used up, or soon will be. [*He goes off.*]

*

[HEGIO *is now on his way back from the harbour, and with him come his ransomed son* PHILOPOLEMUS, *the slave* STALAGMUS, *and* PHILOCRATES.]

HEGIO: Now, my son, let me thank Jove and all the gods, as I must, for restoring you to your father – for granting me this relief from the load of sorrow I have had to bear since I lost you – for bringing this man [*Stalagmus*] back into my sight and power – and for the honourable way in which my trust has been rewarded here [*touching Philocrates*].

PHILOPOLEMUS: For my part, I have had enough misery, enough exhausting anguish and lamentation; and I well understand your grief, from what you have told us already since we landed. Have we not other things to think about?

PHILOCRATES: What have you to say to me, sir, now that I have proved my good faith and brought your son back to you and to freedom?

HEGIO: What you have done for me, Philocrates – what you have done for me and my son – is something for which I can never repay you.

PHILOPOLEMUS: Oh yes, you can, father; you will, and I shall, and the gods will show us the way to make a worthy return to our benefactor for his kindness. And this man [*Stalagmus*] too, father, you will now be able to reward as he deserves.

HEGIO: Well, I can say no more. I cannot find words to refuse you anything you ask.

PHILOCRATES: What I ask, sir, is that you will give me the chance to reward the services of the slave whom I left here with you as my surety; he has always been a better friend to me than to himself.

HEGIO: Yes ... in return for your goodness to us, you shall have your wish ... you shall have that and any other thing you desire. And I hope you will not hold it against me if ... in my anger ... I have treated him harshly.

PHILOCRATES: Why, what have you done to him?

HEGIO: When I discovered how I had been tricked ... I had him put in chains and committed to the quarries.

PHILOCRATES: Oh, horror! Oh, the shame – my life to be saved at the cost of such a fate for that good man!

HEGIO: To make amends, I will surrender him into your hands; he is yours, he is free; and you need not pay me a penny for him.

PHILOCRATES: You are kind indeed, sir. Will you have him sent for at once?

HEGIO: I will. [*To servants in the house*] Anyone there? ... Go at once and bring Tyndarus back here ... Now will you two go in? I want to put some questions to this whipping-post, and find out what became of my younger son. Go in and wash yourselves.

PHILOPOLEMUS: Will you come this way, Philocrates?

PHILOCRATES: Thank you. [*They go in.*]

HEGIO [*to Stalagmus*]: Now then ... step over here, my good man ... my pretty slave ...

STALAGMUS: If a gentleman like you can tell such lies, what am I supposed to do? I may have been good-looking in my time – pretty if you like; but a good man, never; nor good for anything, and never will be. Don't expect me to be any good to you.

HEGIO: At any rate you must have a good idea of what sort of position you are in now. But if you can tell the truth, you may be able to make a bad business slightly better. Speak openly and honestly . . . though I doubt if you ever did an open and honest action in your life.

STALAGMUS: I've admitted it, haven't I? You can't make me blush by harping on it.

HEGIO: Oh, I'll make you blush before I've finished with you! I'll make you blush from head to foot.

STALAGMUS: Ha! That means a flogging, doesn't it? As if I wasn't used to it! You can cut the cackle; just tell me what you're offering, and you may get what you're asking for.

HEGIO: You have a gift of the gab, I see. But I would be obliged if you would restrain it for the present.

STALAGMUS: With pleasure.

HEGIO [aside]: He's certainly not the amenable youth that he was . . . Well, then, to come to the point, give me your attention and answer my questions carefully. And remember that truthful answers will somewhat ameliorate your condition.

STALAGMUS: To hell with that. Do you think I don't know what I deserve?

HEGIO: Maybe, but you have a chance of escaping some, if not all, of the consequences.

STALAGMUS: I shall escape precious little, I know. There'll be consequences enough, and I shall have earned them. I ran away, I kidnapped your son, and I sold him.

HEGIO: To whom?

STALAGMUS: To Theodoromides Polyplusius, in Elis, for six hundred drachmas.

HEGIO: Theo . . .? Gods in heaven! That's the father of my prisoner, Philocrates!

STALAGMUS: Of course he is; I know the young man better than you do – seen him dozens of times.

HEGIO: Jove Almighty, save me, and give me back my son! [He runs to the house] Philocrates! Come here, for your sweet life's sake! Come out here, I want you!

[PHILOCRATES appears.]

PHILOCRATES: Here I am, sir; what do you want?

HEGIO: This man says he sold my son to your father in Elis for six hundred drachmas.

92

PHILOCRATES: How long ago was that?

STALAGMUS: It'll be nearly twenty years now.

PHILOCRATES: He's lying.

STALAGMUS: One of us is. It's a fact, anyway, that your father gave you a four-year-old boy for your very own, when you were about the same age.

PHILOCRATES: What was the boy's name? Tell me that, if your story is true.

STALAGMUS: He was generally known as Laddie; and later your family gave him the name of Tyndarus.

PHILOCRATES: How is it I don't know you?

STALAGMUS: People usually forget, or pretend not to know, someone whose acquaintance they don't value.

PHILOCRATES: Are you telling me that the boy you sold to my father, and the boy who was given to me, are one and the same person?

STALAGMUS: That's right; this gentleman's son.

HEGIO: And do you know if the poor fellow is still alive?

STALAGMUS: I got my money for him: I never bothered what happened to him after that.

HEGIO [to Philocrates]: What do you think?

PHILOCRATES: Well, of course, it's my slave Tyndarus who is your son, if this man's story is to be believed! Tyndarus and I grew up together; from boy to man he had a decent and honourable upbringing.

HEGIO: If you are right, then I am at once the happiest and unhappiest of men. I cannot bear to think of the terrible thing I have done to him, if he is my son! To have done so much more, yet so much less, than I had the right to do! My heart bleeds for what I have made him suffer; oh that I could undo what has been done! . . . And here he comes . . . in what a state for a brave and honest man!

[TYNDARUS *is brought in by guards, shackled and carrying a crowbar; he is allowed a moment to rest and recover at the far side of the scene.*]

TYNDARUS: I've often seen pictures of the tortures of the damned in hell; but there's no hell to equal the place where I've been, in those quarries. Down there they make a man work till he's incapable of feeling tired any more. As soon as I got there, they gave me this crow to amuse myself with – like the dicky-birds and

ducklings that rich men's children are given to play with! ...
Hullo, there's the master outside the house ... and ... why, it's
my young master back from Elis!

HEGIO: My son ... my long awaited son ... welcome!

TYNDARUS: Son? Why son, for God's sake? ... Oh yes, I get it ...
you call yourself my father, because like a parent you are bringing
me into the daylight.

PHILOCRATES: Welcome, Tyndarus.

TYNDARUS: Welcome to you, the cause of all this misery.

PHILOCRATES: But now, I promise you, you're going to be a free
man and a rich man. This is your father. And this ... is the slave
who stole you from your father when you were four years old,
took you away and sold you to my father, for six hundred drachmas. It was then that my father gave you to me, a little slave of
my very own, and of my own age. We have just brought this man
back from Elis, and he has told us the whole story.

TYNDARUS [hardly taking this in]: But ... what of Hegio's son, whom
you went to –

PHILOCRATES: He's here, in the house ... your own brother ...

TYNDARUS: You mean ...? You've brought him back ... Hegio's
captive son?

PHILOCRATES: We have; as I say, he's in the house now.

TYNDARUS: Thank God; you've done a fine job, sir.

PHILOCRATES: But listen: Hegio is *your* father too. This thief stole
you from here when you were a child.

TYNDARUS: Did he? I'll get him hanged for that, now we're both
grown up.

PHILOCRATES: He deserves it.

TYNDARUS: He does, and I'll serve him as he deserves, by God! ...
So [now looking more closely at Hegio] is it really true ... you are my
father?

HEGIO: I am indeed, my son.

TYNDARUS: I seem to remember now ... yes, now it's coming back
to me ... I think I can remember, vaguely, hearing people call
my father Hegio.

HEGIO: I am Hegio ... [He embraces his son.]

PHILOCRATES: But look at those chains, sir; isn't it time you took
the weight off your son and put it on ... your son's slave?

HEGIO: Of course, that is the first thing we must do. Come in, and we'll send for the blacksmith, to get the chains off you and present them to this fellow.

STALAGMUS: I shall appreciate that; they'll be the only thing I possess in the world!

EXEUNT

*

EPILOGUE

Spectators, you have seen today
A highly edifying play:
No sex, no secret love affairs,
No baby smuggled in backstairs.
Here is no fraud or knavery,
No boy buys girl from slavery
Behind his father's back. Such plays
Are far from common nowadays.
Playwrights no longer use the pen
To improve the minds of decent men.
If we have pleased, not wearied you,
   If you think virtue worth reward,
Kind friends, you all know what to do . . .
   Just let us know it – and applaud.

THE BROTHERS MENAECHMUS
(MENAECHMI)

INTRODUCTORY NOTE TO
THE BROTHERS MENAECHMUS

As the prototype of Shakespeare's *The Comedy of Errors*, the *Menaechmi* of Plautus has gained a special place in the attention of English readers, a place of privilege perhaps rather higher than is justified by its merits. Neither play, needless to say, is the brightest jewel in its author's crown, but their existence provides the closest link of which we have evidence between our own poet and the father of European comedy. The fact that no English version of *Menaechmi* is known to have existed prior to the production of *The Comedy of Errors* leaves enticingly open the question whether Shakespeare's acquaintance with Plautus was direct or indirect. It is more than likely that he had the opportunity, and ability, at least to dip into the Latin; on the other hand, there is nothing in his version of the comedy that could not have been derived from a mere second-hand hearing of the plot of *Menaechmi*.

Be that as it may, critics have employed themselves in comparing, and coming to different conclusions about, the merits of these two comedies. Shakespeare enlarged the scope of the play by providing the twin masters with twin servants (taking a cue perhaps from the *Amphitryo* of Plautus) and by adding a note of gravity or pathos in the situation of the wives and of Aegeon. Plautus is content with one pair of twins and the merely farcical possibilities of the impossibly identical resemblance between them; he was right, it may be felt, in thinking that any concession to serious reflection would make the improbabilities of the affair all the more conspicuous. It is, however, something of a weakness in the comedy that both the brothers are equally callous in their treatment of the women; there is no hint of censure upon the infidelity of Menaechmus, and Sosicles first appears as a staid and virtuous young man, only to be easily tempted into debauch and theft.

The character of the 'parasite' (for which see some remarks in the foreword to *Captivi*) is here effectively employed as a link in the chain of events, and not merely as a mouthpiece for the traditional 'gluttony' jokes. His name, Peniculus (*pencil*), means 'little brush', i.e. a crumb-brush for sweeping a table clean; I call him 'Sponge', which may convey the appropriate suggestion of his nature and occupation.

The Prologue bears signs of confusion and incompleteness. For this reason I have thought it a permissible improvement to transfer its last five lines (72–6) to an earlier place (after 55) where the speaker is interrupting his narrative with humorous asides about himself and the stage-setting.

CHARACTERS

MENAECHMUS   *a young married man living in Epidamnus*

SOSICLES   *his twin brother, also generally known by the name Menaechmus*

PENICULUS   *nicknamed The Sponge, a cadging friend of Menaechmus*

EROTIUM   *Menaechmus's mistress*

MESSENIO   *slave of Sosicles*

CYLINDRUS   *cook in the house of Erotium*

A MAID   *in the house of Erotium*

THE WIFE   *of Menaechmus*

THE FATHER   *of Menaechmus's wife*

A DOCTOR

Slaves and baggage-porters

*

The scene is at Epidamnus, outside the houses of Menaechmus and Erotium.
A Prologue is spoken by an unnamed character.

THE BROTHERS MENAECHMUS

PROLOGUE:

First, friends, a hearty welcome to you all –
And to myself. My business is to call
Plautus before your . . . ears, not eyes, today;
So please attend to what he has to say.
And please attend to me, while I unfold,
Briefly, the tale that here is to be told.

You know our comic writers have a way
Of claiming that what happens in the play
Takes place in Athens, that it may appear
To have a truly Grecian atmosphere.
For this play's setting – you must take my word
It happened in . . . the place where it occurred.
The story breathes a Grecian air, you'll see,
Though not of Attica, but Sicily.
So much for preface to my argument.
Now for the argument – which I present
In generous measure, bags and bushels packed
And running over, a whole barn in fact,
Because I have so much to *give away*
In setting out the story of the play.

In Syracuse a merchant, it appears,
Begat twin sons, who from their earliest years
Were so alike that neither nurse nor mother
Could ever tell one baby from the other,
So little was the difference between them,
As I was told by somebody who'd seen them –
I never saw them, I would have you know.
Now, when the boys were seven years old or so,

Their father planned a business trip abroad,
Loaded a ship and, with one child aboard,
Sailed to Tarentum, leaving the twin brother
At home, in Syracusa, with his mother.
Tarentum was *en fête* when they got there;
Hundreds of folk had come to see the fair.
And wandering in the crowd, the little lad
One day got separated from his dad.
An Epidamnian trader found the child
And took him off to Epidamnus. Wild
With desperate grief at losing his dear son,
The father, ere a few more days were done,
Fell sick and died upon Tarentine land.
When in due course the tidings came to hand
At Syracuse, and the grandfather knew
His son was dead, his grandson missing too,
He changed the name of the surviving brother
(Because, in fact, he much preferred the other)
And *Sosicles*, the one at home, became
Menaechmus – which had been his brother's name.
That was the name of the grandfather too
(I do know that, from hearing much ado
About a debt he owed). I hope that's clear . . .
But don't forget . . . the twins, when they appear,
Will both be called Menaechmus. Now again
I move to Epidamnus [*He takes a few steps*] to explain
The rest of this affair . . . [*He breaks off, and
continues prosaically.*]

Anybody got any commissions for me in Epidamnus? Now's the
time to say so, if you have. Don't be afraid. Give me your orders –
and of course the necessary funds for the business. No money, no
business. And what happens to your money if you give it me is no
business of yours either ! . . . [*Indicating the scene on the stage*] All this
is Epidamnus – as long as this play lasts, anyway. In another play
it will be another place, I expect. Same with the houses – they may
be occupied by a young man one day, an old man the next; rich
man, poor man, beggarman, king, client, or clairvoyant . . . But to
get back to where I was – while still remaining where I am ! . . .

This Epidamnian trader, he who stole
The boy, was childless; money was his whole
Life and existence, but he had no son
To leave it to when his day's work was done.
So he adopts the boy, and when of age
Gives him a wife, dowry, and heritage.
He died. While on a country walk, they say,
Outside the city, on a stormy day,
Trying to cross a torrent, in he fell;
And thus the thief was carried off to hell,
Who carried off the boy! The adopted heir
Inherited a large estate, and there [*showing the house*]
Menaechmus lives today. Now watch; for here
You'll see the twin from Syracuse appear
In Epidamnus, with one slave behind him,
To search for his twin brother – and to find him.

*

[PENICULUS *enters from the town, about to pay a visit to the house of Menaechmus.*]

PENICULUS: My name is Peniculus – or Sponge, as the young
fellows call me – Sponge, because whenever I eat I wipe the table
clean! . . .

You know, it's ridiculous for people to throw prisoners into
chains and put fetters on runaway slaves – at least I think so; because
if a man is in trouble, and you give him more trouble, he'll be all
the more anxious to escape and commit more crimes. They always
get themselves out of their chains by some means or other; if
they're in fetters, they file away the ring or smash the bolt off with
a stone; it's child's play. If you really want to keep a man from
running away, the best way to do it is with food and drink; keep
his nose down to a full table; give him anything he asks for, every
day; I guarantee he'll never run away then, not even if he's on a
capital charge; you'll have no difficulty in keeping him, as long as
you keep him in that sort of confinement. Food – it's a marvellously
effective kind of strait-jacket; the more you stretch it the closer it
clings . . .

Take me, now; I'm just on my way to my friend Menaechmus. I've been his bond-slave for some time now, and I'm still offering myself voluntarily to imprisonment. I tell you, that man doesn't just give you a meal; he builds you up, makes you a new man; there isn't a doctor to touch him. That's the sort of host he is; has a tremendous appetite himself, gives banquets fit for Harvest Festival, piles the tables so high with culinary contraptions, you have to stand on your couch to reach anything off the top.

But alas, as far as I am concerned, there has been an intermission for many days past. All this time I have been housebound and homebound in the company of my own dear ones – and everything I buy or eat comes *very* dear, I can assure you! Moreover, I'm now running out of my dearly bought supplies. So I'm paying a call on my dear patron . . . Ah, the door's opening . . . and it's Menaechmus himself coming out . . . [*He retires to a corner.*]

[MENAECHMUS, *a young man, appears at the door of his house, finishing off an altercation with his wife, who is just inside.*]

MENAECHMUS: . . . And if you weren't such a mean, stupid, obstinate, and impossible female, you wouldn't want to do anything that you see your husband dislikes . . . If you go on like this any longer, I'll divorce you and pack you off to your father . . . Every time I choose to go out of doors you try to stop me and call me back, pester me with questions, what am I going to fetch, what have I brought back, what did I do when I was out. I might as well have married an immigration officer, the way I have to declare every blessed thing I've done or am doing . . . I've spoiled you, that's what it is. But I give you due warning: in consideration of my providing you with servants, food, clothes, jewellery, household linen, and finery, everything you could possibly need, you will kindly behave yourself or there'll be trouble – and you will cease spying on your husband's movements . . . [*Turning away from the door*] Come to that, if you want something to spy on, you can have it . . . I'm going to take my girl out tonight and get an invitation to supper somewhere.

PENICULUS: He may think it's his wife he's telling off, but I'm the one he's getting at. If he's not going to be home for supper, that's one in the eye for me, not his wife.

MENAECHMUS: Good; that's done it! My language has frightened her from the door. Now then, all you *loving* husbands ... aren't you going to load me with gifts and congratulations for my heroic fight? ... [*He now reveals that he is wearing one of his wife's gowns under his cloak*] Look, I've just stolen this gown of my wife's and I'm taking it to my girl! That's the way to treat 'em ... that's a slap in the face for the sharp-eyed wardress! A beautiful, neat, ingenious masterly trick, my friends! That's going to cost the wretched woman something – or cost me, for that matter, since I've got to say goodbye to it ... Ah well, let's say I've filched some booty from the enemy for the benefit of my friends.

PENICULUS: What about me, boy? Do I get a share of the booty?

MENAECHMUS [*hearing but not seeing him*]: Damn it! Someone else spying on me?

PENICULUS: No, someone protecting you; don't be alarmed.

MENAECHMUS: Who's there?

PENICULUS: Me.

MENAECHMUS: Oh, it's you, my old friend On-the-Spot, my dear Mr Come-in-Time. How are you?

PENICULUS: Very well, thanks, how are you? [*They shake hands.*]

MENAECHMUS: What are you doing now?

PENICULUS: Holding my guardian angel by the hand.

MENAECHMUS: You couldn't have found me at a more favourable moment.

PENICULUS: I know. I'm like that. I can tell a favourable moment to the nearest second.

MENAECHMUS: Would you like to see a sight to gladden your eyes?

PENICULUS: It depends who cooked it. Show me the leavings and I'll tell you if there was anything wrong with the cooking.

MENAECHMUS: Did you ever see a mural painting ... the eagle abducting Ganymede, or Venus seducing Adonis?

PENICULUS: Often. But why should such paintings interest me particularly?

MENAECHMUS [*posing in a graceful attitude in the female gown*]: Behold ... do I look like anything like them?

PENICULUS: What on earth are you dressed up like that for?

MENAECHMUS: Say I'm a smart fellow.

PENICULUS [*ignoring the inexplicable eccentricity*]: Where are we going to eat?

MENAECHMUS: First say what I told you to say.

PENICULUS [*obediently*]: You're a smart fellow.

MENAECHMUS: Is that all you can say?

PENICULUS: And a most amusing fellow.

MENAECHMUS: Anything else?

PENICULUS: Good Lord, no, nothing else – until I know what it's in aid of. You've got some quarrel with your wife, I suspect, so I shall have to be careful where I tread.

MENAECHMUS: Don't worry; we're going to bury our troubles and burn up the day in some place the wife doesn't know about.

PENICULUS: Come on, then; now you're talking sense. Say the word and I'll light the pyre; the day's already dead down to the waist. What are we waiting for?

MENAECHMUS: Only for you to stop talking.

PENICULUS: Knock my eye out if I utter another word except at your orders.

MENAECHMUS: Come away from this door.

PENICULUS [*moving a little, but keeping an anxious eye on the house door*]: All right.

MENAECHMUS [*also cautiously watching the door*]: Farther this way.

PENICULUS: If you like.

MENAECHMUS: Come on, there's nothing to be afraid of. You can turn your back on the lioness's den.

PENICULUS: What about you? You'd do well as a chariot-racer.

MENAECHMUS: Why a chariot-racer?

PENICULUS: The way you keep looking over your shoulder to see if the enemy is gaining on you . . .

MENAECHMUS: Look, tell me something –

PENICULUS: Me? I'll tell you anything you like, or deny it if you prefer.

MENAECHMUS: Are you good at smelling? Can you identify a thing by its scent?

PENICULUS: Why? Do you want to propose me for the College of Augurs?

MENAECHMUS: Smell this dress . . . What does it smell of? [*Offering him the skirt of the gown*] You don't want to?

PENICULUS: I'd rather smell the upper part of a woman's garment; elsewhere the nose detects a somewhat unwashed odour.

MENAECHMUS: Smell this part, then ... Oh, you *are* a fussy man.

PENICULUS: I should hope so.

MENAECHMUS: Well, what does it smell of?

PENICULUS: It smells of ... [*knowing Menaechmus's intentions*] stolen goods, secret amours, and a free lunch. I hope there'll be –

MENAECHMUS: Right you are! Lunch is the word. This gown is going to my girl Erotium, and I'll have lunch laid on at her place, for her, for me, and for you.

PENICULUS: Good enough.

MENAECHMUS: There we will carouse until tomorrow's dawn.

PENICULUS: Grand! It's a pleasure to listen to you. Shall I knock at the door? [*That is, of the neighbouring house where Erotium lives.*]

MENAECHMUS: Please do ... No, wait.

PENICULUS [*disappointed*]: Oh, now you've pushed the loving cup a mile off.

MENAECHMUS: Knock gently.

PENICULUS: Why? The doors aren't made of Samian pottery, are they? [*He thumps the door.*]

[*The door immediately opens and* EROTIUM *is seen to be about to come out.*]

MENAECHMUS: Wait, wait, for goodness sake! Here she comes herself ... Oh, see how the sun is dimmed beside the radiance of that lovely person!

EROTIUM: Menaechmus, my sweetheart! Welcome!

PENICULUS: No welcome for me?

EROTIUM: You don't count.

PENICULUS: Like on the battlefield – camp-followers don't count.

MENAECHMUS: That's right; and today I have planned an engagement for myself at your house.

EROTIUM: You shall have it.

MENAECHMUS: He and I are going to have a drinking battle; and whichever proves himself the superior fighter on the bottle-field, becomes your conscript. You shall be umpire and choose which you will have for your – night. Oh my darling, when I look at you, how I hate my wife!

EROTIUM: Meanwhile you apparently feel compelled to wear her clothes. What is this?

MENAECHMUS: Spoils from my wife for your adornment, my rose.

EROTIUM: That puts you head and shoulders above any other of my suitors, darling.

PENICULUS: Just like her sort, to talk pretty when she sees something to get her hands on . . . If you loved him, my dear, you ought to have bitten his nose off by now.

MENAECHMUS [removing his cloak to get rid of the gown]: Hold this, Peniculus. I must hand over my promised gift.

PENICULUS: Give it here. But wait a bit; won't you give us a dance in that thing?

MENAECHMUS: Me dance? Are you out of your mind?

PENICULUS: One of us is, I'm not sure which. All right, if you won't dance, take it off.

MENAECHMUS: I risked my life getting hold of this today . . . I doubt if Hercules ran such a risk when abstracting Hippolyta's girdle . . . Here you are, a present for the only girl in the world who likes to do what I like.

EROTIUM [taking the gown]: You set an example to all true lovers.

PENICULUS: All who are hell-bent to ruin themselves.

MENAECHMUS: I bought it for my wife a year ago; four hundred drachmas it cost me.

PENICULUS: Four hundred down the drain, as I figure it.

MENAECHMUS: Now then, do you know what I want you to do for me?

EROTIUM: I know. I'll see to it.

MENAECHMUS: Good. Tell your people to prepare lunch for the three of us – and send to the market for something toothsome . . . say, pork kidneys, or smoked ham, or pig's head . . . something of that kind, a nicely done dish to give me a vulture's appetite. And the sooner the better.

EROTIUM: You shall have it, my love.

MENAECHMUS: We'll get off to town. We shan't be long; and then we can do some drinking while the things are cooking.

EROTIUM: Come back as soon as you like. We'll be ready for you.

MENAECHMUS: Don't waste any time, then. Come along, Sponge . . . [He hurries off.]

PENICULUS: I'm with you ... and watching you. I wouldn't lose sight of you today for all the treasures of heaven. [*He follows.*]

EROTIUM [*at her door*]: Tell Cylindrus I want him out here at once, please.

[CYLINDRUS, *her cook, appears.*]

Take a basket, and some money. Here ... here's three pounds for you.

CYLINDRUS: Three pounds ... that's right, ma'am.

EROTIUM: Get us something to eat; enough for three, please; not too little, and not too much.

CYLINDRUS: Three. What kind of three?

EROTIUM: I and Menaechmus and his table-companion.

CYLINDRUS: That's more like ten. These table-companions can easily do the work of eight men each.

EROTIUM: I've told you how many guests there are; go and do your business.

CYLINDRUS: Very good, ma'am. Consider the meal cooked, call the guests in.

EROTIUM: Don't be long.

CYLINDRUS: I'll be back in two shakes.

[*He hurries off to market.* EROTIUM *goes indoors.*]

*

[*The twin* MENAECHMUS, *who exactly resembles his brother and was originally called* SOSICLES (*as we shall call him*), *has now arrived by sea and comes from the harbour with his slave* MESSENIO *and other slaves carrying baggage.*]

SOSICLES: Messenio, I don't believe sea-farers can ever enjoy a greater pleasure than their first sight of land from the ocean.

MESSENIO: For my part, I'd say the pleasure would be greater if it were your own homeland you were sighting. Can you tell me, sir, what we're doing now in Epidamnus? Are we going to circulate round all the islands, like the sea itself?

SOSICLES: I have come to look for my twin brother.

MESSENIO: And how long do you propose to go on looking for him? We've been at it now for six years. The Danube, Spain, Massilia, Illyria, all over the Adriatic, the Greek colonies, and the

III

entire coast of Italy – we've visited the lot. You would have found a needle by this time, long ago, if it were there to find. We're looking for a dead man among the living; if he were alive, we should have found him long before this.

SOSICLES: Very well, then, I am looking for someone who can give me certain news, someone who can say he knows for certain that my brother is dead. If it be so, I shall search no longer; but short of that, I shall never give up the quest as long as I live. No one but I knows how much I love him.

MESSENIO: Might as well look for a knotted bullrush ... Why don't we go home, master? We're not writing a book of our travels, are we?

SOSICLES: Kindly do what you're told, eat what you're given, and mind your manners. I don't want any more of your impudence; and I'm not arranging my plans to suit you.

MESSENIO [aside]: There you are, you see. That's to remind me I'm a slave. He puts it in a nutshell. All the same, I can't hold my tongue ... Sir, Menaechmus, I've just been looking at our purse, and I must say there's a bit of a drought in the reservoir. As far as I can see, if you don't make tracks for home, you'll be down to nothing, and then ... looking for your brother ... will be rather a bother. Do you know what sort of people live here? In Epidamnus you'll find all the worst drunkards and debauchees; the place is full of sharks and swindlers; and as for the harlots, I'm told they're the most seductive in the world. That's why it's called Epidamnus – anyone that lands up here is doomed to damnation.

SOSICLES: I'll be careful. Give me that purse.

MESSENIO: What do you want with the purse?

SOSICLES: I don't trust you after what you just said.

MESSENIO: Me? What are you afraid of?

SOSICLES: Lest you see me damned in Epidamnus. You're rather too fond of the women, Messenio; and I'm rather quick-tempered, and not always responsible for my actions. If I take charge of the money, it'll save us from both dangers – you from putting a foot wrong, and me from having to be angry with you.

MESSENIO: Take it, and welcome. Mind you don't lose it.

[CYLINDRUS *returns from market with his provisions.*]

CYLINDRUS: I've done some good shopping ... got just what I

wanted. I shall have a nice meal to offer the party ... Hullo, there *is* Menaechmus! Oh dear, I shall catch it ... guests waiting outside the door before I can get back with the provisions. I'd better go and speak to him ... Good morning, sir.

SOSICLES: Who in the world may you be?

CYLINDRUS: Who am I? Don't you know me, then?

SOSICLES: I swear I don't.

CYLINDRUS [*passing this off with a grin*]: Are your fellow-guests with you?

SOSICLES: What fellow-guests?

CYLINDRUS: Your table-companion.

SOSICLES: My table-companion?

CYLINDRUS [*aside*]: The man is surely off his head.

MESSENIO: Didn't I tell you the place was swarming with swindlers?

SOSICLES: Who is this table-companion of mine you're expecting, young fellow?

CYLINDRUS: Your ... Sponge.

MESSENIO: Sponge? I've got that here in the kitbag.

CYLINDRUS: I'm afraid you're a bit early for lunch. I've only just got back from market.

SOSICLES [*kindly, thinking he has to do with a lunatic*]: I say, young man, can you tell me how much a pig costs here – a perfect one, suitable for sacrifice?

CYLINDRUS: About ... two drachmas.

SOSICLES: Here's two drachmas for you ... go and make the offerings and get yourself absolved, at my expense. It's clear you must be a lunatic, whoever you are, to come pestering a perfect stranger.

CYLINDRUS: Well! I'm Cylindrus. Surely you know me by name?

SOSICLES: You may be Cylindrus or Coriendrus or what you please, but go to hell. I don't know you and I don't want to know you.

CYLINDRUS: Well, I know you; your name is Menaechmus.

SOSICLES: Now you're talking like a sane man, I will say. That is my name. But where have you met me?

CYLINDRUS: Where have I met you? Aren't you the lover of my mistress Erotium?

SOSICLES: I certainly am not, and I haven't the slightest idea who you are.

CYLINDRUS: Not know who I am, after all the times I've served you with drink at your parties at our place?

MESSENIO: God help me! Why haven't I got something to break this fellow's head with?

SOSICLES: How can you have served me with drink, when I've never seen or set foot in Epidamnus till this day?

CYLINDRUS: You haven't?

SOSICLES: I swear I haven't.

CYLINDRUS: Aren't you the occupant of that house there?

SOSICLES: May the gods damn the occupants of that house there!

CYLINDRUS [aside]: It's he that's off his head, cursing himself like that ... Excuse me, Menaechmus –

SOSICLES: What now?

CYLINDRUS: If you want my advice, I think you should take that two drachmas you offered me just now ... it's you that must be out of your mind, sir, calling down curses on your own head ... the best thing would be to buy a pig for yourself ...

MESSENIO: By all the gods, this fellow's unbearable. I'm sick and tired of him.

CYLINDRUS [chatting on cheerfully to the audience]: It's just his way; he often pulls my leg like this. He can be ever so amusing – when his wife's not there ... I say, Menaechmus ... Menaechmus!

SOSICLES: Well?

CYLINDRUS: Do you think I've got enough food here for the three of you – or should I get some more – for you and the lady and your table-companion?

SOSICLES: What lady, what table-companion are you talking about?

MESSENIO: What devil has got into you, man, to pester my master like this?

CYLINDRUS: I'm not concerned with you. I don't know you. I'm talking to this gentleman. I know him.

MESSENIO: I know you're a raving lunatic, and that's a fact.

CYLINDRUS: Anyway, I must go and get these things cooked. It won't take long, so don't go far away. With your leave, sir –

SOSICLES: You have my leave to go and be hanged.

CYLINDRUS: And you'd better go and ... lie down, while I apply the powers of Vulcan to these articles. I'll go in, then, and let Erotium know you're standing out here ... then she can ask you in . . . so you needn't hang about outside the door . . . [*He goes into the house.*]

SOSICLES: Has he gone at last? He has. Upon my word, Messenio, I begin to perceive that you spoke only too truly.

MESSENIO: You'll have to be careful, sir. I shouldn't wonder if this is some harlot's house, from what that mad fellow said.

SOSICLES: But how extraordinary that he should know my name!

MESSENIO: Bless you, no, nothing extraordinary in that. It's a way these women have; they send their slave boys or girls down to the port, and if there's a foreign ship in, they find out where she's from, and the master's name and everything; then they freeze on to him, and never let him out of their sight; and once they've got him hooked they send him home squeezed dry. And if I'm not mistaken, there's a pirate ship in *that* port at this moment [*pointing to Erotium's house*] and we'd do well to give her a wide berth.

SOSICLES [*sceptical*]: I'm sure that's very good advice.

MESSENIO: I'll believe it's good advice when I see you taking good heed of it.

SOSICLES: Say no more now, I hear the door opening. Let's see who comes out. [*He hides in some corner.*]

MESSENIO: I'll get rid of this meantime [*the bag he is carrying*]. Hey, galley-slaves, look after this stuff. [*He joins* SOSICLES.]

[EROTIUM *appears at the door, speaking to someone within.*]

EROTIUM: No, don't shut the door; leave it as it is. See that everything is ready in there; make sure we have all that we need. Spread the couches and burn some perfumes; a gentleman likes to have things nice and comfortable. The more comfortable they are, the worse for his pocket, and the better for us! . . . The cook said my friend was waiting out here; where has he got to, I wonder? . . . [*Spying Sosicles*] Ah, there he is – my most valuable and helpful friend! And of course he gets the consideration he deserves here; he's quite at home in this house . . . I'll go nearer and speak first . . . Darling! Why in the world are you standing out in the street, when the door's wide open for you? You know this house is more of a home to you than your own. We've got everything ready as you ordered, just as you like it; you won't be kept waiting. Lunch is prepared as you wished; we can sit down to it as soon as you like.

SOSICLES: Who is the woman talking to?

EROTIUM: She is talking to you, of course.

SOSICLES [*coming further into view*]: And what have you, or did you ever have, to do with me?

EROTIUM: Is it not you, above all other men, whom by the will of Venus I must most honour and worship, as you well deserve, since it is to you alone and to your generous hand I owe all my good fortune?

SOSICLES: The woman is either insane or intoxicated, Messenio. I've never seen her before, and she greets me as her dearest friend.

MESSENIO: What did I tell you? That's the way things are here. This is only a shower of leaves; you'll have trees falling on your head if we stay here three days. She's just like all the harlots here, experts at wheedling the money out of you. Let me have a word with her . . . Hey, woman, listen to me.

EROTIUM: I beg your pardon?

MESSENIO: Where have you seen this gentleman before?

EROTIUM: In the same place where he has often seen me, here, in Epidamnus.

MESSENIO: Here in Epidamnus? A man who has never set foot in the place till this day?

EROTIUM: Huh! Very funny! . . . Won't you come in, Menaechmus darling? You'll be much more comfortable inside.

SOSICLES: Blest if she doesn't call me by my right name too! I'm hanged if I know what this means.

MESSENIO: It means she's got wind of that purse you're carrying.

SOSICLES: Yes, that's very thoughtful of you, by Jove. Here, you take it. I'll soon find out whether it's me or my purse she's in love with.

EROTIUM: Come along, let's go in to lunch.

SOSICLES: It's very kind of you; but . . . please excuse me.

EROTIUM: Then why did you ask me to cook a lunch for you, not an hour ago?

SOSICLES: I? Asked you to cook lunch for me?

EROTIUM: Of course you did; for you and your table-companion.

SOSICLES: Damn it, what table-companion? . . . The woman is undoubtedly mad.

EROTIUM: Your friend The Sponge.

SOSICLES: Sponge? The one I clean my shoes with?

EROTIUM: Oh you know, the man who was with you just now –
when you brought me the robe you'd stolen from your wife.

SOSICLES: What *is* all this? I gave you a robe – stolen from my wife?
Are you in your right mind? . . . This woman must be dreaming
on her feet, like a horse.

EROTIUM: Why do you have to mock at everything I say, and deny
everything you've done? ·

SOSICLES: Just kindly tell me what it is that I am supposed to have
done and am denying.

EROTIUM: You denied that you had given me, this very morning, a
robe belonging to your wife.

SOSICLES: And I still deny it. What's more, I haven't got a wife and
never had one, and I have never before in the whole of my life
put a foot inside the gate of this town. I have had lunch on board
my ship, then I came ashore and here I've met you.

EROTIUM [*now thinking he must be mad*]: Oh, just think of it! Oh dear,
this is terrible . . . What do you mean by a ship?

SOSICLES [*explaining whimsically*]: Well, it's a sort of a wooden
affair . . . gets a lot of knocking about, nailing and banging with a
hammer . . . full of bolts and pegs, like a furrier's drying-frame.

EROTIUM: Oh for heaven's sake, stop joking and come in with me.

SOSICLES: My good woman, it's someone else you're looking for,
not me.

EROTIUM: As if I didn't know you perfectly well! You're Menaechmus, son of Moschus; born, by all accounts, in Sicily, the country
which was ruled first by Agathocles, then by Phintias, then by
Liparo, and after his death by Hiero who is the present king.

SOSICLES: All that is perfectly correct, madam.

MESSENIO: Jupiter! Do you think she comes from those parts? She
seems to know all about you.

SOSICLES: Upon my word, I don't think I can go on refusing her
invitation.

MESSENIO: Mind what you're about. You're done for if you cross
that doorstep.

SOSICLES: Shut up. This is going to be all right. I'll agree to everything she says, in return for a little hospitality . . . [*He returns to
Erotium, confidentially*] Look, my dear, I had a good reason for
contradicting you just now. I was afraid this man of mine might

tell my wife about the dress and about our lunch party. I'm ready to come in as soon as you like.

EROTIUM: Are you going to wait for your friend?

SOSICLES: I am not; he can go to blazes; and if he does come I don't want him admitted.

EROTIUM: That'll suit me all right! But there's something else I'd like you to do for me, darling.

SOSICLES: Anything you say, beloved.

EROTIUM: That robe you've given me – could you take it to a dressmaker to have it refashioned with some improvements which I would like added?

SOSICLES: Of course I will. That's a good idea; it'll make it look different and my wife won't know it if she sees you wearing it in the street.

EROTIUM: You can take it away when you go.

SOSICLES: I'll do that.

EROTIUM: Let's go in, then.

SOSICLES: I'll be with you directly. I just want to have a word with my man first.

[EROTIUM *goes in.*]

Messenio! Come here.

MESSENIO: What are you up to? You ought to think what you're doing.

SOSICLES: Why ought I?

MESSENIO: Because –

SOSICLES: All right, I know; you needn't tell me.

MESSENIO: More fool you, then.

SOSICLES: I've captured a prize; so far so good. Get along and find a billet for those men, as soon as you can. Then come back and meet me here before sunset.

MESSENIO: You don't know what you're letting yourself in for, master – those women . . .

SOSICLES: That's quite enough, now. It's my funeral, not yours, if I make a fool of myself. This woman is the fool, an ignorant fool; from what I've seen so far, there's booty waiting for us here. [*He goes into the house.*]

MESSENIO: No, you're not going in there? . . . Oh, damn and blast it, he's properly done for now. That pirate ship has got our little boat in tow for destruction. I'm the fool, though, to expect to be able to control my master; he bought me to obey orders, not give them ... [*He turns to the slaves*] Come on, you lot; let's be off, so that I can get back here at the time he said. [*He takes them off with the baggage.*]

*

[*An hour or two later,* PENICULUS *returns from the town.*]
PENICULUS: Well, that was the most stupid and fatal thing I have ever done in all the thirty odd years of my life – to go and get myself mixed up in that public meeting, fool that I was. While I was standing there gaping, Menaechmus must have slipped off and gone back to his mistress – not wanting to take me with him, of course. Gods confound the man who first invented public meetings, that device for wasting the time of people who have no time to waste. There ought to be a corps of idle men enrolled for that sort of business, every one of them to answer his name when called or pay a fine on the spot. After all, there are plenty of men who don't need more than one meal a day and have nothing else to do – never get invited out to eat, or invite their friends in; they could very well spend their time on meetings and committees. If things were managed that way, I wouldn't have lost that lunch today; I'm pretty sure he meant to give it me, sure as I'm alive. I think I'll go in, anyway; there's always the attractive prospect of left-overs ... [*The door opens and* SOSICLES *is about to come out, carrying the gown, and wearing a garland at a rakish angle on his head.*] But what's this? Menaechmus is coming out, with a garland on his head. They've cleared away, then, and I'm just in time to escort him home. I'll see what he's up to first, then I'll go and speak to him.
    [SOSICLES *is speaking back to Erotium within.*]
SOSICLES: Now you go and have a nice sleep, there's a good girl. I'll see that you get this back in plenty of time today, all nicely cleaned and altered. In fact it'll look so different you won't know it's the same one.
PENICULUS: Well, I'll be blowed, and he's off to the dressmaker's with that gown! Eaten all the lunch and drunk all the wine, and his table-friend left outside all this time! I'll jolly well get even

with him for this treatment or I'm not the man I think I am. Just you wait, young man.

SOSICLES [*coming out*]: Oh gods above, did ever a man expect less of your bounty and receive more in one day than I have? Lunch, drinks, a woman, and . . . this for a prize, which its rightful owner is not going to see again.

PENICULUS: I can't quite catch what he's saying from here. Is it about the trick he's played me, now that he's got his belly full?

SOSICLES: The girl says I stole this from my wife and gave it to her! I could see there was some mistake, but I immediately agreed with her, as if we were on familiar terms; anything she said, I fell in with it. In short . . . I never had a better time at less expense.

PENICULUS: I'm going to talk to him. I'm dying to have a scrap with him.

SOSICLES: Now who's this coming my way?

PENICULUS: And what have you got to say for yourself, you base, vain, fickle and flighty, false and faithless, crooked and inconstant man? What have I done to deserve such infamous treatment at your hands? I know how you gave me the slip down in town not an hour ago, how you put away a luncheon without me there to assist at the obsequies. How dare you? Had not I as much right to be at the graveside as you?

SOSICLES: I don't know what business you have to be pitching into me, young fellow, when you don't know me and I've never seen you before. Unless you want me to give you the punishment your impudence deserves.

PENICULUS: As if you hadn't punished me enough already, by Jupiter!

SOSICLES: Perhaps you will be good enough to tell me your name at any rate?

PENICULUS: Is that your idea of a joke, pretending not to know my name?

SOSICLES: I swear I've never seen or met you till this minute, to the best of my knowledge. All I can say is, whoever you are, I shall be obliged if you will cease to annoy me.

PENICULUS: Come on, Menaechmus; wake up.

SOSICLES: I am quite awake, thank you.

PENICULUS: Do you mean to say you don't know me?

SOSICLES: If I did, I wouldn't deny it.

PENICULUS: You don't know me – your table-companion?

SOSICLES: It's quite clear to me, your brain is out of order.

PENICULUS: Tell me, didn't you steal that gown from your wife today and give it to Erotium?

SOSICLES: Damn it, I haven't got a wife and I never stole a gown and never gave one to Erotium.

PENICULUS: Have you gone mad? Oh dear, this is the end. Didn't I see you come out of your house this morning wearing that gown?

SOSICLES: God blast you, do you think we're all pansies like you? You mean to say you saw me wearing a woman's gown?

PENICULUS: I do, so help me.

SOSICLES: Oh go to . . . where you belong. Or go and get yourself certified, lunatic.

PENICULUS: That settles it. I'm going to tell your wife everything that's happened, and no one shall stop me. You'll find this high-handed treatment will recoil on your own head. I'll make you pay for eating up that lunch, you see if I don't. [*He goes into Menaechmus's house.*]

SOSICLES: What *does* all this mean? It seems that everyone I set eyes on is determined to make a fool of me . . . I hear someone coming.

[*A MAID comes out of Erotium's house.*]

MAID: Oh, Menaechmus, my mistress asks if you will be so very kind as to take this bracelet to the jeweller's at the same time and get him to add an ounce of gold to it and have it remodelled.

SOSICLES: With pleasure; tell her I'll do that and anything else she wants me to do – anything she wants.

MAID: You know this bracelet, of course?

SOSICLES: I don't know anything about it, except that it's a gold one.

MAID: It's the one you stole, so you said, some time ago from your wife's chest when she wasn't looking.

SOSICLES: I certainly never did.

MAID: Goodness, don't you recognize it? You had better give it back to me, in that case.

SOSICLES: No, wait a minute. Yes, of course I remember now. Yes, it is the one I gave her. This is it all right. And where are the armlets I gave her at the same time?

MAID: You never gave her any armlets.

SOSICLES: Didn't I? No, you're quite right. This was all I gave her.

MAID: Shall I say you'll look after it?

SOSICLES: Yes, you can say I'll look after it. I'll get the gown and the bracelet back to her at the same time.

MAID: If you'd like to do something for me, love, you could get me some gold earrings made – say about two pounds worth of gold – pendants, you know – then I'd be glad to see you next time you visit us, wouldn't I?

SOSICLES: I'll do that with pleasure – if you can give me the gold. I'll pay for the making.

MAID: Oh – I thought you could provide the gold. I can pay you back later.

SOSICLES: No, you provide the gold, and I'll pay you back – with interest.

MAID: But I haven't any gold.

SOSICLES: Then give it me when you have some.

MAID: I'd better be going, then –

SOSICLES: Say I'll take care of these things ... [*The* MAID *goes in.*] ... and get them sold as soon as possible for what they'll fetch! Has she gone? Oh yes, the door's shut ... How all the gods love, aid, and exalt me! But I mustn't stop here. I must get away while I can from this den of vice. Get moving, Menaechmus! About turn, quick march. I'd better get rid of this garland too ... I'll throw it away ... over on this side ... so that if anyone is after me they'll think I've gone that way. Now I'll go and find that man of mine, if I can, and tell him how good the gods have been to me. [*He goes away to the town.*]

   [PENICULUS *and the* WIFE *of Menaechmus come out of the neighbouring house.*]

WIFE: How much longer am I expected to put up with this kind of marriage, I'd like to know, with my husband quietly robbing me of all I possess to make presents to his mistress?

PENICULUS: Don't say any more now. You're about to catch him red-handed, I promise you. Come this way. I've just seen him, drunk and with a garland on his head, taking your stolen gown to the dressmaker's ... Oh look, here is the very garland he was wearing ... now do you believe me? He must have gone this way, then, so you can follow his tracks if you want to. [*Looking in the opposite direction to that taken by Sosicles.*] Here he is too, by Jove, on his way back ... that's fine! He hasn't got the gown, though.

WIFE: How shall I deal with him?

PENICULUS: Just as usual; give it him hot. That's what I would do. Come over here and stalk him from cover.

[*They retire into an alley.* MENAECHMUS *comes along the street.*]

MENAECHMUS: What fools we are to cling to this idiotic and supremely boring custom! Yet we do, and the more important we are, the more we cling to it. To have a large following of clients is everybody's ambition. Whether the clients are honest men or worthless, is immaterial; nobody bothers about that; a client's wealth is what matters, not his reputation for honesty. A decent poor man is of no account at all, but a rich rogue is considered a most desirable client. Yet look at the trouble a lawless and un-scrupulous client can cause his patron. He will deny his debts, and be for ever going into court; he is avaricious, fraudulent, having made his fortune by usury and perjury; his whole mind is bent on such things. When his day of trial comes, it's a day of trial for the patron too (for we have to plead for the malefactors), whether the case is before a jury or judge or magistrate. That is the way I have been worried to death by a client today, and prevented from getting on with anything I wanted to do. The man button-holed me and wouldn't let me go. I had to put up a defence in court of all his countless crimes; I offered all kinds of involved and complicated terms of settlement; and just when I had more or less succeeded in getting the parties to agree to a decision by wager, what must the fellow do but demand a guarantor? Oh dear! ... and a more manifest villain I have never seen exposed; there were three un-shakeable witnesses for every one of his misdeeds. Gods curse the wretched man, for spoiling my day! Curse me too, for ever going near the forum this morning. A perfectly good day wasted – lunch ordered, and my mistress no doubt anxiously awaiting me. I've hurried away from town as soon as I possibly could; and now, I suppose, she will be angry with me – unless the gift of the gown has placated her; the one I stole from my wife, you remember, and gave to Erotium.

PENICULUS [*to the Wife*]: What do you think of that?

WIFE: I am cruelly married to a cruel husband.

123

PENICULUS: You heard what he said all right?

WIFE: I heard all right.

MENAECHMUS: My best plan will be to go in and join the party and have a good time.

PENICULUS [coming forward]: Just a minute. You're going to have a bad time first.

WIFE: Yes, indeed you are. You're going to pay heavy interest on that property you've borrowed.

PENICULUS: There's a nice surprise for you.

WIFE: Did you think you could get away with a mean trick like that?

MENAECHMUS: I don't know what you're talking about, my dear.

WIFE: You don't?

MENAECHMUS: Shall we ask him to explain? [Taking her hand.]

WIFE: Take your dirty hands off me, please.

PENICULUS: That's the way to talk to him.

MENAECHMUS: What have you got against me?

WIFE: As if you didn't know.

PENICULUS: He knows all right, but he pretends he doesn't, the scoundrel.

MENAECHMUS: What are you talking about?

WIFE: A robe –

MENAECHMUS: A robe?

WIFE: Yes, a robe, a wrap, which somebody –

MENAECHMUS: A wrap?

PENICULUS: What are you trembling at?

MENAECHMUS: I'm not trembling at anything.

PENICULUS: Well, you look as if you'd taken the rap! And who ate up the lunch behind my back? [To Wife] Let him have it.

MENAECHMUS: I wish you'd shut up. [Trying to make signals to Peniculus.]

PENICULUS: I certainly won't shut up. [To Wife] He's trying to tip me the wink to keep quiet, you see.

MENAECHMUS: Damn it, I'm not tipping you any winks or nods.

PENICULUS: There's boldness for you – to deny what's plainly visible.

MENAECHMUS: Woman, I swear by Jupiter and all the gods – if that will satisfy you – that I did not wink or nod at that man!

PENICULUS: All right, you didn't nod at 'that man'; she'll take your word for it. Now let's get back –

MENAECHMUS: Back where?

PENICULUS: Back to the dressmaker's, I suggest, and get that gown back.

MENAECHMUS: What gown?

PENICULUS [*after looking at the Wife, who is too upset to reply*]: It's no use my saying any more, if she's not going to play.

WIFE [*sobbing*]: I'm ... so ... unhappy ...

MENAECHMUS: What are you unhappy about, my dear? Tell me, please. Has one of the servants been troublesome? Have the men or women been answering you back? If so, please tell me, and I'll have them punished.

WIFE: Stupid man!

MENAECHMUS: She *is* upset about something. I don't like to see her –

WIFE: St ... stupid man!

MENAECHMUS: There's someone in the house you're angry with, I'm sure.

WIFE: *Stupid man!*

MENAECHMUS: It surely can't be me ... can it?

WIFE: Oh? Sense at last, then?

MENAECHMUS: But I've done nothing wrong.

WIFE: Stupid man again!

MENAECHMUS [*trying to fondle her*]: My dear, do tell me what is troubling you.

PENICULUS: Trying to play the sweet hubby with you now!

MENAECHMUS [*to Peniculus*]: Can't you mind your own business? I'm not talking to you, am I?

WIFE: Take your hands off me, please.

PENICULUS: Serve you right. Let's see you again eating up the lunch in my absence, and playing the drunken fool with me in front of the house with a garland on your head.

MENAECHMUS: Heavens above! I tell you I haven't had any lunch, nor put a foot inside that house this day!

PENICULUS: You haven't?

MENAECHMUS: By the head of Hercules, I haven't.

PENICULUS: He's the most brazen liar I've ever known ... Haven't

125

I just seen you out here in the street with a wreath of roses on your head – when you told me my brain was out of order, pretended you didn't know me, and said you were a stranger here?

MENAECHMUS: But, good heavens, I parted from you some time ago, and have only just now come home.

PENICULUS: Go on, you can't fool me. And you didn't reckon on my being able to pay you out, did you? Well, I have. I've told your wife all about it.

MENAECHMUS: What have you told her?

PENICULUS: Oh, I forget. You'd better ask her yourself.

MENAECHMUS: What is it all about, my dear? What has he told you? What has been happening? Can't you speak? Can't you tell me what it is?

WIFE: Still asking me that? As if you didn't know.

MENAECHMUS: I wouldn't ask, would I, if I knew?

PENICULUS: What a double-faced scoundrel the man is! . . . You'll never get away with it, my lad. She knows all about it. I gave her all the details myself.

MENAECHMUS: *What* details?

WIFE: Very well, since you have no shame and no wish to confess voluntarily, just listen to this. I'll tell you why I am angry, and what this man has told me. A gown has been stolen and taken out of the house.

MENAECHMUS: A gown? I've been robbed of a gown?

PENICULUS: The rascal's still trying to twist you, you see . . . No, *you've* not been robbed, *she* has. If you've been robbed, we shall never see it again, that's certain.

MENAECHMUS: You keep out of this . . . Explain to me, my dear.

WIFE: A gown, I repeat, is missing from the house.

MENAECHMUS: Who can have taken it?

WIFE: The man who removed it can best answer that, I should think.

MENAECHMUS: And who would he be?

WIFE: His name is Menaechmus.

MENAECHMUS: Really? What a rotten thing to do. Who is this Menaechmus?

WIFE: *You* are this Menaechmus.

MENAECHMUS: Am I?

WIFE: You are.

MENAECHMUS: And who is my accuser?

WIFE: I am.

PENICULUS: So am I. And I add that you gave it to your mistress Erotium.

MENAECHMUS: I gave it to her?

WIFE: Yes, *you* did, *you* did.

PENICULUS: If you like, we'll bring on an owl to keep repeating 'yoo, yoo'; we're tired of it.

MENAECHMUS: No, no, my dear, I never gave it away. By Jupiter and all the gods I swear –

PENICULUS: You'd much better swear that we are telling the truth.

MENAECHMUS: I didn't give it outright; I only lent it.

WIFE: Did you indeed? And have you ever known me lend your cloaks or tunics outside the house? It's a woman's place to lend out women's clothes, and a man's the men's. Perhaps you will kindly bring the gown back.

MENAECHMUS. I will certainly see that it comes back.

WIFE: It will certainly be in your interest to do so. You're not coming into this house again until you bring the gown with you. I'm going home.

PENICULUS: And what do I get for what I've done for you in this business?

WIFE: I'll do as much for you, when something is stolen from your house. [*She goes into her house.*]

PENICULUS: That'll be never; there's nothing in my house that I'm likely to lose. May the gods blast you both, wife and husband! I'll get along to town; it's obvious I'm no longer a friend of this family. [*He goes off.*]

MENAECHMUS: She thinks she's got her own back, does she – shutting me out of the house? As if I didn't know of another place, and a better one, where I shall be welcome. All right, my lady, if you don't want me, I shall have to grin and bear it. Erotium will want me; she won't shut me out; she'll shut me in, both of us together. I'll go now, and beg her to let me have the gown back – tell her I'll buy her a better one. [*He knocks at her door.*] Hey there! Is there a doorkeeper here? Open please, and let someone ask Erotium to come out here.

127

EROTIUM [*within*]: Who is asking for me?

MENAECHMUS: Someone who loves you more than his own life. [EROTIUM *comes out*.]

EROTIUM: Menaechmus, my dear! Don't wai† outside, come in.

MENAECHMUS: No, stay. Let me tell you what I've come for.

EROTIUM: I know quite well what you've come for – so that you and I may enjoy ourselves.

MENAECHMUS: The fact is . . . darling, will you please let me have that gown back, the one I gave you this morning. My wife has found out all about the whole affair. I'll buy you another one worth twice as much, any kind you like.

EROTIUM: But I have just given it you, not half an hour ago, to take to the dressmaker; and the bracelet you were to take to the jeweller to be re-made.

MENAECHMUS: You gave me the gown and a bracelet? You're mistaken; you never did any such thing. After giving it you this morning, I went off to town, and now I have just come back; this is the first time I've seen you since then.

EROTIUM: Oh? I can see through that little game all right. I put the things into your charge and now you've thought up a nice way to do me out of them.

MENAECHMUS: Good heavens, no! I'm not trying to do you out of anything, by asking for it back. I told you, my wife has found out –

EROTIUM: And I never asked for it in the first place, did I? It was your idea to bring it to me; you said it was a present for me; now you want it back. It's all the same to me; you can keep it, take it back, wear it yourself, let your wife wear it, or lock it up in a cupboard for all I care. If that's all you think of me, after all I've done for you, you're not coming into this house any more, I give you my word – not without ready money in your hand. You can't muck about with me like that, young man. You can go and find someone else to make a fool of. [*She goes in.*]

MENAECHMUS: Oh, no, please, you can't be as angry as all that. Please, wait, listen, come back! You're not going? Oh do come back, just for my sake! . . . She's gone. The door's locked. Now I'm properly locked out. No one will believe a word I say, either at home or at my mistress's. I don't know what I'm going to do

128

now . . . I shall have to go and find a friend somewhere to advise me. [*He goes off to the town.*]

*

[*Later.* SOSICLES *returns from town, with the gown under his arm.*]

SOSICLES: I was a fool to let Messenio have the purse and money this morning. He'll have gone to ground in some grog-shop by now, I expect . . .

[*The* WIFE *looks out of her house.*]

WIFE: I wonder if there's any sign of my husband coming home . . . Oh yes, there he is. I'm saved! He's bringing the gown back.

SOSICLES: I wish I knew where the man had got to.

WIFE: I'll go and give him a suitable welcome . . . Well, you sinner, aren't you ashamed to appear in my sight with that thing on you?

SOSICLES: I beg your pardon? Is anything the matter, madam?

WIFE: Heartless creature! Are you still daring to bandy words with me?

SOSICLES: Why shouldn't I address you, pray? Have I committed any crime?

WIFE: Still asking me that? Oh, you're utterly shameless.

SOSICLES: Have you ever heard, madam, why the Greeks used to call Hecuba a bitch?

WIFE: I certainly haven't.

SOSICLES: It was because Hecuba used to do exactly what you are doing, pour every kind of abuse on anyone she came across. So she came to be called The Bitch – and rightly too.

WIFE: Oh! I won't put up with this infamous conduct any longer. I'd rather live and die without a husband than endure such outrageous behaviour.

SOSICLES: And what business is it of mine, whether you can endure your married life or intend to part from your husband? Is it perhaps the custom here to babble your affairs to any stranger that comes along?

WIFE: Babble! I tell you I won't stand it any longer. I'll get a divorce sooner than suffer such treatment for the rest of my life.

SOSICLES: Well, bless me, I've no objection. Get a divorce, and remain divorced, for the rest of your life, or as long as Jupiter is king.

WIFE: An hour ago you denied having stolen that gown, and here you are with it before my eyes. Aren't you ashamed of that?

SOSICLES: Oh my goodness, woman, what wicked impudence! Do you really claim that this gown was stolen from you, when it was given to me by another lady for me to take to the repairer's?

WIFE: Oh! I shall . . . I shall send for my father and tell him all about your wicked doings. [*She goes to the door.*] Decio! Go and find my father, and bring him back with you. Tell him it's urgent . . . I'll soon expose all your evil practices!

SOSICLES: I think you must be mad. What are these evil practices of mine?

WIFE: Stealing my clothes, and stealing my jewels, your wife's property, out of the house, and carrying them off to your mistress! Isn't that something to 'babble' about?

SOSICLES: My good woman, if you know of any medicine that would help me to swallow your venomous insults more easily, I should be glad if you would tell me of it. I haven't the faintest idea who you think I am; and I know no more of you than I do of Hercules's grandfather-in-law.

WIFE: Mock me if you like; you won't mock him so lightly – my father, who will be here in a minute. [*Looking down the street.*] There he is, do you see? Perhaps you know him?

SOSICLES: Oh yes, I know him as well as Calchas! I met him that day when I first met you.

WIFE: Not know me indeed! Not know my father!

SOSICLES: Bring me your grandfather if you like; I shan't know him either.

WIFE: Huh! Just like you too. Just what I would expect from your conduct.

[*The Wife's* FATHER *comes slowly along the street. As he is assumed to be still some way off, he has time for a good grumble before reaching the others.*]

FATHER: I'm coming, I'm coming, as fast as an old man can, and as fast as the need may be . . . but it isn't easy . . . don't I know it? I'm not as nippy as I used to be . . . the years tell on me . . . more weight to carry and less strength. Yes, age is a bad business, a dead

loss. It brings you nothing but troubles, and plenty of them. I
could tell you what they are, but it would take far too long. . . .
What chiefly worries me at this moment is, what on earth does my
daughter want, suddenly sending for me like this? She hasn't given
me the least idea what she wants me for. Why should she demand
my presence so urgently? . . . I think I've a pretty good idea what
it's all about, though. She's had some quarrel with her husband, I
expect. They're like that – these women who expect their husbands
to be at their beck and call; with a good dowry behind them, they're
terrors. Not that the husbands are always blameless, if it comes to
that. Still, there are limits to what a wife should have to put up
with; and you can be sure a woman doesn't send for her father
without good reason – some misconduct on the husband's part or a
serious quarrel. Well, we shall soon know . . . Ah yes, there she is
outside the house . . . and her husband, in no good temper by the
looks of him. Just as I thought. I'll get a word with her first. [*He
beckons to her.*]

WIFE: I'll go to him . . . Oh, father, I'm glad to see you.

FATHER: I'm glad to see you. I hope you're well. All well here, eh?
Nothing wrong, I hope, to bring me over here? You look a bit
downcast, though; why is that? And why is he standing over there
looking so grumpy? I believe you've been having a bit of a tiff
over something or other. Have you? Come on, out with it, tell
me whose fault it was, and don't make a long tale of it.

WIFE: It is not I that have done anything wrong, you can make
your mind easy on that, father. But I cannot live here any longer;
I simply cannot stand it; you must take me away.

FATHER: What's the trouble, then?

WIFE: I am being treated like dirt.

FATHER: By whom?

WIFE: By my husband, the husband you found for me.

FATHER: So that's it – a bit of a squabble. How many times have I
told you that I won't have you, either of you, running to me with
your complaints?

WIFE: How can I avoid it, father?

FATHER: Do you want me to tell you?

WIFE: If you please.

FATHER: I've told you dozens of times; it's your business to try to please your husband, not keep spying on everything he does, always wanting to know where he's going and what he's up to.

WIFE: What he's up to is making love to the harlot next door.

FATHER: I don't blame him; and I warrant he'll go on loving her all the more, the more you keep on at him like this.

WIFE: Drinking there too.

FATHER: And do you think you have a right to stop him drinking, there or anywhere else he chooses? I never heard such impudence, girl. I suppose you think you can also stop him accepting invitations to supper, or inviting friends to his own house? Do you expect a husband to be your slave? You might as well expect him to do the housework for you, or sit with the women and spin.

WIFE: I see I've brought you here to plead for my husband, not for me. My advocate has gone over to the other side.

FATHER: My dear girl, if he commits any criminal offence, I shall have a lot more to say to him than I have said to you. He keeps you in clothes, jewellery, and all the servants and provisions you could possibly need; your best plan is to accept the situation sensibly.

WIFE: Even if he robs me, steals my clothes and jewels out of my cupboards, empties my wardrobe behind my back to make presents to his strumpets?

FATHER: Ah well, he has no right to do that – if that is what he is doing. But if he isn't, you have no right to accuse an innocent man.

WIFE: I tell you, father, at this very moment he has a gown and a bracelet of mine, which he had given to that woman, and which he is only now bringing back because I found out about it.

FATHER: Oh dear ... I'd better learn the truth about this, from his own lips. I'll have a word with him ... Now then, Menaechmus, what's this that you two are quarrelling about? I want to know. Why are you moping over here, and she in a temper over there?

SOSICLES: Whoever you are, old gentleman, and whatever your name may be, I swear by Jupiter and all the gods above –

FATHER: Good heavens, what's coming?

SOSICLES: – that I have never done the slightest wrong to that woman who keeps accusing me of having stolen and abstracted a garment from her house –

WIFE: A wicked lie!

SOSICLES: – and if I have ever put a foot inside that house, may I be the damnedest of all damned creatures on earth!

FATHER: Why, you imbecile, have you taken leave of your senses, to utter such a curse upon yourself, and say you have never set foot inside the house you live in?

SOSICLES: Are you now saying that I live in that house too?

FATHER: Well, do you deny it?

SOSICLES: I most certainly deny it.

FATHER: Then you are telling a flat lie – unless you've moved out of the house since yesterday ... Daughter, come over here ... have you and your husband moved out of this house?

WIFE: Where in the world should we move to, and why, for goodness sake?

FATHER: I'm hanged if I know.

WIFE: He's pulling your leg, of course. Can't you see that?

FATHER: Come now, Menaechmus, that's enough of your joking; let's come to the point.

SOSICLES: What point? What has my business got to do with you? I don't know who you are or where you come from or how I am supposed to be concerned with you or with this woman who has done nothing but insult me ever since I met her.

WIFE [in alarm]: Look at him, father! His eyes are turning green; all his face is turning green; and that glitter in his eyes – look!

SOSICLES [aside]: If they are going to declare me insane, the best thing I can do is to pretend to be insane; perhaps that will frighten them off. [He acts accordingly.]

WIFE: Now he's gaping and flinging himself about. Oh father, what ever shall I do?

FATHER: Come away, my dear, come away as far as possible from him.

SOSICLES [raving]: Euhoe! Euhoe! Bacchus ahoy! Wilt thou have me go hunt in the woods away? I hear thee, I hear thee, but here I must stay. I am watched by a witch, a wild female bitch, on my left, and behind her a smelly old goat, a lying old dotard whose lies have brought many an innocent creature to ruin ...

FATHER: Ay, ruin on you!

SOSICLES: Now the word of Apollo commands me, commands me to burn out her eyes with firebrands blazing ...

133

WIFE: Ah!! Father, father, he is threatening to burn out my eyes!

SOSICLES: Woe is me, when madmen themselves call me mad.

FATHER: Here, girl!

WIFE: Yes?

FATHER: What are we going to do? Shall I get some servants here? Yes, that's it; I'll get some men here to carry him home and tie him up before he can do any worse harm.

SOSICLES: Now what am I going to do? They'll have me carried off to their house if I don't think of something quickly ... [*Making to attack the Wife*] I hear thee, Apollo, bid me strike this woman's face and spare not, if she will not speedily avoid my sight and begone to whatever hell she chooses. Thy will be done, Apollo!

FATHER: Go inside, girl, go inside at once before he murders you!

WIFE: I'm going. Watch him, father. Don't let him get away. Oh! What terrible things for a poor wife to hear! ... [*She escapes into the house.*]

SOSICLES: That's got rid of her nicely. Now for this wicked whiskered tottering Tithonus, so-called son of Cygnus ... At thy command, Apollo, I shall pound his body to bits, smash every bone and limb with his own walking-stick ...

FATHER: You dare touch me, or come a step nearer, and you'll be sorry for it.

SOSICLES: I obey, Apollo. With a two-edged axe I will mash this old man's flesh and bones to mincemeat ...

FATHER: My goodness, I must look out for myself, or I'm afraid he really will do me as much harm as he threatens.

SOSICLES: More commands, Apollo? Ay, now thou biddest me harness my fierce wild horses and mount my chariot to ride down this aged toothless stinking lion ... So be it ... now I am in my chariot, now I hold the reins, here is the goad in my hands ... Gallop apace, my steeds! Let me hear the ring of your hoofs! Swift be the flight of your feet on your tireless courses!

FATHER: You keep your horses away from me!

SOSICLES: Apollo, Apollo! Still thou art bidding me charge on the foeman who stands in my path and destroy him ... [*The old man stands his ground and grapples with the madman.*] ... Ah! Who is this who seizes me by the hair and drags me from my car? Who is this who defies and obstructs thy orders, thy royal commands, O Apollo! . . . [*He gives up the battle and falls to the ground.*]

FATHER: Well I never! He must have had a terribly sudden and serious stroke. He was perfectly well a few minutes ago, and now raving mad. I've never seen a man taken so suddenly. Good gods, what ever shall I do? I'd better go and find a doctor as quick as I can . . . [*He hurries off.*]

SOSICLES: Have they gone at last? Have I got rid of those two pests who have turned a sane man into a raving lunatic? . . . My best plan now is to get back to my ship while the going's good. You won't tell him, friends, will you? Don't tell the old man, if he comes back, which way I've gone. Goodbye. [*He goes.*]

*

[*Later. The* FATHER *returns, wearily.*]

FATHER: All this time I've been waiting for the doctor to get back from his rounds. My bottom's numb with sitting, and my eyes sore with watching out for him. At last the tiresome fellow finished with his patients and came home. Tells me he had to set a broken leg for Aesculapius and mend an arm for Apollo – whatever he meant by that . . . Oh, now I come to think of it, I wonder if I've summoned a stonemason instead of a doctor? Anyway, here he comes now . . . Hurry up, man; can't you move faster than an insect?

[*The* DOCTOR *arrives.*]

DOCTOR: Now, sir, what did you say was the nature of the illness? Is it a case of possession or hallucination? Are there any symptoms of lethargy or hydropsical condition?

FATHER: I've brought you here to tell me that, and to cure him.

DOCTOR: There'll be no difficulty about that; we'll cure him all right, I can promise you.

FATHER: I want him to have the most careful attention.

DOCTOR: I'll care for him most carefully. I shall be sighing over him every minute of the day.

FATHER: Look, here he comes. Let's watch his behaviour.

[*They stand aside.* MENAECHMUS *comes from the town.*]

MENAECHMUS: Upon my word, I don't know when I spent a more

135

fatal and frustrating day. All my carefully concealed schemes have
been exposed by that satellite of mine. Like a Ulysses, he has plotted
against his lord, and made me look a cowering guilty fool. I'll
get even with the fellow, if I live; I'll put an end to his life – if you
can call it his life – my life, I should say, since it's my food and
money he's been living on! Anyway, I'll stop his breath. As for that
woman, she has behaved just as you would expect from her kind.
I ask her to let me have the gown returned to my wife, and she
says it was a gift to her. Oh dear, what a life!

FATHER: Do you hear what he's saying?

DOCTOR: He's saying what an unhappy creature he is.

FATHER: Go and speak to him, do.

DOCTOR: Good afternoon, Menaechmus. Oh dear me, you shouldn't
have your arm uncovered like that. Don't you know that is the
worst possible thing for your complaint?

MENAECHMUS: Why don't you go and hang yourself?

FATHER: Do you notice anything?

DOCTOR: I should think I do! It'll take bushels of hellebore to get the
better of this malady . . . Tell me, Menaechmus –

MENAECHMUS: Tell you what?

DOCTOR: Just one question – do you drink white wine or red?

MENAECHMUS: Oh go to blazes!

DOCTOR [to Father]: Yes, indeed, the fit is coming on him again.

MENAECHMUS: Why don't you ask me whether I eat pink, purple,
or yellow bread? Whether I eat birds with scales or fish with
feathers?

FATHER: Ts, ts! Listen to his raving. Can't you give him a dose of
something immediately to save him from going completely mad?

DOCTOR: All in good time. I'll ask him some more questions.

FATHER: You'll kill us all with your rigmarole.

DOCTOR: Tell me, young man, do you ever feel your eyes scaling
over?

MENAECHMUS: Imbecile, do you take me for a lobster?

DOCTOR: And another thing: have you noticed any rumbling in the
bowels?

MENAECHMUS: They don't rumble when I'm full; they rumble
when I'm empty.

DOCTOR: Well, I don't see anything unreasonable in that answer.

Do you sleep all night? Do you fall asleep easily when you get into bed?

MENAECHMUS: I sleep soundly enough – if I've paid all my bills. Oh, Jupiter and all the gods blast you and your silly questions!

DOCTOR: Madness coming on again. Be careful when he talks like that.

FATHER: He's talking as sanely as Nestor, compared with what he was a little time ago; then he was calling his wife a crazy bitch.

MENAECHMUS: I was?

FATHER: You certainly were – in your madness, of course.

MENAECHMUS: I was mad?

FATHER: You were; you threatened to run me down with a chariot and four. I saw you. I can bring eye-witness evidence against you.

MENAECHMUS: Oh, can you? And I can prove you stole the sacred crown off Jupiter's head and were put in prison for it; I have evidence that when you were let out you were flogged at the stake; and I know how you murdered your father and sold your mother. Take that slander back in your teeth to convince you I'm a sane man.

FATHER: For heaven's sake, doctor, whatever you're going to do, do it quickly. You can surely see he's out of his mind.

DOCTOR: Yes ... well ... this is what I would advise you to do. Have him brought over to my house.

FATHER: Do you think that will be best?

DOCTOR: I certainly do. There I shall be able to supervise his treatment.

FATHER: Just as you please.

DOCTOR [to Menaechmus]: I'll put you on to hellebore for three weeks.

MENAECHMUS: I'll put you on to a rack and have you pricked with goads for a month.

DOCTOR: Go and find some men to carry him to my house.

FATHER: How many men will it take, do you think?

DOCTOR: Judging by his present condition of insanity, not less than four.

FATHER: I'll have them here directly. You keep an eye on him, doctor, meanwhile.

DOCTOR: Oh, I must go home and see to the necessary preparations. You tell your men to bring him along.

FATHER: Very well. We'll get him to your house immediately.
DOCTOR: I'll go, then.
FATHER: Goodbye.

[*They go their ways.*]

MENAECHMUS: Exit doctor. Exit father-in-law. Now I am alone.
Jupiter! Whatever can have possessed those two to pronounce me
insane? Me – who have never had a day's illness in my life! I'm
not insane at all, nor am I looking for a fight or a quarrel with
anybody. I'm just as sane as every other sane man I see; I know my
friends when I see them, I talk to them normally. Then why are
they trying to make out that I am insane – unless it's they who are
insane? Now what do I do? I'd like to go home, but wife says no.
Next door there's no welcome for me either. What a damnable
business! I shall just have to wait here; they'll let me in at nightfall,
I should hope. [*He sits down at his own doorstep.*]

[MESSENIO *comes from the town.*]

MESSENIO: It's the mark of a good slave, I always say – one who can
be trusted to watch and provide for his master's welfare, plan and
organize his affairs – that he attends to his master's business just as
well in his master's absence as in his presence, or better. Every
right-thinking slave ought to value his own back more than his own
throat, look after his shins rather than his belly. He'll remember, if
he has any sense, how their masters reward worthless, idle, and
dishonest slaves: floggings, chains, the treadmill, sweating, starving, freezing stiff – that's what you get for laziness. I'd rather take
the trouble to keep out of that sort of trouble. That's why I've
decided to be a good slave, not a bad one. I can bear a lash of the
tongue more easily than a lash of the whip; and I'd much rather
eat corn than grind it. So I do as my master tells me, carry out his
orders in an efficient and orderly manner; and I find it pays me.
Others can do as they think best; I'm going to do my duty. That's
my resolution – to play safe, do no wrong, and always be where
I'm wanted. The way to be a useful slave is to be afraid of trouble
even when you've done no wrong; the ones who are not afraid
of anything, even when they *have* deserved trouble – they've got
something to be afraid of! I shan't have much to fear. It won't be
long before my master rewards me for my services. Anyway, that's
my idea of service – making sure my own back doesn't suffer.

So now I've done everything he told me, seen the baggage and the slaves settled at an inn, and come back here to meet him. I'll knock at the door and let him know I'm here, so that I can rescue him safely out of this den of thieves. Although I'm very much afraid the struggle may be over and I have come too late.

[*As he goes up to Erotium's door, the* FATHER *comes back with four strong slaves.*]

FATHER: Now you men, you have your orders and I repeat them again, and by heaven and earth I charge you to observe them diligently. I want that man picked up and carried at once to the doctor's house; see to it, unless you care nothing for the comfort of your own legs and sides. And don't, any of you, take the slightest notice of anything *he* may threaten to do to you. Well? Jump to it. What are you waiting for? He ought to be on your backs and away by now. I'll go along to the doctor's; I shall be ready to meet you there when you arrive.

[*He goes. The slaves grapple with Menaechmus.*]

MENAECHMUS: Help! Murder! What's happening? Why am I being set on like this? What do you want? Have you lost something? Why are you attacking me? Where are you dragging me? Where are you carrying me? Help, help, people of Epidamnus! Citizens, help! Let me go, can't you!

MESSENIO: Almighty gods! What do I see? My master man-handled and carried off by a gang of ruffians!

MENAECHMUS: Won't anyone come to my aid?

MESSENIO: I will, master. I'll fight 'em. Oh, men of Epidamnus, look at this horrible wicked outrage – my master being kidnapped in the street, in broad daylight, a freeborn visitor abducted in your peaceful city! Drop him, you villains!

MENAECHMUS [*taking Messenio for a stranger*]: Oh thank you, my man, whoever you are; help me, for goodness sake; don't let them do this outrageous thing to me.

MESSENIO: I'll help you, I'll defend you, I'll put up a fight for you. I'll not see you die – sooner die myself. Go on, sir, knock his eye out – that one that's got you by the arm. I'll plant a crop of fisticuffs among these other faces ... You try to carry this man off and it will be the worse for you. Drop him!

MENAECHMUS: I've got my fingers in this one's eye.

MESSENIO: Leave him with an empty socket in his head. You villains! You robbers! You thugs!

SLAVES: Murder! Help!

MESSENIO: Let him go!

MENAECHMUS: How dare you attack me! [*To Messenio*] Tear the skin off them!

[*The slaves are by this time routed, and decamp.*]

MESSENIO: Get out of it, the lot of you; off with you to hell. [*Clouting the last of them*] And here's one for you ... a prize for being the last ... I gave their faces a good doing over, didn't I? Gave 'em all I wanted to. By jingo, sir, it was a lucky thing I got here just in time to help you.

MENAECHMUS: May the gods bless you, my good fellow – [*aside*] whoever you may be. But for you, I doubt if I should have lived to see this day's end.

MESSENIO: I'm sure you can't refuse to give me my freedom after this, master.

MENAECHMUS: I? Give you your freedom?

MESSENIO: Surely, after I've saved your life, master.

MENAECHMUS: What *do* you mean? You're under some misapprehension, my good man.

MESSENIO: I am? Why?

MENAECHMUS: I'll take my oath, by Jupiter above, you're not one of my servants.

MESSENIO: Don't talk –

MENAECHMUS: I mean it. No slave of mine ever did so much for me as you have done.

[MESSENIO *is puzzled for a moment; then, taking Menaechmus at his word:*]

MESSENIO: You mean ... ? I'm no longer a slave of yours? I can go free, then?

MENAECHMUS: You have my permission to go free and to go wherever you please.

MESSENIO: Is that an order, sir?

MENAECHMUS: It's certainly an order, so far as I have any power to give you orders.

MESSENIO: Hail, one time master, now my patron! [*Shaking hands with himself, as if being congratulated by his master's friends*] 'Congratulations, Messenio, on your freedom' ... 'Thank you, sir, it's very kind of you' ... But I say, master ... please, to please me, just go on giving me orders the same as when I was your slave. I still want to go on living with you. I'll go home with you when you go.

MENAECHMUS: Indeed you won't!

MESSENIO: I'll pop round to the inn and collect the baggage and your purse and bring them back here. The purse with our travelling money is safely sealed up in the trunk; I'll have it back here in a jiffy.

MENAECHMUS [*amused*]: Do, by all means.

MESSENIO: You'll find the money's all there just as you gave it to me. Wait here for me. [*He dashes off.*]

MENAECHMUS: This is a day of wonders and no mistake! First I'm told I'm not myself, then I'm shut out in the street, and now comes this fellow saying he's my slave, so I set him free and he says he's going to bring me a purse full of money! If he does, I shall certainly tell him to clear off and be as free as he likes and go wherever he likes. I don't want him coming to claim the money back again when he comes to his senses. And that doctor and my father-in-law said *I* was out of my senses. It makes no sense to me. It's like a bad dream ... However, I'll go and call on my mistress again, even if she is in a bad temper with me, and see if I can get her to let me have my wife's gown back. [*He knocks at Erotium's door, and is admitted.*]

[MESSENIO *had not gone far when he met his real master again, and back they come.*]

SOSICLES: Have you the impudence to tell me you have met me anywhere else today since we parted here and I told you to come back to find me here?

MESSENIO: What, and haven't I just rescued you from four men who were trying to carry you off, here in front of this house? And you were howling for help to heaven and earth, and up I came and by force of my own fists got you away safe in spite of the lot of them. And for having saved your life you gave me my freedom. And then I said I was going to fetch the money and our baggage, and meanwhile you, it seems, took a short cut to intercept me and try to pretend none of this ever happened.

SOSICLES: Are you telling me I have given you your freedom?

MESSENIO: Of course you have.

SOSICLES: Oh dear, no. You can rest assured I would rather become a slave myself than ever let you out of my hands.

[MENAECHMUS *comes out of Erotium's house, with a parting shot at someone within.*]

MENAECHMUS: I have *not* taken a gown and a bracelet from here today; swear if you like by your own bright eyes that I have, it won't alter the fact – bitches!

MESSENIO: Gods preserve us! What do I see?

SOSICLES: What do you see?

MESSENIO: Your living image.

SOSICLES: What do you mean?

MESSENIO: Your double. As like as two peas.

SOSICLES: There is certainly a remarkable resemblance – so far as I can tell what I look like.

MENAECHMUS [*seeing Messenio*]: Oh there you are again, my preserver, whoever you are.

MESSENIO: If you please, young sir, be good enough to tell me your name ... for heaven's sake ... if you have no objection.

MENAECHMUS: Well, bless me, I can't grudge you that much after what you've done for me. My name is Menaechmus.

SOSICLES: But that is my name!

MENAECHMUS: I am a Sicilian – from Syracuse.

SOSICLES: That is my home town.

MENAECHMUS: No, really?

SOSICLES: It's the truth.

MESSENIO [*now thoroughly confused, aside*]: Of course, I know him [*Menaechmus*] now; he's my master; I'm his slave, but I thought I was the other man's. [*To Menaechmus*] The fact is, sir, I thought this man was you ... and I'm afraid I've caused him a bit of trouble. [*To Sosicles*] I hope you'll pardon me, sir, if I unwittingly said anything stupid to you.

SOSICLES: You seem to me to be talking utter nonsense. Don't you remember coming ashore here with me today?

MESSENIO: Did I? Yes, you're quite right. You must be my master, then. [*To Menaechmus*] You'll have to find another slave, sir. [*To Sosicles*] Pleased to meet you, sir. [*To Menaechmus*] Good day to you, sir. This is Menaechmus, of course.

MENAECHMUS: But *I* am Menaechmus.

SOSICLES: What *are* you talking about? You Menaechmus?

MENAECHMUS: Certainly I am. Menaechmus, son of Moschus.

SOSICLES: Son of my father?

MENAECHMUS: No, sir, son of my own father. I don't want to claim yours or deprive you of him.

MESSENIO: Gods above! [*He goes aside*] Oh gods, make what I think I expect come true – more than could ever be hoped for! If I'm not mistaken, these are the twin brothers. They both claim the same father and home. I'll speak to my master alone ... Menaechmus!

MENAECHMUS *and* SOSICLES: Yes?

MESSENIO: No, not both of you. The one that came here with me by sea.

MENAECHMUS: Not me.

SOSICLES: No, me.

MESSENIO: You then. Come here, sir, please.

SOSICLES: Here I am. What do you want?

MESSENIO: That man, sir, is either an impostor or your twin brother. I've never seen two men more alike; you and him – he and you – water is not more like water nor milk like milk than you two are. What's more, he says he's from the same country and has the same father as you. We must go and ask him some more questions.

SOSICLES: By the gods, Messenio, that's a wonderful idea. Thank you. Go on, and stand by me, do. If you find that he is my brother, you are a free man.

MESSENIO: That's what I hope.

SOSICLES: And I.

MESSENIO [*to Menaechmus*]: Excuse me, sir; I think you said your name was Menaechmus?

MENAECHMUS: I did.

MESSENIO: Well, this gentleman's name is Menaechmus too. And you said you were born in Syracuse, I believe; so was he. And your father was Moschus, you said? So was his. Now, this is where you can both do something for me, and for yourselves too.

MENAECHMUS: You have earned the right to ask, and be granted, any favour you desire. I am a free man, but I am willing to serve you as your bought slave.

MESSENIO: I have every hope, sir, of finding that you two are twin brothers, owning one father, one mother, and one birthday.

MENAECHMUS: That sounds like a miracle. I hope you can make your promise good.

MESSENIO: I am sure I can; if you will both be good enough to answer my questions.

MENAECHMUS: Ask away. I'll tell you anything I know.

MESSENIO: Your name is Menaechmus?

MENAECHMUS: It is.

MESSENIO: And yours the same?

SOSICLES: It is.

MESSENIO: And your father, you say, was Moschus?

MENAECHMUS: That is correct.

SOSICLES: So was mine.

MESSENIO: You are a Syracusan?

MENAECHMUS: Yes.

MESSENIO: And you?

SOSICLES: You know I am.

MESSENIO: Good. So far all the indications agree. Now for some further points. Can you tell me what is the earliest thing you remember about your life at home?

MENAECHMUS: I remember my father taking me to Tarentum on a business trip, and how I lost my father one day in the crowd and so got kidnapped.

SOSICLES: Jupiter Almighty, preserve me!

MESSENIO: No exclamations, please. Wait your turn to speak ... How old were you when you left home with your father?

MENAECHMUS: Seven years old. I was just beginning to lose my first teeth. That was the last time I saw my father.

MESSENIO: Next question: how many sons did your father have at that time?

MENAECHMUS: To the best of my recollection, two.

MESSENIO: You and another one – which was the elder?

MENAECHMUS: Neither.

MESSENIO: Neither? How could that be?

MENAECHMUS: We were twins – both of us.

SOSICLES: Gods be praised, I am saved!

MESSENIO: If you keep interrupting, I shall stop talking.

SOSICLES: No, please, I'll keep quiet.

MESSENIO: Tell me now, were you and your twin brother both given the same name?

MENAECHMUS: Oh no; I was called Menaechmus, as I still am; my brother was called Sosicles.

SOSICLES: That settles it! I cannot refrain any longer from embracing him. Brother, my twin brother, greeting! I am Sosicles.

MENAECHMUS: Then how have you since got the name of Menaechmus?

SOSICLES: After the news reached us that you were lost and our father dead, our grandfather changed my name and had me called Menaechmus after you.

MENAECHMUS: That sounds possible. Tell me one thing more.

SOSICLES: What?

MENAECHMUS: What was our mother's name?

SOSICLES: Teuximarcha.

MENAECHMUS: It's true! Bless you, my brother! Given up for lost, and found again after all these years!

SOSICLES: Bless you, brother. At last my sad and weary search is ended and I rejoice to have found you.

MESSENIO: Now I see why that woman called you by your brother's name, and invited you to lunch. She must have thought you were he.

MENAECHMUS: Gad, yes, that's quite right. I did ask to be given lunch here today. I was eluding my wife, having just borrowed one of her gowns to give to my mistress.

SOSICLES: Is this the gown you are referring to?

MENAECHMUS: That's the one. How did you get hold of it?

SOSICLES: Your mistress insisted on my going in to lunch with her, and said I had given her the gown. I had an excellent lunch, enjoyed myself with wine and woman, and came away with the gown and a gold bracelet.

MENAECHMUS: I am delighted to have put a bit of good luck in your way. The woman obviously thought it was me she was entertaining.

MESSENIO: Well, sir, does the offer of freedom which you made to me still stand?

MENAECHMUS: Of course, a very fair and just request. Brother, will you grant it, for my sake?

SOSICLES: Messenio, you are a free man.

MENAECHMUS: Messenio, I congratulate you on your freedom.

MESSENIO: Thank you, sirs ... [*aside*] but it'll need more than congratulations to keep me a free man for life.

SOSICLES: Well, brother, after this satisfactory solution of our troubles, shall we return home together?

MENAECHMUS: I shall be happy to do so, brother. But first I shall hold an auction and sell all I have here. Let me welcome you to my house meanwhile.

SOSICLES: I shall be delighted.

MESSENIO [*seizing a good chance*]: May I ask you one other thing, gentlemen?

MENAECHMUS: What is that?

MESSENIO: Let me be your auctioneer.

MENAECHMUS: You shall.

MESSENIO: Shall I announce the sale immediately?

MENAECHMUS: Let us say a week today.

MESSENIO [*proclaiming*]: Sale by auction – this day week in the forenoon – the property of Menaechmus – sale will include – slaves, household effects, house, land, etcetera – and a wife, should there be any purchaser. All to be sold at an agreed price, cash down. [*Confidentially*] And I doubt if the whole lot will fetch more than – fifty thousand.

So farewell, friends; let's hear your loud applause.

EXEUNT

THE SWAGGERING SOLDIER
(MILES GLORIOSUS)

INTRODUCTORY NOTE TO
THE SWAGGERING SOLDIER

An incidental allusion in this play (at line 211) to the imprisonment of a 'foreign', i.e. Roman, poet may plausibly be connected with the fate of the dramatist and poet Naevius, who suffered punishment for his political views, and who died about 200 B.C. This clue, together with stylistic indications – the absence of metrical variety, for instance – places the play among the earliest of its author's productions; and it is acknowledged (in the 'delayed prologue' spoken by Palaestrio) as a translation from a Greek original entitled *Alazon* (The Braggart). But, however early and however derivative it may be, it can be set beside *Pseudolus*, one of the latest plays, near the summit of Plautus's achievement.

We cannot say how much the actual shape of the play owes to its model, but it has some unusual features. The main action is divided into two almost unrelated parts; the first consists of a plot to deceive the slave Sceledrus and enable the girl Philocomasium to masquerade as her own twin sister; the second is a campaign to prick the pomposity of the swaggering philanderer Pyrgopolynices. Left in this shape, the play would have given the soldier too little prominence and delayed its main theme for too long. The introduction of a preliminary scene, sketching the character of Pyrgopolynices as a braggart and as a woman-chaser, provides us with the expectation of the downfall prepared for him, and this introduction, together with the 'prologue' supplied by Palaestrio, ensures that during the first part of the play our attention is engaged not so much by the bamboozling of Sceledrus as by the situation which is being built up to facilitate the release of Philocomasium from Pyrgopolynices.

The bridge-passage between the two main stages of the action contains an unnecessary, but nevertheless entertaining digression in the discourse of Periplectomenus on his own virtues and the pleasures of bachelorhood; it also serves to establish the character of the young lover Pleusicles – a brother to many other Plautine youths, compliant and invertebrate.

It has been pointed out by many critics that the figure of the professional soldier, the careerist interested only in his own exploits in the service of any cause or employer, was common in Alexandrine Greece but could hardly have been a familiar phenomenon in the Rome of Plautus's time. This would not necessarily prevent the Roman public from enjoying the caricature of a foreign type; nor need we suppose that they were unacquainted with the vices of boastfulness, self-conceit, and lechery, whether in soldiery or any other walk of life. In the main, it is not the military braggadocio of Pyrgopolynices but his amatory pretensions that are subjected to Plautus's scathing attack. And it is this theme that gives the play a sharper satirical bite than can be found anywhere else in his work; nowhere else does the comedy of intrigue and light-hearted mischief work up to such a savage and damnatory finale.

CHARACTERS

PYRGOPOLYNICES	*a handsome and conceited soldier*
ARTOTROGUS	*his satellite*
PALAESTRIO	*his confidential slave*
SCELEDRUS	*another slave*
PERIPLECTOMENUS	*an elderly neighbour of the soldier*
PHILOCOMASIUM	*the soldier's concubine*
PLEUSICLES	*a young man in love with Philocomasium*
ACROTELEUTIUM	*a courtesan*
MILPHIDIPPA	*her maid*
LURCIO	*under-slave in the soldier's house*
CARIO	*a cook in Periplectomenus's house*

Other slaves of Pyrgopolynices and Periplectomenus

*

The scene is at Ephesus, outside the houses of Pyrgopolynices and Periplectomenus.

· THE SWAGGERING SOLDIER

[*The houses of Periplectomenus and Pyrgopolynices are adjacent, in such a way that, as we shall hear, a secret passage can be cut in the party wall between them; their front doors, however, are fairly widely distanced apart, and some kind of ornamental masonry or shrubbery obstructs the view from one to the other and provides a screen for eavesdroppers.*

PYRGOPOLYNICES, a military man of handsome and impressive appearance, is either just emerging from his house or arriving at it from another part of the town; during his opening words, he is relieved of the heavier parts of his accoutrement by slaves or soldiers, who take them away for cleaning. He is accompanied by his satellite ARTOTRO-GUS.]

PYRGOPOLYNICES: My shield, there – have it burnished brighter than the bright splendour of the sun on any summer's day. Next time I have occasion to use it in the press of battle, it must flash defiance into the eyes of the opposing foe. My sword, too, I see, is pining for attention; poor chap, he's quite disheartened and cast down, hanging idly at my side so long; he's simply itching to get at an enemy and carve him into little pieces ... Where's Arto-trogus?

ARTOTROGUS: Here, at his master's heels, close to his hero, his brave, his blessed, his royal, his doughty warrior – whose valour Mars himself could hardly challenge or outshine.

PYRGOPOLYNICES [*reminiscent*]: Ay – what of the man whose life I saved on the Curculionean field, where the enemy was led by Bumbomachides Clytomestoridysarchides, a grandson of Nep-tune?

ARTOTROGUS: I remember it well. I remember his golden armour, and how you scattered his legions with a puff of breath, like a wind sweeping up leaves or lifting the thatch from a roof.

PYRGOPOLYNICES [*modestly*]: It was nothing much, after all.

ARTOTROGUS: Oh, to be sure, nothing to the many more famous

deeds you did – [*aside*] or never did. [*He comes down, leaving the Captain attending to his men.*] If anyone ever saw a bigger liar or more conceited braggart than this one, he can have me for keeps ... The only thing to be said for him is, his cook makes a marvellous olive salad ...

PYRGOPOLYNICES [*missing him*]: Where have you got to, Artotrogus?

ARTOTROGUS [*obsequiously*]: Here I am, sir. I was thinking about that elephant in India, and how you broke his ulna with a single blow of your fist.

PYRGOPOLYNICES: His ulna, was it?

ARTOTROGUS: His femur, I should have said.

PYRGOPOLYNICES: It was only a light blow, too.

ARTOTROGUS: By Jove, yes, if you had really hit him, your arm would have smashed through the animal's hide, bones, and guts.

PYRGOPOLYNICES [*modestly*]: I'd rather not talk about it, really.

ARTOTROGUS: Of course, sir; you don't need to tell me anything about your courageous deeds; I already know them all. [*Aside*] Oh dear, what I have to suffer for my stomach's sake. My ears have to be stuffed lest my teeth should decay from lack of use. I have to listen to all his tall stories and confirm them.

PYRGOPOLYNICES [*fishing for more flattery*]: Let me see, didn't I – ?

ARTOTROGUS [*promptly*]: Yes, that's right, I remember – you did. By Jove, yes ...

PYRGOPOLYNICES: What are you referring to?

ARTOTROGUS: That ... whatever it was ...

PYRGOPOLYNICES: Have you got a – ?

ARTOTROGUS: Notebook? Yes, sir, and a pencil. [*Producing them.*]

PYRGOPOLYNICES: You are as good as a thought-reader, my dear man.

ARTOTROGUS: Well, it's my job, isn't it, sir, to know your mind? I've trained myself to anticipate your wishes by instinct.

PYRGOPOLYNICES: I wonder if you remember ... [*He seems to be vaguely calculating.*]

ARTOTROGUS: How many? Yes, a hundred and fifty in Cilicia, a hundred in Scytholatronia, Sardians thirty, Macedonians sixty – killed, that is – in one day alone.

PYRGOPOLYNICES: How many does that make altogether?

ARTOTROGUS: Seven thousand.

PYRGOPOLYNICES: Must be at least that. You're an excellent accountant.

ARTOTROGUS [*showing his blank tablets, with a grin*]: And I haven't any of it written down. All done from memory.

PYRGOPOLYNICES: A prodigious memory, by Jove.

ARTOTROGUS: Nourished by a prodigious appetite.

PYRGOPOLYNICES: Go on as you are doing, my man, and you will never go hungry. I give you the freedom of my table.

ARTOTROGUS: And what about Cappadocia, sir, when you slaughtered five hundred at one fell swoop – or would have done if your sword hadn't got blunted first?

PYRGOPOLYNICES: They were only poor footsloggers; I decided to spare their lives.

ARTOTROGUS: Need I say, sir – since the whole world knows it – that the valour and triumphs of Pyrgopolynices are without equal on this earth, and so is his handsome appearance? The women are all at your feet, and no wonder; they can't resist your good looks; like those girls who were trying to get my attention yesterday.

PYRGOPOLYNICES: What did they say to you?

ARTOTROGUS: Oh, they pestered me with questions. 'Is he Achilles?' 'No, his brother,' I said. And the other girl said, 'I should think so, he's so good-looking and so charming; and hasn't he got lovely hair? I envy the girls who go to bed with him.'

PYRGOPOLYNICES: Did they really say that?

ARTOTROGUS: They did; and they begged me to bring you past their house today – as if you were a travelling show!

PYRGOPOLYNICES: It really is a bore to be so good-looking.

ARTOTROGUS: I'm sure it is. These women are a perfect pest; always begging and wheedling and imploring for a chance to see you. They keep asking me to arrange an introduction; I simply can't get on with my proper work.

PYRGOPOLYNICES: Well, I suppose it's time we went to the forum, to pay those recruits I enlisted yesterday. King Seleucus was most insistent that I should round up and sign on some troopers for him, and I mean to oblige him this very day.

ARTOTROGUS: Let's go, then.

PYRGOPOLYNICES: Escort, fall in; and follow me. [*He resumes his equipment, and marches off with his bodyguard.*]

    [PALAESTRIO, *a young, artful, and sophisticated slave, comes out of the Captain's house, to address the audience in the manner of a Prologue.*]

PALAESTRIO:

Now, friends, if you will kindly pay attention,
I will kindly explain the plot of this invention ...
[*To an interrupter*] If you don't want to listen, you'd better get up and go,
And leave room for those who do. All right? ... very well, then ....
Now you're all settled, I'll tell you about the plot
And explain the title of the play you're about to see
On this happy and festal occasion.
In the Greek this play is entitled *Alazon – The Braggart*;
Which in Latin we have translated by *Gloriosus*.
This town is Ephesus. The soldier you saw just now
Going off to the forum – he's my lord and master;
He is also a dirty liar, a boastful, arrogant,
Despicable perjurer and adulterer.
He thinks all women are after him, but in fact
Wherever he goes he's an object of derision.
Even the girls who smile their allurements at him
Are usually making mouths behind his back.
I've only recently become his slave,
And I'd like to tell you how it came about
That I fell into his hands after serving another master.
Listen, then. This is where the story begins.
    My master at Athens was a young man of excellent character.
He loved an Athenian woman, and she loved him;
Which is love as it should be. But while he was away
On his country's service – a diplomatic mission
To Naupactus – a highly responsible post –
This soldier man turned up at Athens, and there
Began paying attentions to my master's mistress,
And currying favour with her mother, with gifts
Of wine and jewels and delicacies for the table;
And so obtained the freedom of the old bawd's house.

But of course the Captain took the first chance that offered
Of playing a dirty trick on the poor old woman,
My master's mistress's mother. He abducted the girl
When the mother wasn't looking, put her on board
And shipped her, like a prisoner, back to Ephesus.
Well, when I heard of my master's girl being stolen,
As soon as I possibly could, I obtained a boat
And set off to carry the news to him at Naupactus.
But the gods were against me; we hadn't been long at sea
Before we fell into the hands of pirates.
Our ship was captured – and that was the end of me.
I never got to my master as I had intended.
The pirate who took me prisoner gave me as a present
To this soldier man. On arriving at his house, here,
Whom should I see but my master's girl from Athens!
As soon as we met, she warned me with a wink
Not to say a word; and later, when we got the chance,
She told me the whole sad story, and how she longed
To get out of that house and back to Athens – still loving
My former master, and heartily loathing the Captain.

   So, having made sure that this was how she felt,
I wrote a secret letter, carefully sealed it,
And gave it to a merchant to carry to my master,
The poor girl's former lover, now at Athens.
The letter was to beg him to come to Ephesus.
It worked. He came. And here he is today,
Staying with the kind old gentleman next door.
And the kind old gentleman, an old friend of his father,
Is being very obliging to his lovelorn guest,
And helping us with advice and encouragement
And willing cooperation. Accordingly,
I've devised a wonderful scheme, back there in the house,
To enable the lovers to meet whenever they want to.
The Captain had given the girl a room to herself,
Which no one else was allowed to enter; and there
I have cut an opening through the party wall
Into the adjoining house. So now the girl
Can come and go as secretly as she pleases!

The old man knows about it; in fact he suggested it.
For one of my fellow-slaves, a very dull creature,
Has been told off by the Captain to act as the poor girl's jailer;
And we're going to play some laughable tricks on him –
Oh, some very ingenious japes – and throw dust in his eyes,
And persuade him he hasn't seen what he thinks he has seen.
But we don't want *you* to be deceived; so don't forget,
One girl is going to pretend to be *two* girls,
One from this house and one from that: same girl,
But pretending to be a different one – all right?
That's how the jailer is going to be bamboozled.
Now there's somebody coming out of the old man's house . . .
Yes . . . this is the kind old gentleman I told you about.

[*He stands aside.*]

[PERIPLECTOMENUS *comes from his house, in a violent rage, and shouting orders to his slaves within.*]

PERIPLECTOMENUS: Mind what I say now. Next time you see an intruder climbing about on the roof, break his legs; unless you want me to whip your backs into ribbons. My neighbours seem to think they have a right to come spying on me from the tiles. Do you hear, all of you? If you catch any of the Captain's men on my roof, just throw him into the street – anyone except Palaestrio, that is. Never mind if they say they're up there looking for a hen or a pigeon or a monkey, you just mash them into mortal mincemeat, if you value your own lives. Whoever they are, don't leave them a whole bone between them – that'll save them from breaking the law by bringing their knuckle-bones to a party!

PALAESTRIO [*aside*]: It sounds as if someone from our place has been getting up to mischief next door . . . all this talk about breaking bones! I'm excluded, however, so I don't have to worry about what happens to the rest. I'll go and speak to him.

PERIPLECTOMENUS: Is that Palaestrio?

PALAESTRIO: It is. How are you today, Periplectomenus?

PERIPLECTOMENUS: You're the one man I want to see.

PALAESTRIO: Oh, why? Some trouble with our people?

PERIPLECTOMENUS: We're sunk.

PALAESTRIO: What has happened?

PERIPLECTOMENUS: The cat's out of the bag.

PALAESTRIO: What cat?

PERIPLECTOMENUS: Someone, I don't know who, someone from your house, has been peeping through our skylight and seen Philocomasium and my young guest inside – kissing each other.

PALAESTRIO: Who could he be?

PERIPLECTOMENUS: One of your fellow servants.

PALAESTRIO: Which one?

PERIPLECTOMENUS: That's what I don't know. He nipped off double quick.

PALAESTRIO: Oh dear. That looks like trouble for me.

PERIPLECTOMENUS: I shouted after him. 'Hey you,' I said, 'what are you doing on my roof?' 'Chasing a monkey,' he said, and vanished.

PALAESTRIO: Just my rotten luck, if I'm to be hung for a damned dumb animal. Is she still there, then? Philocomasium – is she in your house now?

PERIPLECTOMENUS: She was when I came out.

PALAESTRIO: Look, sir, go and tell her to skip across as quick as she can, and let everyone see she's at our place – unless she wants her love affair to send all us slaves to join a gallows party.

PERIPLECTOMENUS: Done. Anything else?

PALAESTRIO: Yes, there is. Tell her not to forget she's a woman, and to keep using all her womanly arts and devices.

PERIPLECTOMENUS: Such as what?

PALAESTRIO: She must convince the slave who saw her – talk him into believing he didn't see her. She may have been seen a hundred times but she must deny it all the same. She's got a tongue, hasn't she, and eyes, and cheek, and naughtiness and nerve and bluff and blarney and guile? She can swear any accuser into silence. She can speak lies, act lies, swear lies, as if she was born to it; she's got craft, cunning, and deceit at her fingers' ends. Don't they say an artful woman doesn't need to go to market – she grows her own spice and stuffing for cooking up any dish of mischief?

PERIPLECTOMENUS: I'll tell her all that, if she's still there ... What are you pondering over now, Palaestrio?

[PALAESTRIO *has gone into a brown study*.]

PALAESTRIO: Hush a moment, while I put on my thinking cap and consider what to do to get even with that colleague of mine who saw her kissing the young man – make him unsee what he saw.

PERIPLECTOMENUS: All right, go on with your thinking. I'll get out of your way ...

[PALAESTRIO *goes into a pantomime of deep cogitation;* PERIPLECTOMENUS, *watching him, comments to the audience on his gestures and attitudes.*]

PERIPLECTOMENUS: Watch him, do. Look at his attitude ... scowling brow, deep in thought ... knocking at his breast – to see if his wits are at home! Turning away now ... left hand on left hip ... doing sums with his right ... slap, right hand on right thigh – a hard slap too, he's having trouble with his thinking machine. Snapping his fingers – that means he's at a loss ... keeps changing his attitude ... shaking his head, 'no, that won't do'. He's got something cooking but doesn't want to serve it up half-baked – wants it done to a turn. Hullo, what now? He's building something ... the façade supported on a column. [PALAESTRIO *has his chin resting on his hand.*] I don't much like the look of that kind of building; I seem to have heard there's a writer in a certain foreign country with his head supported on a stone block and two warders holding him down day and night. Hah! now that's better ... that's a fine attitude ... just what a slave in a comedy ought to look like. He'll go on like this all day, you know, and never rest till he's found what he's looking for ... I believe he's got it ... Come on, get on with it, whatever it is. [PALAESTRIO *is frozen in a trance.*] Wake up, you can't go to sleep now ... unless you want to be whacked awake with a bundle of birches. Hey, I'm talking to you. Were you drinking last night? Palaestrio, I'm talking to you. Wake up. Show a leg. It's morning.

PALAESTRIO: I know.

PERIPLECTOMENUS [*in a playful reminiscence or parody of a martial ballad*]:

Then awake and beware, for the foeman is near;
He is laying an ambush to cut off your rear.
Look alive and take thought how to counter the host,
Do not sleep at your ease, there's no time to be lost.

Make a march, intercept him, get men up and doing,
Outflank the invader and save us from ruin.
Starve out your besiegers but save your supplies,
And protect your own lines of defence from surprise . . .

Hurry up, old chap, this is urgent. Think, devise, invent, some crafty plan of campaign, and be quick about it. Show us how to make what was seen unseen and what was done undone . . . Yes, he's got some big idea in his head now . . . he's erecting a mighty bastion. Come on, man, tell us you've got it all under control and we shall be confident of victory.

PALAESTRIO: I have got it all under control.

PERIPLECTOMENUS: Splendid; then everything will go as you wish.

PALAESTRIO: Bless you for those kind words.

PERIPLECTOMENUS: Well, am I to hear the result of your deliberations?

PALAESTRIO: Listen, and I will conduct you into the purlieus of my ingeniosity; you shall be privy to my purposes.

PERIPLECTOMENUS: I shall not betray a word of them.

PALAESTRIO: My master, let me tell you, is a man wrapped up in an elephant's hide; he has no more intelligence than a stone.

PERIPLECTOMENUS: I am aware of that.

PALAESTRIO: So this is the way I am going to work. This is the master plan. I shall say that Philocomasium has a twin sister who has just arrived from Athens with a man who is in love with her; and the two sisters, I shall say, are as alike as two drops of milk; and the visitors, I shall say, are being bedded and boarded at your place.

PERIPLECTOMENUS: Splendid! Wonderful! Congratulations! An excellent idea!

PALAESTRIO: Thus if my colleague takes it into his head to report the matter to the Captain, saying he saw Philocomasium kissing a strange man, I shall say it was her sister making love with her gentleman friend.

PERIPLECTOMENUS: Good; perfect. And I'll tell the Captain the same story if he asks me.

PALAESTRIO: Don't forget to say they are exactly alike. And of course we must put Philocomasium up to it, so that she doesn't make any slip if the Captain asks her.

PERIPLECTOMENUS: It's a brilliant idea, it really is. But I say, what if the Captain asks to see them both together? What do we do then?

PALAESTRIO: Oh, easy. We can think of dozens of excuses – she's not at home, she's gone for a walk, she's asleep, she's dressing, she's having a bath, she's gone out to lunch, she's at a party, she's busy, she won't want to be disturbed, she's not available. You can go on putting him off as long as you like, once we've got him on the right road, in the mood to believe any lie we tell him.

PERIPLECTOMENUS: Very well; all right.

PALAESTRIO: You go in, then; and if she's there, tell her to get back home at once. And put her wise to this scheme about the twin sister; explain it all to her, and make sure she understands what we're going to do.

PERIPLECTOMENUS: I'll send her over thoroughly primed and coached. Anything else?

PALAESTRIO: Only go.

PERIPLECTOMENUS: I'm going. [*He hurries into his house.*]

PALAESTRIO: And I'm going too – to employ a little subtlety on the problem of finding out which of our lads went chasing a monkey this morning. It shouldn't be difficult; he's sure to have let some of his mates into the secret about the master's girl and how he caught her kissing a strange man next door. I know what they're like – 'I was never one to keep a secret to myself'. And when I've found the culprit, I'll bring up all my assault weapons –

> The fight is on, with martial might and main
> I am resolved to see my foeman slain . . .

If I don't find him, well . . . if I don't find him, I'll have to put my nose to the earth like a foxhound, scent him out and track him down . . . Sh! the door's opening . . . this is the slave who has been told off to watch Philocomasium.

[*From the Captain's house comes* SCELEDRUS, *an honest but slow-witted slave. He wanders towards the next house, looking cautiously at the door and up at the roof.*]

SCELEDRUS: Either I was walking in my sleep on the roof this morning, or I surely saw my master's girl Philocomasium in there; and looking for trouble, from what I saw.

PALAESTRIO [*aside*]: That's it, then! He's the one that saw the kissing going on.

162

SCELEDRUS: Who goes there?

PALAESTRIO: Friend and colleague. What's doing, Sceledrus?

SCELEDRUS: Oh, Palaestrio, I'm glad you're here.

PALAESTRIO: Are you indeed? What can I do for you?

SCELEDRUS: I'm afraid –

PALAESTRIO: Afraid? Of what?

SCELEDRUS: I'm horribly afraid, Palaestrio, that the whole lot of us are heading for mortal death and damnation.

PALAESTRIO: You may be; no headers or high dives of that sort for me, thank you.

SCELEDRUS: I suppose you don't know of the latest horrible happenings in our household?

PALAESTRIO: What horrible happenings?

SCELEDRUS: Shocking things.

PALAESTRIO: Then I don't want to hear of them. Keep your knowledge to yourself.

SCELEDRUS: But you're going to hear of them. This morning, I was up on the roof, looking for our monkey.

PALAESTRIO: Useless man chases mischievous monkey.

SCELEDRUS: You go to hell.

PALAESTRIO: And you go – on with your story.

SCELEDRUS: Well, in passing I happened, just by chance, to look down into the courtyard of the next house; and there was Philocomasium, in the arms of some unknown youth, kissing him!

PALAESTRIO: Impossible! Incredible!

SCELEDRUS: Well, that's what I saw.

PALAESTRIO: You did?

SCELEDRUS: I did, with these two very eyes.

PALAESTRIO: Ah, go on. You're lying; you never saw any such thing.

SCELEDRUS: Do you think there's something wrong with my eyesight?

PALAESTRIO: I don't know; you'd better ask a doctor. But I wouldn't take responsibility for that story, if I were you; you'll only be putting your own head and heels in mortal danger. You're in it already, twice over, if you don't keep your silly mouth shut.

SCELEDRUS: Why twice over?

PALAESTRIO: Because – *one*, if your accusation against Philocomasium is false, they'll kill you for that; and *two*, if it's true, you're her keeper and they'll kill you for your carelessness.

SCELEDRUS: I don't know what'll become of me, then. I'm perfectly certain I saw her.

PALAESTRIO: You're sticking to your story, then, you poor idiot?

SCELEDRUS: I'm only telling you what I saw. What else can I do? What's more, she's still in there now.

PALAESTRIO: In there? Not in our house?

SCELEDRUS: Go in and see for yourself. I don't expect you to take my word for it.

PALAESTRIO: I certainly will.

[*He goes into Periplectomenus's house.*]

SCELEDRUS: I'll be waiting for you here ... And meanwhile I'll watch out for the young heifer and catch her on the way back from her grazing. I don't know what I'm going to do, though. The Captain made me her keeper; if I report her, I'm a dead man. So I am if I don't and he finds out about it. Women will be up to any daredevilment, curse them. She must have slipped out of doors while I was up on the roof, the audacious little minx. If the Captain hears of it, he'll hang the whole household on a gallows and me with them. Oh damn it all, I'll hold my tongue and hope to escape a miserable death. I can't be expected to look after a wench who goes out looking for customers, can I?

[PALAESTRIO *comes back.*]

PALAESTRIO: Oh Sceledrus, Sceledrus, if you aren't the most unblushing liar in the world; and the most ill-starred, misbegotten, god-forsaken –

SCELEDRUS: What's the matter now?

PALAESTRIO: Go and get your eyes gouged out, will you, for seeing what was never there to see.

SCELEDRUS: What do you mean, never there?

PALAESTRIO: I wouldn't give a rotten nut for your life now.

SCELEDRUS: Why, what's wrong?

PALAESTRIO: As if you didn't know.

SCELEDRUS: Of course I don't know; that's why I'm asking.

PALAESTRIO: Go and get your clacking tongue cut off.

SCELEDRUS: Why should I?

PALAESTRIO: Philocomasium is at home, and you say you've just seen her making love with a man next door.

SCELEDRUS: Why do you eat so much darnel? Wheat's cheap enough.

PALAESTRIO: What are you talking about?

SCELEDRUS: Darnel; it's bad for the eyes; you're not seeing clearly.

PALAESTRIO: You're stone blind, never mind seeing clearly. She's at home, I tell you; in there [*the Captain's house*]; in that house.

SCELEDRUS: At home? She can't be.

PALAESTRIO: I tell you she is.

SCELEDRUS: Get away. You're pulling my leg.

PALAESTRIO: I wouldn't soil my hands —

SCELEDRUS: What!

PALAESTRIO: — touching such dirty objects.

SCELEDRUS: Go and hang yourself.

PALAESTRIO: That may happen to you, unless you get yourself some new eyes and a new line of talk ... St! someone coming from our place ...

SCELEDRUS: Well, I'm going to keep my eye on *this* door. [*That is, Periplectomenus's house*] There's no way of getting from this house to that except through this door.

PALAESTRIO: But she's there already, I tell you. Really, Sceledrus, I don't know what's come over you.

SCELEDRUS: I know what I see, I know what I think, and if I trust anyone I trust myself. Nobody can make me believe she's not in this house. I'm stopping here, and she can't slip across without my knowing it. [*He plants himself in front of Periplectomenus's door.*]

PALAESTRIO [*aside*]: Now I'll get him. I'll shoot him down at his post ... Would you like me to prove that you're imagining things?

SCELEDRUS: Prove it, then.

PALAESTRIO: And that you're dumb-witted as well as cross-eyed?

SCELEDRUS: Anything you like.

PALAESTRIO: You stick to it that the Captain's girl is in there?

SCELEDRUS: Yes, I do. I know for a fact that I saw her there kissing a stranger.

PALAESTRIO: And you're certain there's no thoroughfare between our house and this?

SCELEDRUS: Of course I am.

PALAESTRIO: No balcony or garden path – no way at all, except over the roof?

SCELEDRUS: That's right.

PALAESTRIO: Very well, then. If she is in our house, and if I bring her out here before your eyes, will you own you deserve a flogging?

SCELEDRUS: I will.

PALAESTRIO: Watch that door, and mind she doesn't nip across when you're not looking.

SCELEDRUS: That's what I intend to do.

PALAESTRIO: I'll have her out here in front of you in two shakes.

SCELEDRUS: Do it, then.

[PALAESTRIO *goes into the Captain's house.*]

Now we shall know whether I really saw what I did see, or whether he'll be able to do what he says he's going to do and prove that she's at home. I've got my own eyes, haven't I? I don't need the loan of anyone else's. Of course that fellow's her favourite; he's always making up to her; he's the one who gets the first pick at the food and the best bits going. He's only been with us – what, three years perhaps – and now he's got the best position in the household ... But I must keep my mind on this job, and my eye on this door. [*He plants himself squarely across the door with arms outstretched, facing the door.*] I'll stand this way. Nobody's going to make a mug of me.

[PALAESTRIO *comes out of the Captain's house, with the girl* PHILOCOMASIUM.]

PALAESTRIO: Remember what I told you, now.

PHILOCOMASIUM: How many times do you think I want telling?

PALAESTRIO: The question is whether you're clever enough to do it.

PHILOCOMASIUM: I've enough cleverness to spare to teach ten innocent girls a few tricks. Go on with your scheme; I'll stay over here.

[PALAESTRIO *crosses to Sceledrus.*]

PALAESTRIO: Well, Sceledrus? Sceledrus!

SCELEDRUS [*not looking*]: I've a job to do here; but say what you want, I'm not deaf.

PALAESTRIO: You're just in the right position to be spread-eagled on a cross outside the gate – and soon will be, I think.

SCELEDRUS: Will I? Why?

PALAESTRIO: Look this way; do you know that woman?

SCELEDRUS [*looking round*]: Gods have mercy! It's the Captain's girl!

PALAESTRIO: That's what I think. Now perhaps you'll –

SCELEDRUS: Do what?

PALAESTRIO: – prepare for immediate death.

PHILOCOMASIUM: Where is the faithful slave who has been laying a monstrous false charge against an innocent girl?

PALAESTRIO: There he is. There is the man who told me what I reported to you.

PHILOCOMASIUM [*to Sceledrus*]: You did, did you, villain? You saw me in that house kissing a man?

PALAESTRIO: A strange man.

SCELEDRUS: I did, so help me –

PHILOCOMASIUM: You saw me yourself?

SCELEDRUS: By Herc'les I did, with these two eyes.

PALAESTRIO: Which you won't have much longer, since they see what isn't there.

SCELEDRUS: You can't tell me that I didn't see what I saw.

PHILOCOMASIUM: The man's mad; and I'm a fool to waste my time talking to him. I'll have him put away.

SCELEDRUS: You can save your threats, miss. I know I'm going to end up on a cross; that's where I shall follow my ancestors – father, grandfather, great-grandfather, great-great-grandfather. You can't threaten me with loss of eyes either ... Here, Palaestrio, come here a minute ... How the devil did she get out here?

PALAESTRIO: She came from our house, of course.

SCELEDRUS: From *our* house?

PALAESTRIO: Can you see *me*?

SCELEDRUS: I can see you all right; but what I can't see is how *she* can have got across from *here* to *there*. There's certainly no balcony or garden path, or window that isn't barred ... I know I saw you in this house, young lady.

PALAESTRIO: Damn you, are you going to persist in your allegations?

167

PHILOCOMASIUM: Oh, of course! This is the dream come true, which I dreamt last night!

PALAESTRIO: What did you dream last night?

PHILOCOMASIUM: I'll tell you. Fancy! Last night I dreamt that my twin sister had come to Ephesus from Athens with her lover. And the two of them spent the night here next door to us. That is what I dreamt.

PALAESTRIO [aside]: That is what I dreamt . . . Go on.

PHILOCOMASIUM: Well, I was delighted to see my sister, but her coming resulted in my being exposed to a scandalous suspicion. Because one of my servants – this is what I dreamt – alleged – as you are doing now – that I had been making love with a strange young man, and all the time it was my twin sister with her friend! So I found myself – in my dream – charged with this horrible false accusation.

PALAESTRIO: And now all that you dreamt has come true, hasn't it? What a remarkable coincidence! You'd better go in and thank the gods. And I think you ought to tell the Captain all about it.

PHILOCOMASIUM: I certainly will. I don't propose to let a wicked calumny like that go unpunished.

[She returns to the house.]

SCELEDRUS: Oh dear, I tremble to think of what I've done. My back is itching all over.

PALAESTRIO: You realize you're for it now?

SCELEDRUS: Anyway, she's at home now. And as long as she's there, I'm not going to take my eyes off this door.

[He mounts guard over the Captain's door.]

PALAESTRIO: Wasn't it extraordinary, Sceledrus, her dreaming exactly what happened, and you thinking you saw her with that young man?

SCELEDRUS: I don't know how to trust myself any more, if I didn't see what I thought I saw.

PALAESTRIO: Well, you had better come to your senses before it's too late; if the master hears of this first, you'll be nicely caught.

SCELEDRUS: Of course I realize now I was wrong; I must have been half blind.

PALAESTRIO: That's obvious – always was, since the girl must have been at home all the time.

SCELEDRUS: I don't know ... it's funny ... I couldn't have seen her, yet I did.

PALAESTRIO: Good god, man, your stupidity has almost put us all on the spot; trying to show what a loyal servant you were, you nearly dished yourself. But look out, someone is coming from next door.

[*Periplectomenus's door opens again, and* PHILOCOMASIUM *is seen, giving instructions to slaves within; she looks exactly the same as before, but adopts the manner of a different person.*]

PHILOCOMASIUM: Light the fire on the altar, please; I must render my joyful and grateful thanks to Diana of Ephesus and pay her homage with fragrant Arabian incense for having preserved me alive when I was hard pressed by the angry waves in Neptune's storm-tossed realm and dominion.

SCELEDRUS: Palaestrio, Palaestrio!

PALAESTRIO: Sceledrus, Sceledrus, what's the matter now?

SCELEDRUS: That woman just coming out there – is she or isn't she our master's mistress?

PALAESTRIO: Upon my word, I believe she is. But how in the world can she have got from *here* to *there* – if it is really the same woman?

SCELEDRUS: Don't you believe it's the same woman?

PALAESTRIO: She certainly looks like it.

SCELEDRUS: We'd better go and speak to her ... What are you doing here, Philocomasium? What right or business have you in this house? Philocomasium, I'm talking to you.

[*She takes no notice.*]

PALAESTRIO: You might as well talk to yourself. She has evidently got nothing to say to you.

SCELEDRUS: I'm talking to you, you shameless and wicked girl, wandering about the place like this.

PHILOCOMASIUM: To whom are you speaking, my man?

SCELEDRUS: To you, of course.

PHILOCOMASIUM: And why should you be speaking to me? Who are you?

SCELEDRUS: Who am I?

PHILOCOMASIUM: Yes, who are you? I don't know you.

PALAESTRIO: Perhaps you don't know who I am either?

PHILOCOMASIUM: Whoever you are, you are very impertinent, both of you.

SCELEDRUS: You don't know either of us?

PHILOCOMASIUM: I don't.

SCELEDRUS: Oh dear, oh dear, it looks as if –

PALAESTRIO: As if what?

SCELEDRUS: As if we've mislaid ourselves somewhere; she says she doesn't know either of us.

PALAESTRIO: We must get to the bottom of this, Sceledrus, and find out whether we are ourselves or somebody else's selves. Somebody round here may have changed us into other people when we weren't looking.

SCELEDRUS: I'm myself, all right.

PALAESTRIO: Well, so am I. [*He addresses Philocomasium again*] I think you're asking for trouble, young woman. You, Philocomasium! I mean you.

PHILOCOMASIUM: Are you out of your senses? Why do you call me by a stupid name I've never heard of?

PALAESTRIO: What should I call you, then?

PHILOCOMASIUM: Honoria is my name.

SCELEDRUS: That can't be right. That's no name for you, Philocomasium. You don't know what honour means; and you're dishonouring my master.

PHILOCOMASIUM: I am?

SCELEDRUS: You are.

PHILOCOMASIUM: I don't know what you mean. I only arrived at Ephesus from Athens last night with my friend, a young Athenian gentleman.

PALAESTRIO: Indeed? And what brings you to Ephesus, may I ask?

PHILOCOMASIUM: I heard that my twin sister was living here, and I have come to look for her.

SCELEDRUS: You're up to no good.

PHILOCOMASIUM: I'm certainly doing no good talking to you two. I'll leave you.

SCELEDRUS: Oh, no you don't. [*He detains her forcibly.*]

PHILOCOMASIUM: Take your hands off me.

SCELEDRUS: You're fairly copped this time, woman.

PHILOCOMASIUM: You let me go or my hands and your face will come to blows.

SCELEDRUS [*to Palaestrio*]: Don't just stand there, you fool. Catch hold of her from your side.

PALAESTRIO: I don't want my side or back involved in this. For all I know, she may not be Philocomasium but her double.

PHILOCOMASIUM [*struggling*]: Are you going to let me go?

SCELEDRUS: No. You come quietly, or I'll drag you home by force whether you like it or not.

PHILOCOMASIUM: My home is in Athens and so is my master. This house is where I am a guest. I don't know what home you are talking about; I don't know either of you and I've never seen you before.

SCELEDRUS: You can have the law on us, then. I'm not letting you go, unless you promise on your honour you'll go back home – in there. [*Indicating the Captain's house.*]

PHILOCOMASIUM: Well, you're too strong for me, whoever you are. Very well, I promise, if you'll let me go, I'll go home as you tell me.

SCELEDRUS [*releasing her*]: There, then, you're free.

PHILOCOMASIUM: Thank you; now I'm free, and now I'll go.
    [*She pops back into Periplectomenus's house.*]

SCELEDRUS: Trust a woman!

PALAESTRIO: The bird has flown, Sceledrus! At any rate, it's as plain as can be, she's the master's girl. Would you like to help me make a thorough job of it?

SCELEDRUS: By doing what?

PALAESTRIO: Go and fetch me a sword out of the house.

SCELEDRUS: What do you want with a sword?

PALAESTRIO: I'm going to storm my way into that house, and if I find any man there cuddling with Philocomasium, chop his head off on the spot.

SCELEDRUS: You think it is her, then?

PALAESTRIO: Not a doubt of it.

SCELEDRUS: She did her best to fool us, didn't she?

PALAESTRIO: Go and get the sword.

SCELEDRUS: I'll have it here in two shakes ... [*He goes into the Captain's house.*]

PALAESTRIO: There's not a man on horse or foot can make a braver show or put up a bolder fight than a woman can. Did you see how artfully she spoke her part in both characters? And how she bediddled my conscientious colleague her keeper? Thank heaven for that bolt-hole through the party wall!

[SCELEDRUS *comes back, more mystified and awestruck than ever.*]

SCELEDRUS: I say, Palaestrio. You won't need that sword after all.

PALAESTRIO: Why? What's happened now?

SCELEDRUS: The girl's at home. I've just seen her.

PALAESTRIO: At home? She can't be.

SCELEDRUS: She is, lying on a bed.

PALAESTRIO: Oh my goodness, if that's so, you're in a proper mess now.

SCELEDRUS: Why am I?

PALAESTRIO: You have assaulted the woman from next door.

SCELEDRUS: Oh dear, that makes it worse than ever, doesn't it?

PALAESTRIO: There's no denying now that the woman is our girl's twin sister; it was she you saw kissing a man.

SCELEDRUS [*partly comforted*]: Yes, that's true enough. I should have done for myself, shouldn't I, if I had told the master?

PALAESTRIO: You would, and if you've any sense you'll say no more about it. No slave need tell all he knows. Anyway I don't want to have any more to do with it and I don't fancy getting mixed up in any more of your problems, so I'll leave you. I'm going to see the gentleman next door; that's where I'll be if the master wants me; you can let me know if he comes.

[*He goes into Periplectomenus's house.*]

SCELEDRUS: So he's off; he might never be the master's slave at all for all he cares about the master's business. Anyhow the wench is safe indoors now, that's certain, since I've just seen her lying down. I'll keep a careful watch from now on. [*He rivets his attention on the Captain's door.*]

[PERIPLECTOMENUS *now comes out of his house, again in an angry temper; but this time it is a calculated pretence.*]

PERIPLECTOMENUS: By Hercules, these men of the Captain's seem to take me for an old woman, the tricks they play on me. Someone has been assaulting and insulting my guest, a free and honest

young girl who came here from Athens, with the young man who
is visiting me.

SCELEDRUS: Now I'm for it. It's me he's making for; and it sounds
as if there's a pack of trouble coming to me over this business.

PERIPLECTOMENUS: I'll have a word with this fellow ... Hey
you, Sceledrus, you arch-villain, was it you that was impertinent
to my guest just now in front of this house?

SCELEDRUS: Listen, please, mister –

PERIPLECTOMENUS: Listen to you? Why should I?

SCELEDRUS: I'd like to explain –

PERIPLECTOMENUS: Explain indeed? What explanation can there be
for such rude and disgusting behaviour? You lawless troopers think
you can take the law into your own hands, do you, rope's end?

SCELEDRUS: May I speak, sir?

PERIPLECTOMENUS: By all the gods and goddesses above, if I'm not
allowed to give you the punishment you deserve, twelve hours
continuous flogging from morning till night, for having broken
down my tiles and gutters, while chasing your partner in crime, that
monkey of yours, and having peeped from up there on a guest of
mine affectionately embracing her sweetheart, and having accused
your master's innocent mistress of misconduct and me of abomin-
able iniquity, and having assaulted my lady guest before my own
front door – if I can't take the rope to you myself, I'll see that your
master is swamped in a tide of ignominy as high as the high seas
at the height of a tempest.

SCELEDRUS: The truth is, sir, I'm that bothered I don't know how
to reason with you ... unless ... if *this* one isn't *that* one, and *that*
one isn't *this* one ... you may think there's some excuse for me ...
the fact is I don't know what I saw ... that lady of yours is either
exactly like ours ... or else they're the same person ...

PERIPLECTOMENUS: Go in and see for yourself, then.

SCELEDRUS: May I?

PERIPLECTOMENUS: That's what I am telling you to do. Have a
good look and make up your mind.

SCELEDRUS: Well, I will, then.

[*He goes into Periplectomenus's house. In the time it takes him to
reach the door, knock, and obtain admission,* PERIPLECTOMENUS
has crossed to the Captain's door to whisper to Philocomasium within.]

PERIPLECTOMENUS: Philocomasium! Skip across to my house, immediately. And when Sceledrus has come out again, skip back double quick ... I bet she'll bungle it ... If he doesn't find her in there, it'll be – ah, here he comes.

[SCELEDRUS *returns, dumbfounded.*]

SCELEDRUS: Almighty powers! It would pass the wit of gods to make one woman more exactly like another, without she's the same person.

PERIPLECTOMENUS: Now what do you say?

SCELEDRUS: I'm a poor miserable sinner.

PERIPLECTOMENUS: Do you still think she's your girl?

SCELEDRUS: She is, and yet she isn't.

PERIPLECTOMENUS: You saw the one in my house?

SCELEDRUS: I did, and your friend with her, kissing and cuddling.

PERIPLECTOMENUS: And is she your master's girl?

SCELEDRUS: I don't know.

PERIPLECTOMENUS: Would you like to make sure?

SCELEDRUS: I would indeed.

PERIPLECTOMENUS: Go into your house, then, quickly, and see whether she's still there.

SCELEDRUS: Yes, that's a good idea. I will. I'll be back in a jiffy.

[*He goes into the Captain's house.*]

PERIPLECTOMENUS [*chuckling*]: Oh dear, oh dear, I never saw a man more neatly bamboozled. It's marvellous ... Here he comes.

[SCELEDRUS *back again, nearly demented.*]

SCELEDRUS: Oh Periplectomenus, for pity's sake, by gods and men and my silly head and your merciful knees –

PERIPLECTOMENUS: What, what? You needn't grovel.

SCELEDRUS: Have mercy on my ignorance and foolishness. Now I know I was blind, daft, and brainless. Philocomasium is in there!

PERIPLECTOMENUS: So, you miserable scoundrel, you've seen them both now, have you?

SCELEDRUS: Yes, I've seen them both.

PERIPLECTOMENUS: And now I'd like to see your master.

SCELEDRUS: Truly, sir, I confess I deserve the severest punishment; I admit I have committed an offence against your guest. But really I thought she was my master's girl, and the Captain had made me her keeper. They're so much alike, she and your young lady, two

174

buckets of water out of the same well couldn't be more alike. And it was me, too, that looked down into your house from the roof, I admit it.

PERIPLECTOMENUS: I should hope you do admit it, since I saw you myself. And there you saw my two guests, the lady and the gentleman, kissing each other, did you?

SCELEDRUS: I did. Well, I can't deny what I saw, can I? But I thought it was Philocomasium I had seen.

PERIPLECTOMENUS: And is that what you think of me? Do you take me for such a despicable scoundrel as to allow an insult of that kind to be offered to my friend and neighbour in my own house, with my knowledge?

SCELEDRUS: Well, no, sir; now that I see how things really are, I realize I acted foolishly. I meant no harm.

PERIPLECTOMENUS: You acted very presumptuously. A slave ought to keep his eyes, hands, and tongue under control.

SCELEDRUS: I promise you, if I ever again breathe a word about anything, even what I know for certain, you can give me to the hangman. I put myself in your hands, and beg you to forgive me this time.

PERIPLECTOMENUS: Well ... I will do my best to believe you meant no harm ... I forgive you.

SCELEDRUS: God bless you, sir.

PERIPLECTOMENUS: And by Jupiter, if you want the gods to bless you, you'll keep a watch on your tongue from now on, and make sure you don't know whatever it is you do know, and haven't seen whatever you have seen.

SCELEDRUS: That's good advice, sir; that's just what I will do. Am I quite forgiven, then?

PERIPLECTOMENUS: Yes, yes; be off with you.

SCELEDRUS: There's nothing else you want, sir?

PERIPLECTOMENUS: Only to see the last of you.

SCELEDRUS [aside]: He's only having me on, I believe – pretending so kindly not to be angry with me. I know what he's up to; he's going to get me arrested at home as soon as the Captain comes back from town. It's a plot between him and Palaestrio to have me thrown out and sold. I knew it; I've known it for some time. I can see the bait in that trap and I'm not touching it. I'll do a bunk and lie doggo for a day or two, until tempers have cooled and all this commotion died down. I know I've earned enough punishment to pay for the sins of a whole people. However, for the time being, I'll get back to where I belong. [*He returns to the house.*]

PERIPLECTOMENUS: So much for him. Upon my word, the man has less brains than a dead pig, the way he allowed himself to be persuaded that he didn't see what he did see! He has capitulated to us now, at all events – eyes, ears, and mind. So far so good. The girl did her part in fine style too. Now I must get back to the council chamber, while Palaestrio is in my house, and Sceledrus has been disposed of. We shall have a quorum ... but I must be there before the assignment of jobs begins or I might miss something. [*He hurries back to his house.*]

*

[*After an interval,* PALAESTRIO *appears from Periplectomenus's house; he is looking out cautiously, restraining his friends from following.*]

PALAESTRIO: Don't come out just yet, sir, nor you, Pleusicles; let me scout around first, to make sure there's no enemy lurking anywhere to overhear our conference. [*He chatters on, while elaborately scrutinizing any possible hiding place.*] Must make certain the ground is absolutely safe from surprise ... can't have any intruder pinching our plans. A well-laid plan is worse than no plan at all, if the enemy can make use of it. If it's of any use to the enemy, it's no use to you. People often have a perfectly good plan stolen under their noses, if they haven't chosen the venue for their conference with sufficient care and circumspection ... Oh yes, if the enemy gets to know your plan of campaign, he can use your plan of campaign to bind and gag you, and you find he has turned the tables on you. I'm just going to see if there's anyone on this side ... or on that side ... laying a snare of ears about our deliberations ... No, all's well ... an empty vista down to the far end of the street. I'll call them out. Now then, Pleusicles and Periplectomenus, you can come out.

[*They come out.*]

PERIPLECTOMENUS: At your command.

PALAESTRIO: A pleasure to command such loyal subjects. But, in the first place, are we to act on the plan we have just been discussing?

PERIPLECTOMENUS: It's by far the most practicable plan.

PALAESTRIO: What do you think, Pleusicles?

PLEUSICLES: If you're agreed, who am I to object? I couldn't have any better counsellor than you, Palaestrio.

PALAESTRIO: That's very nice and obliging of you, sir.

PERIPLECTOMENUS: He couldn't say less, I'm sure.

PLEUSICLES: But I must say the prospect distresses me terribly, pains me heart and soul.

PERIPLECTOMENUS: What distresses you, I should like to know?

PLEUSICLES: That you, at your age, should be involved in a juvenile escapade of this sort; that I should be asking you to lend your efforts to save my face, to help me in my love affair; that you should be engaged in the sort of business which a man of your age should turn his back on, not encourage. I am ashamed to give you all this trouble at your age.

PALAESTRIO: You're a very unusual kind of lover, if you're ashamed of what you're doing. You're no lover at all, sir; nothing but a shadow of a lover.

PLEUSICLES: Do *you* think I ought to bother him, at his age, with my love affair?

PERIPLECTOMENUS: Good God, man! Do you think I've got one foot in the grave already? You think I've lived long enough, do you, and ought to be in my coffin? I'm only fifty-four, let me tell you; I can see without spectacles, I'm nimble on my pins, and I can turn my hand to anything.

PALAESTRIO [*to Pleusicles*]: That's true, you know; apart from his white hair, he doesn't show a sign of age; he has all his faculties as good as new.

PLEUSICLES: I know that, Palaestrio, from my own experience. He has been as kind to me as any friend of my own age.

PERIPLECTOMENUS: I should hope so; and the more you try me, the better you'll learn how helpful I can be to a young man in love.

PLEUSICLES: I have no need to learn what I know well already.

PERIPLECTOMENUS: No indeed, you've got the evidence in front

of you and don't need to look any further for it. It takes a man
who has been a lover himself to see into a lover's heart. For that
matter, there's some love in my own heart yet, and sap in my body;
I'm not so dried up as to have said goodbye to all the delights and
pleasures of life. Furthermore I can still be an agreeable table-
companion and join in a witty argument without wanting to lay
down the law or contradict my neighbours. I make a special point
of not being a bore in company; I know how to take my share of
the talking, and my share of silence too when it's someone else's
turn to talk. I never cough, spit, or snuffle. Yes, sir, I'm an Ephesian,
not an Apulian – or Animulian.

PALAESTRIO: A model of middle-aged manners – if his manners
are all he claims them to be; a child of the nursery of Venus!

PERIPLECTOMENUS: Yes, I can show you a better exhibition of
manners than I would care to claim credit for. You won't find me
making a pass at someone else's girl at a party, or snatching plates
of food, or grabbing the cup out of turn, or starting a drunken
quarrel among the company. If anyone annoys me, I simply go
home, have no more to do with him. As long as I am in company,
I like to make myself gracious, friendly, and agreeable.

PALAESTRIO: Grace and good manners are second nature to you, sir.
Find me three such men of your kind and I'll give their weight in
gold for them.

PLEUSICLES: You won't find one, of his age, more charming in
every way, more delightful to have as a friend.

PERIPLECTOMENUS: Yes, I think I can convince you that I still
have the spirit of youth, when you see what a good friend I can
be to you in all circumstances. Do you need a counsellor at law –
serious, forceful? I am at your service. Or one of gentler manner?
I can be gentle as the untroubled sea, speak softer than the whisper
of a summer breeze. A gay companion for the table? I'm your
man. The perfect dinner guest, the most accomplished caterer –
that's me. And at a dance I'll show a leg as light as any ballet-
boy.

PALAESTRIO: What more talents than these could a man ask for,
if he had the choice?

PLEUSICLES: What I would ask for would be the means to express
the gratitude that his kindness deserves – and yours. I realize how

much you are doing for me, and I hate to think how much I am costing you, sir.

PERIPLECTOMENUS: Cost? Don't be a fool, my boy. What you spend on an enemy, or a bad wife, that is cost; what you spend on a good friend, and a welcome guest, is all gain; so is what you spend on your duties to the gods – all gain, to any right way of thinking. Thanks to the good gods, I have the means to give you generous hospitality. Eat and drink, make yourself at home in my house and give yourself a good time. My house is a free house; and I'm a free man, thank God; I like to be alive. I was rich enough, by the grace of heaven, to get myself a rich and well-born wife; but no, thank you; I'm not having any barking bitch in this house.

PALAESTRIO: No? You don't care for the joys of fatherhood, then?

PERIPLECTOMENUS: I much prefer the joys of freedom.

PALAESTRIO: Ah well, no doubt you know what's best for you – as well as for other people.

PERIPLECTOMENUS: Oh yes; to marry a good wife, of course, would be very pleasant – if there were any place on earth where you could find one. But am I to saddle myself with the sort of woman ... well, the sort of woman who'd never say 'If you'll buy me the wool, dear, I'll make you a warm cosy wrap and some good winter vests to keep out the cold' ... as if any wife ever did say such a thing! Instead of that, she'd be waking me up before cock-crow, with 'Darling, it's Mother's Day; can you let me have some money to buy something for mother?' or 'I shall need some money to make jam', 'It's Minerva's day, I shall have to pay the fortune-teller, and the dream-caster and the soothsayer and the horoscopist; and I simply can't not send anything to that woman who tells your character from your eyebrows; and I ought really to tip the wardrobe maid; and the laundry girl has been giving me black looks for some time for not having given her anything. Then there's the midwife complaining that she has not been paid enough, and I hope you're going to send something to the slave-children's foster-mother.' All that sort of expense that women cost you is what keeps me from getting married and having to listen to that kind of talk.

PALAESTRIO: You can count yourself lucky, sir; once let go of your freedom and you don't easily get it back again.

PLEUSICLES: All the same, it's a fine thing for a man who is well off and well born, to raise up children, to perpetuate his own and his family's name.

PERIPLECTOMENUS: What do I want with children? I have plenty of relatives. I'm quite happy as I am, I've got all I want, I live as I please, I do as I like; and on my death my relatives will have my property to carve up between them. They'll soon be all round me, taking care of me, calling to inquire how I am and whether they can do anything for me. They come already, as a matter of fact, before dawn, asking how I've slept. Children? huh! . . . my children are all the people who send me presents . . . people who, when they offer a sacrifice, invite me to the feast and feed me better than they do themselves . . . people who ask me to lunch or dinner. And there's no one so sorry for himself as the poor devil who finds that he has given me less than the rest! So there they are, matching gift against gift, and I'm chuckling to myself; I know it's my property they're fishing for, with all this competition to nurse and coddle me.

PALAESTRIO: You're a wise one, sir, I will say, the way you look after number one. A good life, when all is said and done, is worth a family of twins and triplets.

PERIPLECTOMENUS: Oh my goodness, yes; children, if I had any, would have brought me a peck of trouble. I should never have had a moment's peace. If a child were ill, I should have thought he was dying; if my son fell off his horse, or fell down drunk in the street, I'd be afraid he had broken his leg or his neck.

PLEUSICLES: If ever a man deserved wealth and long life, give me that man who knows how to conserve his wealth and look after his health and be of service to his friends.

PALAESTRIO: Bravo for a fine old gentleman! . . . You know, when I come to think of it, it's a pity, upon my word it is, that the gods didn't allot the gift of life to men on a less impartial scale. In the market, now, an honest overseer fixes the price of goods according to their merits – a good price for good merchandise that deserves it – and cuts down the seller's price for any bad merchandise, in proportion to its deficiencies. In the same way, to be fair, the gods should have allotted to humans their appropriate share of life. A man of pleasant character should be given a long life; the villains and criminals should have their lives cut off short. If the gods had gone about it this way, there would be far fewer wicked men amongst us, and far less audacious law-breaking; and what's more, life wouldn't be so expensive for the honest men.

PERIPLECTOMENUS: No, no; it's only a fool and an ignoramus who would arraign the gods and find fault with their designs. But enough of this; I must get off to market, so that I can provide you, my friend, with such hospitality as shall be worthy of us both, a hearty welcome and good hearty fare.

PLEUSICLES: I am more than satisfied with what you have done for me already. To have a guest, even your dearest friend, planted on you for three days together is something of an affliction; ten days of it must be a whole Iliad of afflictions. Even if the master puts up with it willingly, the servants grumble.

PERIPLECTOMENUS: My dear friend, my servants are taught to serve, not to give me orders or expect me to consider their convenience. If they don't like what suits me – well, I'm skipper and they have to get on with it; they just have to do what they don't like, and get cuffs instead of thanks for it. Now for my shopping.

PLEUSICLES: If you must, sir; but please don't kill the fatted calf; anything will do for me.

PERIPLECTOMENUS: Oh good heavens, you're not going to sing that old song, are you? You're talking like a lower-class person; the sort of person who, when he sits down at your table and food is put in front of him, says 'Oh, you shouldn't have gone to all this expense for me; no, really, it's ridiculous, there's enough for ten people here' – complains of what you've bought for him, and eats it up just the same.

PALAESTRIO: That's it! That's exactly what they do. The wise old bird, he doesn't miss anything!

PERIPLECTOMENUS: And mark you, however high the table is heaped, you'll never hear them say 'No more of that, thank you ... you can take this dish away ... I shan't need the ham, thanks ... nor the pork ... the conger will be very nice cold, you'd better remove it ... go on, take it away.' Oh no, you won't hear anything like that from one of them; they just fall to and sprawl all over the table in their eagerness to help themselves.

PALAESTRIO: You've a good manner of describing bad manners, sir.

PERIPLECTOMENUS: I haven't said a hundredth part of what I could find to say if I had time.

PALAESTRIO: Yes ... well ... perhaps we ought now to turn our attention to the business in hand. Please listen to me, gentlemen. I shall need your help, sir, to carry out the ingenious ruse which I have devised for trimming Captain Curlylocks and assisting our loving friend in his design of abducting and possessing his beloved Philocomasium.

PERIPLECTOMENUS: Let's hear the plan.

PALAESTRIO: Let's have that ring of yours.

PERIPLECTOMENUS: My ring? What do you want that for?

PALAESTRIO: Give it me first, and then I'll expound the structure of my stratagem.

PERIPLECTOMENUS: Very well, then; here it is. [*Giving the ring.*]

PALAESTRIO: And here is my stratagem.

PERIPLECTOMENUS: Our ears are wide open.

PALAESTRIO: The Captain, my master, is the most accomplished seducer that ever was or ever will be.

PERIPLECTOMENUS: I can quite believe that.

PALAESTRIO: His handsome features, he will tell you, surpass those of Alexander; and for that reason, so he says, all the wives of Ephesus are out to get him.

PERIPLECTOMENUS: I expect there are many husbands who sincerely hope you are wrong about him, but I don't doubt what you say for a moment. Continue, Palaestrio, and come to the point as quickly as possible.

PALAESTRIO: Do you think you could find a woman of desirable appearance, with a talent for practical joking and mischief?

PERIPLECTOMENUS: A freeborn woman, or a freed woman?

PALAESTRIO: Whichever you like, provided she has an eye to the main chance, is used to earning her keep by bodily work, and has some sense in her head; sensibility would be too much to expect, no woman has that.

PERIPLECTOMENUS: Ripe, or just budding?

PALAESTRIO: Well ... juicy ... as attractive as possible, and as young as possible.

PERIPLECTOMENUS: I know! ... the very thing ... a young protégée of mine ... in the business. But what do you want her for?

PALAESTRIO: I want you to take her into your house, and produce her as your wife – all dressed up like a married woman, hair suitably done, ribbons and ringlets and so on; and you must coach her in the part.

PERIPLECTOMENUS: I don't see what all this is leading up to.

PALAESTRIO: You will. By the way, has she got a maid?

PERIPLECTOMENUS: Oh yes, a very artful one too.

PALAESTRIO: We shall need her as well. Now listen: you must instruct the woman and her maid to pretend that she is your wife, and that she is swooning for love of this military man, and that she has given this ring to her attendant, and that *she* has given it to *me*, so that *I* can give it to the Captain, acting as a kind of go-between –

PERIPLECTOMENUS: You needn't shout; I'm not deaf . . . The man is breaking my eardrums!

PALAESTRIO: Sorry. As I say, I shall give him the ring, pretending it was conveyed and entrusted to me by your wife as a means of introducing her to him. And being the sort of man he is, he will be in a frenzy to get at her; seducing women is the only thing the wretched man is interested in.

PERIPLECTOMENUS: Right. Set your mind at rest. You couldn't find two more attractive women, not anywhere under the sun, than the pair I shall produce for you.

PALAESTRIO: I'll leave that to you, then. We shall want them as soon as possible. Now, Pleusicles, a word with you.

PLEUSICLES: At your service.

PALAESTRIO: One important thing; when the Captain comes back, you must remember not to call Philocomasium by her real name.

PLEUSICLES: What must I call her?

PALAESTRIO: Honoria.

PLEUSICLES: Oh, of course, that's the name we agreed on, isn't it?

PALAESTRIO: 'Nuff said. Off you go.

PLEUSICLES: I'll remember. Still I don't quite see why –

PALAESTRIO: I'll explain later – when necessary; say no more now. The old gentleman has got his job to do; see that you do yours, when the time comes.

PLEUSICLES: Very well, I'll go, then.

PALAESTRIO: And try to keep your mind on your instructions!

[PLEUSICLES *goes back to the house.*] This is going to be a rare old mix-up! I've got something moving now! If my troops are well trained, I shall get the girl out of the Captain's clutches before the day is over. Now for that fellow Sceledrus. [*He knocks and calls at the Captain's door.*] Sceledrus! Hey, Sceledrus, it's Palaestrio here. Come out here, if you're not too busy.

[*A tipsy slave,* LURCIO, *comes out.*]

LURCIO: You can't have Sceledrus.

PALAESTRIO: Why can't I?

LURCIO: He's asleep . . . and swallowing.

PALAESTRIO: How can he be swallowing if he's asleep?

LURCIO: Well . . . snoring. Snoring is a sort of . . . swallowing.

PALAESTRIO: Has he gone to bed, then?

LURCIO: All except his nose . . . that's wide awake and talking.

PALAESTRIO: He must have helped himself to a cup or two on the sly, while making mulled wine in the cellar . . . Here you, rascal, if you're his assistant cellar-man –

LURCIO: What do you want?

PALAESTRIO: How has Sceledrus managed to fall asleep?

LURCIO: By closing his eyes, I expect.

PALAESTRIO: Idiot! that's no answer. Come here. Tell me the truth or you're a dead man. Did you draw wine for him?

LURCIO: I did not.

PALAESTRIO: You deny it?

LURCIO: Of course I deny it . . . he told me to. I deny I filled a four-pint pitcher for him, and I deny he drank it off hot for his lunch.

PALAESTRIO: And you deny you drank any, I suppose?

LURCIO: So help me gods, I didn't *drink* it. It was that hot, it burned my gullet. I had to toss it down in one gulp.

PALAESTRIO: So some people can soak themselves silly on the best wine, while others have to be content with vinegar-water. A fine cellarman and potboy we've got!

LURCIO: I bet you'd do the same in our place. You're jealous you can't join us.

PALAESTRIO: Has he ever helped himself to wine before? Answer me, scoundrel. And make no mistake, if you tell me a lie you'll be strung up.

LURCIO: So that's it, is it? You want to go and tell everybody what

I told you ... then I'll be sacked from this cellar-tippling job ... and you'll take charge of it ... with another potboy to help you.

PALAESTRIO: No, I won't; indeed I won't. Come on, you needn't be afraid to tell me.

LURCIO: I've never seen him open a jar of wine – honest. It was like this ... he'd tell me to open one for him ... and I'd go and open it.

PALAESTRIO: I thought there seemed to be a lot of jars standing empty on their heads!

LURCIO: Oh, bless you, no ... it wasn't us that knocked so many of them off their feet. It's a bit slippery in some places in that cellar. There was a big two-quart pot there, close to them jars, like that ... and this pot would often get its belly full ten times running ... I've seen it, full, empty, full, empty. So most likely this big pot must have got rolling drunk and knocked over some of the little jars.

PALAESTRIO: Get along with you. You've all been getting rolling drunk in that cellar evidently. I'll have to go myself and fetch the master back from town.

LURCIO: Oh my God! If the master comes home, and hears what's been going on, he'll hang me – for not telling him before. [*Confidentially to the audience*] I'll get away somewhere, by heck, and put off the evil day. Don't tell *him* [*meaning Palaestrio*], will you? ... Promise ... [*He attempts to sneak off.*]

PALAESTRIO: Here, where are you off to?

LURCIO: I've got to go somewhere for somebody. I'll be back.

PALAESTRIO: Who has sent you?

LURCIO: Philocomasium.

PALAESTRIO: Oh; in that case, get along; and come back quickly.

LURCIO: All right ... and [*returning with an afterthought*] if there's any trouble being handed out while I'm away, you can have my share, and welcome.

[*He goes off in the direction of the town.*]

PALAESTRIO: I see now what the girl is up to. With Sceledrus asleep, she has sent her assistant warder off on an errand, so that she can hop across next door. Good enough ... Now here comes Periplectomenus with the woman I asked him to find ... [*Seeing them come out of the house*] a good looker, by Jove! The gods are with us all right this time. She walks and dresses more like a lady than a paid woman. Everything's turning out beautifully!

[PERIPLECTOMENUS *has brought the girl* ACROTELEUTIUM *and her maid* MILPHIDIPPA *out of his house.*]

PERIPLECTOMENUS: Now then, Acroteleutium, and you too, Milphidippa, I think I've explained the whole scheme to you. If you haven't understood anything in the plan or the part you have to play, I'll go over it again to make sure you've got it right. If you have, let us talk of something else.

ACROTELEUTIUM: I should be a dim-witted fool, sir, to hire myself out and offer to help you, if I didn't know all the tricks of my trade.

PERIPLECTOMENUS: It's always best to get your instructions quite clear.

ACROTELEUTIUM: Oh yes, a girl like me must have her instructions, everyone knows that. Still, it was I, wasn't it, that told you the best way to cook the Captain's goose, the moment you started to speak to me?

PERIPLECTOMENUS: Yes . . . well . . . two heads are better than one. I've known people miss the best line of country through never knowing it was there.

ACROTELEUTIUM: You can take it from me, when a woman has mischief to do, her memory is infallible and indestructible. But for doing a good turn or keeping a promise, she'll suddenly become so forgetful she can't remember a thing about it.

PERIPLECTOMENUS: It's the latter I'm afraid of, since you will be doing both things at once – doing me a good turn, and making mischief for the Captain.

ACROTELEUTIUM: As long as we don't think about the good we're doing, we'll be all right!

PERIPLECTOMENUS: Oh, the wickedness of women!

ACROTELEUTIUM: Don't you worry; it's nothing to the wickedness of the men we have to deal with.

PERIPLECTOMENUS: I'm sure you're equal to it. Come this way, please.

PALAESTRIO [*aside*]: I'd better go and join them . . . Ah, sir, I'm glad you've got back . . . and with two such charming acquisitions.

PERIPLECTOMENUS: Ah, Palaestrio, you're just the man we want to see. [*Aside to him*] I've got the girls you wanted, all present and correct.

PALAESTRIO: You're a genius, sir . . . [*He greets the women*] Palaestrio presents his compliments to Acroteleutium.

ACROTELEUTIUM: Who is this, please? He seems to know my name already.

PERIPLECTOMENUS: This is our master-planner.

ACROTELEUTIUM: Good morning, master-planner.

PALAESTRIO: Good morning to you, my dear. Now tell me, has this gentleman given you full instructions?

PERIPLECTOMENUS: They have both been thoroughly coached in their duties.

PALAESTRIO: I'd like to check that. I don't want you making any mistakes.

PERIPLECTOMENUS: I haven't added a word to the instructions you gave me.

ACROTELEUTIUM: You want me to take your Captain down a peg, don't you?

PALAESTRIO: That's exactly it.

ACROTELEUTIUM: Then everything's ready; everything is neatly, completely, precisely, and properly provided for.

PALAESTRIO: You will pretend that you're this gentleman's wife?

ACROTELEUTIUM: That is correct.

PALAESTRIO: And you will pretend you've taken a fancy to the Captain?

ACROTELEUTIUM: I will.

PALAESTRIO: And you will pretend to be using me and your maid as your go-betweens in the affair?

ACROTELEUTIUM: Your prediction is perfect; you ought to be a soothsayer.

PALAESTRIO: And your maid is supposed to have given me this ring, from you, for me to give to the Captain, with your message to him?

ACROTELEUTIUM: That's right.

PERIPLECTOMENUS: What is the point of going through all this again? They know it all well enough.

ACROTELEUTIUM: No, he's quite right, sir. After all, when you've got a good master builder, it's his job to lay the keel well and truly,

187

then it's easy to build the rest of the ship properly, once it has been well and truly laid down. Now *this* ship has been well and truly laid, and by good experienced craftsmen. As long as our provider doesn't let us down, but gives us all we need, I know what we're capable of, we shall soon have everything shipshape.

PALAESTRIO: And do you know my master?

ACROTELEUTIUM: What a question! Who doesn't know that public pest, that big-mouthed menace to women, that scent-reeking hairdresser's delight?

PALAESTRIO: And does he know you?

ACROTELEUTIUM: Of course he doesn't. He has never seen me.

PALAESTRIO: So far, so good. I hope all will be as easy as it sounds.

ACROTELEUTIUM: Why don't you just leave him to me, and stop worrying? If I don't have him done to a turn, it'll be my fault entirely.

PALAESTRIO: Good, then, in you go; and get to work with all your wits.

ACROTELEUTIUM: Trust us for that.

PALAESTRIO: Take them in, Periplectomenus. I'll go and meet the Captain in the forum and give him this ring and say it's from your wife and she's mad about him. As soon as we get back, send the maid to us as if on a confidential errand from her.

PERIPLECTOMENUS: We'll see to that. Off you go.

PALAESTRIO: Watch out, then, and I'll soon have him here thoroughly primed.

PERIPLECTOMENUS: Have a nice walk; and good luck to you!

[PALAESTRIO *goes off to the town.*]

Now then, if I bring off this affair successfully, and work the trick so that my young friend can get the Captain's girl away from him and off to Athens – there'll be a nice present waiting for you, my dear.

ACROTELEUTIUM: Is the girl herself taking any part in the business?

PERIPLECTOMENUS: Oh yes; she's playing up beautifully, indeed brilliantly.

ACROTELEUTIUM: I'm sure everything will be all right, then. When we pool our talents for mischief-making, there will be no fear of our being outwitted by anyone else's low cunning.

PERIPLECTOMENUS: Let us go in, then, shall we, and think it over carefully? We can't afford to make any slip or mistake in what we have to do; there must be no hitch when the Captain turns up. Shall we go in?

ACROTELEUTIUM: I am only waiting for you, sir. [*They return to the house.*]

*

[*A little later.* PALAESTRIO *has met his master in the forum, and now returns with him. As it turns out, he has not yet delivered the message and the ring, but the following scene can be assumed to be taking place at some distance from the house.*]

PYRGOPOLYNICES: Yes, it is very satisfactory when your work goes smoothly and gives you no trouble. I have enlisted my troops to go and help Seleucus defend his kingdom – and I've sent them off in the charge of my dear friend Artotrogus; so now I can take a rest.

PALAESTRIO: What is more, sir, you can stop thinking about Seleucus and think of yourself. I am commissioned to put you in the way of a delightful new proposition.

PYRGOPOLYNICES: Indeed? Very well, I will put all other business aside and hear what you have to say. What is it? Consider my ears entirely at your disposal.

PALAESTRIO: Have a good look round first and see that there are no other ears lying in wait for us. My orders were to handle this affair with the utmost secrecy.

PYRGOPOLYNICES [*having looked*]: There's no one about.

PALAESTRIO: In the first place, then, here is a love token for you. [*Giving him the ring.*]

PYRGOPOLYNICES: What's this? Where did this come from?

PALAESTRIO: From a lovely and charming woman, one who loves you and passionately desires your handsome person. It was her maid that gave me that ring to give to you.

PYRGOPOLYNICES: What sort of woman is she? Freeborn, or a manumitted slave?

PALAESTRIO: Pah! As if I'd be bringing you messages from a freed woman, when you have more freeborn women running after you than you can cope with!

PYRGOPOLYNICES: Is she married?

PALAESTRIO: She is and she isn't.

PYRGOPOLYNICES: She can't be both married and unmarried, can she?

PALAESTRIO: Yes, because she's young and her husband is old.

PYRGOPOLYNICES: Excellent.

PALAESTRIO: She is very charming and quite a lady to look at.

PYRGOPOLYNICES: I hope you are telling me the truth.

PALAESTRIO: She's a perfect match for you, if ever I saw one.

PYRGOPOLYNICES: She must be a beauty indeed, in that case. Well, who is she?

PALAESTRIO: She is the wife of Periplectomenus, the old gentleman who lives next door to us. She's dying of love for you, and wants to get away from her husband; she can't stand the old man, and she has just told me to beg and implore you to give her the chance and the means to escape from him.

PYRGOPOLYNICES: By Hercules, I've a good mind to take her, if that is what she wants.

PALAESTRIO: Oh, she wants it all right.

PYRGOPOLYNICES: What can we do with that girl we've got at present?

PALAESTRIO: Tell her to clear off, of course. Tell her to go where she likes. As it happens, there's this twin sister of hers, just arrived in Ephesus, with her mother; they're looking for her.

PYRGOPOLYNICES: What? Is her mother in Ephesus?

PALAESTRIO: So I have heard, on good authority.

PYRGOPOLYNICES: Well, by Hercules, that's a splendid opportunity to get rid of the girl.

PALAESTRIO: But you'd want to do it as nicely as possible, I suppose?

PYRGOPOLYNICES: How do you mean?

PALAESTRIO: I mean you'd want to remove her immediately but without any hard feelings on her part?

PYRGOPOLYNICES: Yes, I would.

PALAESTRIO: Then this is what I suggest you should do. You're rich enough; tell her to keep all the jewellery and stuff you've provided for her. Tell her she can have them as a gift, and she's free to go wherever she likes.

PYRGOPOLYNICES: Yes, that's a good idea. But mind, I don't want to let her go, and then have the other one changing her mind and giving me the slip.

PALAESTRIO: Oh go on, sir! As if she would. She'd give her eyes for you.

PYRGOPOLYNICES: Venus, I am yours!

[*By this time they are near the Captain's house.*]

PALAESTRIO: Look out now! Someone is coming from next door. Keep out of sight over here ... [*They conceal themselves, as* MIL-PHIDIPPA *approaches.*] This is the lady's despatch-boat.

PYRGOPOLYNICES: Despatch-boat?

PALAESTRIO: The go-between. This is the maid who brought me the ring which I gave you.

PYRGOPOLYNICES: She's a pretty little piece, too.

PALAESTRIO: But an ape, an ugly duckling, compared to her mistress. Look at her, all eyes and ears, like a hunter stalking his prey.

MILPHIDIPPA [*perceiving that she is being watched*]: So here is the arena; this is where I shall have to go through my tricks. I'll pretend I haven't seen them yet nor know they are here.

PYRGOPOLYNICES: Don't say anything. Let's listen first, and see whether she mentions my name.

MILPHIDIPPA [*soliloquizing with the obvious intention of being heard*]: I hope there are no busybodies around here, watching to see what I'm doing – people with all day to spare and nothing better to do. I don't want any person of that sort upsetting or interfering with my plans by popping out just when my mistress happens to be popping over to next door to visit the young gentleman she's hoping to sleep with, the one she is breaking her poor heart over, that ever so attractive and ever so handsome Captain Pyrgopoly-nices.

PYRGOPOLYNICES: Do you think this one loves me too? She admires my appearance. Her language certainly needs no scrubbing.

PALAESTRIO: What do you mean by that, sir?

PYRGOPOLYNICES: She expresses herself so nicely – not an inelegant word.

PALAESTRIO: No description of you, sir, could contain any inelegant word.

PYRGOPOLYNICES: She is certainly a most charming and attractive girl. By Hercules, I feel tempted already, Palaestrio.

PALAESTRIO: What, before you've seen the other one?

PYRGOPOLYNICES: Ah, well, I take your word for her without seeing her. But this little . . . despatch-boat – I could easily fall in love with her, failing the other one.

PALAESTRIO: Oh no, you don't! She is engaged to me. You marry the mistress today and this one becomes mine the same moment.

PYRGOPOLYNICES: In that case, why don't you go and speak to her?

PALAESTRIO: Follow me, then.

PYRGOPOLYNICES: I am at your heels.

MILPHIDIPPA: What wouldn't I give for a chance to meet the man I have come out to see!

[*The men step back again into concealment, and* PALAESTRIO *speaks in a loud mysterious tone.*]

PALAESTRIO: Fear not, be of good cheer, and your wish shall be granted. There is one near you who knows where you can find that which you are seeking.

MILPHIDIPPA: Who's that? [*Pretending to be startled.*]

PALAESTRIO: One who is a co-partner in your councils and conversant with your counsels.

MILPHIDIPPA: Oh dear, then my secret is no longer a secret.

PALAESTRIO: Nay, secret it is, though secret it isn't.

MILPHIDIPPA: How can that be?

PALAESTRIO: Your secret is safe from any untrustworthy ear. I am your trusted friend.

MILPHIDIPPA: If you are an associate of our sisterhood, give me the password.

PALAESTRIO: 'I know a lady loves a man.'

MILPHIDIPPA: I know plenty.

PALAESTRIO: But they don't all send gift-rings.

MILPHIDIPPA: Now I understand; that explains everything. But is . . . anyone else . . . hére?

PALAESTRIO: He is and he isn't.

MILPHIDIPPA: Let me speak to you alone.

PALAESTRIO: Will it take long?

MILPHIDIPPA: Just a couple of words.

PALAESTRIO [*to Pyrgopolynices, keeping him out of sight*]: I'll be back in a moment.

PYRGOPOLYNICES: And what am I supposed to do? Stand here doing nothing, like a heroic statue?

PALAESTRIO: Yes, just stand there and be patient, please. I'm doing the best I can for you.

PYRGOPOLYNICES: Well, hurry up. I'm suffering agonies.

PALAESTRIO: This class of goods has to be handled very circumspectly, as you well know.

PYRGOPOLYNICES: All right, all right, do it your own way.

PALAESTRIO [*returning to Milphidippa*]: The man has no more sense than a stone . . . Now then, here I am; what did you want to say?

MILPHIDIPPA [*now inaudible to Pyrgopolynices*]: I want your advice on how this Wall of Troy is to be scaled.

PALAESTRIO: You know – she is supposed to be swooning with love for him –

MILPHIDIPPA: Yes, I know all that.

PALAESTRIO: Tell him how handsome he is; praise his beautiful figure and talk about his noble courage.

MILPHIDIPPA: Oh, I've got my wits about me for that kind of thing, as I've proved to you before now.

PALAESTRIO: The rest is up to you. Keep your eyes open, and take any hint from me when stalking the prey.

PYRGOPOLYNICES [*impatient*]: Am I going to get a look-in any time today? Why don't you come back here?

PALAESTRIO [*returning*]: Coming, sir. Now what do you want?

PYRGOPOLYNICES: What has she been saying to you?

PALAESTRIO: She says her mistress is weeping and wailing, crying her heart out in anguish and misery, poor soul, longing for you and not being able to see you; and now she has sent her maid to you.

PYRGOPOLYNICES: Let her approach me, then.

PALAESTRIO: Now you know what you must do? Show a haughty disdain, as if you were not at all pleased. Pitch into me, for making you common property, as it were.

PYRGOPOLYNICES: Yes, that's a good idea; I'll do that.

PALAESTRIO: Shall I call her, then? She's looking for you.

PYRGOPOLYNICES: Tell her to approach, if she has any business with me.

PALAESTRIO: Approach, woman, if you have any business with my master.

MILPHIDIPPA: My respects to you, handsome Captain.

PYRGOPOLYNICES: She uses a title I am accustomed to ... May the gods give you all you desire, madam.

MILPHIDIPPA: All I desire is life with you –

PYRGOPOLYNICES: No, that is too much to ask.

MILPHIDIPPA: Oh, not for myself, sir – but for my mistress, who dies for love of you.

PYRGOPOLYNICES: As do many others, who cannot have their wish.

MILPHIDIPPA: Ay, indeed it is no wonder if you set a price upon your favours – with those handsome features, that noble figure, that fame for courage and daring deeds. Was ever a man more godlike?

PALAESTRIO [*aside to her*]: He's not a man, my dear; a vulture is more of a man than he is, I should say.

PYRGOPOLYNICES [*aside*]: I'll play high and mighty, since she admires me so.

PALAESTRIO: Look at him – strutting about like an idiot ... Well, sir? Won't you answer her? Her mistress is the one I told you about.

PYRGOPOLYNICES: Which one is she? I get so many invitations, I can't remember them all.

MILPHIDIPPA: I am from the one who robs her fingers to adorn yours. Didn't I bring that ring from her who desires you, to *him*, who handed it to you?

PYRGOPOLYNICES: And what is your wish now, woman? Name it.

MILPHIDIPPA: That you spurn not the one who desires you, the one who has no life but in your life. On you alone it rests whether she is to live or die.

PYRGOPOLYNICES: And what is her wish?

MILPHIDIPPA: To speak to you, to embrace you, to cover you with caresses; if you do not come to her aid, she will die of despair. Oh my hero, my Achilles, grant my prayer, save with your fair hand that fair lady. Great sacker of cities, slayer of kings, show forth your charity!

PYRGOPOLYNICES: Oh ye gods! what a bore it is. [*To Palaestrio*]

You scoundrel, how many times have I forbidden you to offer my services to all and sundry?

PALAESTRIO: You see, woman? I have told you before and I tell you again: without his proper fee, this boar is not at the service of any and every female in the sty.

MILPHIDIPPA: Let him name his fee, and he shall have it.

PALAESTRIO: It will be one golden Philippic talent. He won't take less from anyone.

MILPHIDIPPA: Oh! . . . oh, but . . . I mean, that's too little, surely.

PYRGOPOLYNICES: Avarice was never in my nature. I have riches enough; I possess more than a thousand pecks of golden Philippics.

PALAESTRIO: And other treasure laid away . . . and heaps – no, mountains –. of silver . . . higher than the peaks of Etna.

MILPHIDIPPA: Fancy! . . . What a liar!

PALAESTRIO [aside to Milphidippa]: That's tickled him, eh?

MILPHIDIPPA: I've got him hooked, haven't I?

PALAESTRIO: Nicely.

MILPHIDIPPA: But let me get away soon, for goodness sake.

PALAESTRIO [to Pyrgopolynices]: Won't you give her an answer, sir, yes or no?

MILPHIDIPPA: You cannot torment the poor lady so, who has never done you any harm.

PYRGOPOLYNICES: Please tell her to call on me herself. Say that I will . . . do all that she asks.

MILPHIDIPPA: Ah! now you act as is right and natural, sir. She wants you, so you want her . . .

PALAESTRIO [aside]: Clever girl!

MILPHIDIPPA: . . . and you haven't the heart to scorn my pleading or refuse my request. [To Palaestrio] How am I doing?

PALAESTRIO: I'm laughing fit to burst.

MILPHIDIPPA: I know; I daren't look at you.

PYRGOPOLYNICES: Of course you cannot understand, my girl, how great an honour I am doing your mistress.

MILPHIDIPPA: Oh I do, and I will tell her so.

PALAESTRIO: He could get gold in plenty for his services anywhere else.

MILPHIDIPPA: I'm sure he could.

PALAESTRIO: The children he sires are all born warriors; his sons live for eight hundred years.

MILPHIDIPPA: Go on, you're joking!

PYRGOPOLYNICES: They live out a thousand years, from generation to generation.

PALAESTRIO: Of course I understated it, sir, lest she should think I was telling her a lie.

MILPHIDIPPA: Glory be! If his sons live that long, how long will he live?

PYRGOPOLYNICES: Woman, I was born on the day after Ops gave birth to Jupiter.

PALAESTRIO: If he had been born the day before, he'd be the king of heaven now.

MILPHIDIPPA: Ah, enough, enough, for pity's sake! Only give me leave to depart with my life.

PALAESTRIO: Why not – since you have your answer?

MILPHIDIPPA: I'll go, then, and bring you the lady for whom I have spoken. Have you any further wish, sir?

PYRGOPOLYNICES: Only that I may never grow more handsome than I am; my good looks are my curse . . .

PALAESTRIO: Well, what are you waiting for? Why don't you go?

MILPHIDIPPA: I'm going.

PALAESTRIO: And listen: when you give her the message, use all your art and craft –

MILPHIDIPPA: I'll make her heart beat faster, you'll see!

PALAESTRIO [*more quietly*]: And if Philocomasium is there, tell her to come back home because *he*'s here.

MILPHIDIPPA: Oh yes, she's in there with my mistress: they have been listening to our conversation from cover.

PALAESTRIO: That's fine; that'll put them on the right tack when they take the helm.

MILPHIDIPPA: Don't stop me now; I must go.

PALAESTRIO [*dallying with her*]: I'm not stopping you . . . I'm not touching you . . . I'm not – [*she shakes him off*] all right.

PYRGOPOLYNICES: Tell her to come out here without delay, and I will give her my attention immediately.

[MILPHIDIPPA *goes in.*]

Now, Palaestrio, what do you suggest I should do with that girl of mine? I can't possibly have this other woman in the house until I have got rid of her.

PALAESTRIO: Why ask me what you should do? I've told you already how to do it as kindly as possible. Let her have all the gold and finery you've fitted her out with; tell her to take it, keep it, and remove it. Tell her this is her best chance of getting home because her mother and sister are here and they'll be able to see her home safely.

PYRGOPOLYNICES: How do you know they are here?

PALAESTRIO: Because I have seen the sister myself.

PYRGOPOLYNICES: And has the sister seen her?

PALAESTRIO: Yes, she has.

PYRGOPOLYNICES: H'm ... and this sister ... is she ... a likely wench, would you say?

PALAESTRIO: You want everything that's going, don't you?

PYRGOPOLYNICES: And the mother? Where did the girl say her mother was?

PALAESTRIO: Asleep on board, with bleary and swollen eyes — according to the sailor who brought them here. By the way, he is staying with our neighbours next door too.

PYRGOPOLYNICES: Oh? And what's he? A likely lad, eh?

PALAESTRIO: Come off it, sir. You'd have made a rare stud stallion, the way you gallop after everything male and female. Keep your mind on this business.

PYRGOPOLYNICES: Yes ... well, about your proposed plan, I think you had better have a word with the girl; you know how to talk to her.

PALAESTRIO: Wouldn't it be much more suitable for you to approach her and put your own case for yourself? You could say you felt obliged to take a wife; your family were urging it, your friends were pushing you into it.

PYRGOPOLYNICES: You really think so?

PALAESTRIO: I certainly do.

PYRGOPOLYNICES: Oh, very well, I'll go and see her. You keep watch out here meanwhile, and give me a call when the lady comes out.

PALAESTRIO: I will. You have only to get the other business settled.

197

PYRGOPOLYNICES: It's as good as settled. If she won't go willingly, I'll have her put out into the street.

PALAESTRIO: I wouldn't do that, if I were you. Much better if you can persuade her to go with good grace. And, as I said, give her all those presents; let her take all the jewellery and pretty clothes you've set her up with.

PYRGOPOLYNICES: I hope to goodness she'll agree.

PALAESTRIO: Oh, she'll agree. Go on, then. Don't wait any longer.

PYRGOPOLYNICES: I accept your commands.

[*He goes in, rather reluctantly.*]

PALAESTRIO: Well, what do you think of our amorous Captain now? Does he fit the description I gave you of him? . . . Now it's about time for Acroteleutium to appear, or her maid, or Pleusicles . . . and by Jupiter, coincidence is playing into my hands every time! Here they come – the very people I most want to see.

[ACROTELEUTIUM, MILPHIDIPPA, *and* PLEUSICLES *come out of the house cautiously.*]

ACROTELEUTIUM: Come along, but be careful in case anyone is watching us.

MILPHIDIPPA: I don't see anyone, except the one we want to see.

PALAESTRIO: And I want to see you.

MILPHIDIPPA: How's it going, master-planner?

PALAESTRIO: I'm no master-planner.

MILPHIDIPPA: Ho! What do you mean?

PALAESTRIO: Compared with you I'm not fit to fix a bolt in a wall.

MILPHIDIPPA: What nonsense!

PALAESTRIO: You're the wickedest wittiest word-spinner I ever saw . . . You should have seen how neatly she kidded the Captain.

MILPHIDIPPA: There's more to be done yet.

PALAESTRIO: Don't you worry; everything's going as it should. It's only necessary for you all to lend your kind assistance, as you are doing. Now, the Captain has gone in to persuade his mistress to clear out and go back to Athens with her mother and sister.

PLEUSICLES: Good!

PALAESTRIO: Yes, and he is giving her all the gold and clothes he had provided for her, as a gift, if only she'll go. I thought of that.

PLEUSICLES: There should be no difficulty, then, if she wants to go and he is anxious to get rid of her.

PALAESTRIO: Ah but you know, when you've climbed out of a deep well nearly to the top, that's the time when there's the most danger of your falling down to the bottom again. We're nearly at the top of the well now; but if the Captain smells a rat, we're done for. Now is the time when we need all our art.

PLEUSICLES: As far as I can see, we've got plenty of fighting material on our side: three women, you, I, and the old man, six altogether. With the ingenuity of six brains to draw upon, I am sure we can devise tactics to take any town by storm.

PALAESTRIO: As long as you play your parts carefully.

ACROTELEUTIUM: We are here to receive your instructions.

PALAESTRIO: You are very kind. First, then, Acroteleutium, these are the orders for your department.

ACROTELEUTIUM: They shall be carried out to the best of my ability, colonel.

PALAESTRIO: I want the Captain neatly, sweetly, and completely spoofed.

ACROTELEUTIUM: That'll be no task, but a pleasure, bless you!

PALAESTRIO: Do you know how you're going to do it?

ACROTELEUTIUM: I presume I am to pretend to be devoured with passion for him.

PALAESTRIO: You've got it.

ACROTELEUTIUM: And that I love him so much that I want to marry him and leave my present husband.

PALAESTRIO: All correct. One more thing, though; you had better say that you have already divorced your husband, the old man has gone away, and this house is your own property; otherwise the Captain may have scruples about invading another man's house.

ACROTELEUTIUM: That's a good idea.

PALAESTRIO: Now when he comes out of his own house, where he is now, be rather distant with him, as if you thought little of your own charms compared to his or were overawed by his magnificence; at the same time compliment him on his good looks, his figure, his charm, his beauty.

ACROTELEUTIUM: I've got all that. Will it do if I give a performance so immaculate that you can't find a single fault in it?

PALAESTRIO: That'll do. Now, Pleusicles, here are some instructions for you. As soon as she has done her bit and gone inside, I want you to turn up here in sailor's rig; wear a broad-brimmed dark brown hat, a cloth patch over one eye, and you'd better have a dark brown cloak – that's the usual colour for sailors – fastened on your left shoulder, one arm flapping free, and some sort of tight belt; contrive to look like a ship's pilot. You will find the old man has got all these things in his house; he has fishermen in his employ.

PLEUSICLES: Yes, but what am I to do when I'm got up like that?

PALAESTRIO: You come here with a message for Philocomasium from her mother: if she's going to Athens she is to come back with you to the port at once, and if she wants any luggage put on board, to have it taken to the ship; if she's not coming, you're going to weigh anchor as the wind is just right.

PLEUSICLES: A delightful scene! Anything else?

PALAESTRIO: The Captain will immediately urge her to go, in fact to hurry, and not keep her mother waiting.

PLEUSICLES: You think of everything.

PALAESTRIO: I shall have told the girl to ask if she can have me to help carry the baggage to the harbour. 'Palaestrio,' he'll say, 'go with the girl to the harbour.' Then I – in case you haven't guessed – will be off and away with you to Athens.

PLEUSICLES: Where you won't be a slave for another three days before I give you your freedom.

PALAESTRIO: Off you go and get togged up.

PLEUSICLES: No further instructions?

PALAESTRIO: Only don't forget your part.

PLEUSICLES: I'll go, then. [*He goes into the house.*]

PALAESTRIO: You girls go in too, right away. He'll be out here an minute now.

ACROTELEUTIUM: We'll follow your orders like holy writ.

PALAESTRIO: Hurry, then; go.
  [*They go into the house.*]
And pat, the door's opening, and here he comes, looking very pleased with himself. He has gained his point; and now he's lusting after a phantom, poor fool.
  [PYRGOPOLYNICES *comes out of his house.*]

PYRGOPOLYNICES: I have persuaded Philocomasium to agree to my proposal, just as I wanted, in a friendly and amicable way.

PALAESTRIO: You were a long time about it. Why was that?

PYRGOPOLYNICES: You know, I never realized till now how much the girl loved me.

PALAESTRIO: What!

PYRGOPOLYNICES: I had to talk and talk; she's made of such stubborn stuff. But in the end I gained my point. I gave her all those presents, anything she wanted, anything she asked for. I also gave her you.

PALAESTRIO: Me!! How can I ever live without you, master?

PYRGOPOLYNICES: Cheer up. I'll see that you get your freedom. I tried everything I could think of, to persuade her to go without taking you with her; but it was no use, she got me down.

PALAESTRIO [aside]: So may the gods get you ... Well, after all, sir, bitter blow as it is for me to lose so excellent a master, I cannot but rejoice that the power of your attractive person, aided by my efforts, has brought you the happy association with our lady friend whom I shall now have the pleasure of introducing to you.

PYRGOPOLYNICES: Say no more, my dear fellow. You shall have your freedom, and a substantial sum, if you bring this affair off successfully.

PALAESTRIO: I shall bring it off.

PYRGOPOLYNICES: But hurry; I'm consumed with anticipation.

PALAESTRIO: Take it easy, sir, and control your passions. Ah, here she comes now ... [They retire into hiding.]

[ACROTELEUTIUM and MILPHIDIPPA come out.]

MILPHIDIPPA: There is the Captain, madam, all ready for you.

ACROTELEUTIUM: Where?

MILPHIDIPPA: On your left.

ACROTELEUTIUM: Oh yes, I see him.

MILPHIDIPPA: Don't look straight at him; we don't want him to think we've seen him yet.

ACROTELEUTIUM: Yes, I can see him. Oh dear, now's the time to make our artfulness more artful than ever.

MILPHIDIPPA: You had better begin.

ACROTELEUTIUM [now loudly]: Gracious, my dear, do you mean to say you've actually seen him? ... [Quietly] Speak up now, and let him hear us.

MILPHIDIPPA: I've actually spoken to him, as naturally as you please, and as long as I liked; he put me quite at my ease, I had no difficulty at all.

PYRGOPOLYNICES: Do you hear that?

PALAESTRIO: I do. Your interview must have given her a lot of pleasure.

ACROTELEUTIUM: You are a lucky girl.

PYRGOPOLYNICES: They can't resist me, can they?

PALAESTRIO: Of course they can't.

ACROTELEUTIUM: It's simply incredible that you should have been able to meet him and get him to listen to you. I've always heard he only receives requests in writing or through an ambassador, like a king.

MILPHIDIPPA: Oh, it wasn't easy, I can tell you, to get an appointment and obtain his consent.

PALAESTRIO: What a reputation you have among the women, sir!

PYRGOPOLYNICES: If it is Venus's will, I cannot prevent it.

ACROTELEUTIUM: It is Venus I have to thank, and I beg and beseech her to grant me the man whom I love and long for, and that he will be kind to me and not grudge me my desire.

MILPHIDIPPA: I pray that he will, too, though he is desired by many. But he scorns them all and puts them aside, all save you.

ACROTELEUTIUM: Ay, that is the fear that torments me; he is so hard to please, I dread lest his eyes should change his heart, once he has seen me, and my poor charms fail to satisfy his fastidious taste.

MILPHIDIPPA: You need have no fear of that, madam.

PYRGOPOLYNICES: She does herself little justice.

ACROTELEUTIUM: I hope you didn't exaggerate my attractions.

MILPHIDIPPA: On the contrary, madam, I took care to give him an impression far short of the truth.

ACROTELEUTIUM: If he will not have me, by heaven, I will throw myself at his knees and beg for pity; if that fails and he still refuses me, I shall seek my death, for life without him I know I cannot endure.

PYRGOPOLYNICES: She must not die! I must prevent her. Shall I go to her?

PALAESTRIO: Certainly not. You will only be cheapening yourself if you make the first move. Let her come to you. Let her be the one to ask and hope and wait. Do you want to lose your reputation?

Don't do anything so foolish. Only two men in the world – you and Phaon of Lesbos – ever had the luck to be so passionately loved by woman.

ACROTELEUTIUM: Am I to go in to him, Milphidippa, or will you call him out here?

MILPHIDIPPA: Oh no, madam, we had better wait till someone comes.

ACROTELEUTIUM: I cannot wait. I'm going in.

MILPHIDIPPA: The door will be locked.

ACROTELEUTIUM: I shall break in.

MILPHIDIPPA: No! You're mad!

ACROTELEUTIUM: If he has ever loved, if his understanding is equal to his beauty, he will in his mercy pardon anything I may do for love of him.

PALAESTRIO: To be sure, the poor creature is consumed with love for you.

PYRGOPOLYNICES: The feeling is mutual.

PALAESTRIO: Sh! don't let her hear you.

[ACROTELEUTIUM *has approached the door, but pauses.*]

MILPHIDIPPA: Why don't you knock, then, madam, instead of standing there in a trance?

ACROTELEUTIUM: Because he whom I seek is not within.

MILPHIDIPPA: How do you know that?

ACROTELEUTIUM: My nose tells me so. If he were in, my nose would scent him.

PYRGOPOLYNICES: She is a diviner. Because she loves me, Venus has given her the gift of second sight.

ACROTELEUTIUM [*sniffing*]: Somewhere ... somewhere near us is the man whom I desire to see ... yes, it is his smell ...

PYRGOPOLYNICES: Bless the woman! Her nose is a better guide than her eyes!

PALAESTRIO: Blinded with love.

ACROTELEUTIUM: Ah! For pity, hold me!

MILPHIDIPPA: What is it, madam?

ACROTELEUTIUM: Hold me, or I shall fall ...

MILPHIDIPPA: What ails you?

ACROTELEUTIUM: I cannot stand. My mind reels at what I see ...

MILPHIDIPPA: Then you've seen the Captain, I'll be bound.

ACROTELEUTIUM: Yes, I have seen him.

MILPHIDIPPA: I don't see him. Where is he?

ACROTELEUTIUM: You do not love him, else you would see him.

MILPHIDIPPA: Nay, with your leave, madam, I could love him as much as you do.

PALAESTRIO: You see, sir, there is not a woman but loves you at first sight.

PYRGOPOLYNICES: Perhaps I have never told you, I am a grandson of Venus.

ACROTELEUTIUM: You go, Milphidippa my dear; go to him please, and speak to him.

PYRGOPOLYNICES: Poor thing, she is overawed by my presence.

PALAESTRIO: Here comes the maid . . .

MILPHIDIPPA: If you please, sirs, I would be glad –

PYRGOPOLYNICES: And so would we.

MILPHIDIPPA: As you bade me, sir, I have brought my mistress here.

PYRGOPOLYNICES: So I see.

MILPHIDIPPA: Won't you ask her to come to you?

PYRGOPOLYNICES: Yes. To oblige you, I think I can find her more tolerable than some.

MILPHIDIPPA: She'll be tongue-tied, I'm afraid, when she comes near you. Even at the sight of you, her eyes have struck her dumb.

PYRGOPOLYNICES: We must cure her of that ailment.

MILPHIDIPPA: You saw how she shook with fright the moment she set eyes on you.

PYRGOPOLYNICES: I have seen armed men do the same; it is not to be wondered at in a woman. What does she want me to do for her?

MILPHIDIPPA: To go into her house, sir; she wants to live with you and be yours for life.

PYRGOPOLYNICES: Go to a married woman's house? And let her husband catch me there?

MILPHIDIPPA: She has already turned her husband out for your sake.

PYRGOPOLYNICES: How could she do that?

MILPHIDIPPA: Because the house is hers; it was part of her dowry.

PYRGOPOLYNICES: Is that so?

MILPHIDIPPA: I assure you it is.

PYRGOPOLYNICES: Tell her to go home; I will be with her shortly.

MILPHIDIPPA: I hope you will not keep her waiting long, sir; it will be torture to her.

PYRGOPOLYNICES: Indeed I won't. Away with you.

MILPHIDIPPA: We'll go, then.

[*She returns to her mistress and escorts her back to the house.*]

PYRGOPOLYNICES [*looking down the street*]: Now what do I see?

PALAESTRIO: What do you see?

PYRGOPOLYNICES: Somebody coming this way – a sailor by his appearance.

PALAESTRIO: Yes, he is coming this way. He wants you, I expect. Ah, this will be that shipmaster.

PYRGOPOLYNICES: Coming to look for the girl, eh?

PALAESTRIO: I expect so.

[*They remain in the background, while* PLEUSICLES, *suitably disguised, arrives from the town; he first speaks aside to the audience.*]

PLEUSICLES: If I hadn't heard of the many kinds of shady shifts that love has put men to, I'd have thought twice before walking the streets in this get-up, for love's sake. However, many a man, I've been told, has done worse things than this for love – downright wicked things, too; need I remind you of Achilles leaving all his compatriots to die? . . . Hullo, there's Palaestrio with the Captain. I must disguise my accent. [*He assumes his 'nautical' character.*] Blast it! Women are the born daughters of delay. Lots of other things can keep a man waiting, but no waiting seems as long as waiting for women. Just their habit, I suppose. Now I've got to find this girl Philocomasium. Better knock at this door . . . Hey there, anyone in?

PALAESTRIO: Now then, young fellow, what's to do? What are you knocking there for? Who do you want?

PLEUSICLES: I'm looking for a girl called Philocomasium. I've a message from her mother. She is to come now if she's coming. We're ready to cast off and she's keeping us all waiting.

PYRGOPOLYNICES: We've been ready for you for some time. Palaestrio, go and get some men to help you carry all her baggage to the ship – gold and jewellery, clothes, and all her valuables. Everything I have given her is packed up and she can take the lot.

PALAESTRIO: I will, sir.

PLEUSICLES: And hurry, for God's sake.

[PALAESTRIO *goes into the house.*]

PYRGOPOLYNICES: He won't keep you waiting ... Excuse my asking, but what has happened to your eye?

PLEUSICLES: Nothing's happened to *this* one.

PYRGOPOLYNICES: The left, I mean.

PLEUSICLES: I lost it for love, if you want to know – too much loving, bedad, else it would be as good as the other ... Can't they hurry up?

PYRGOPOLYNICES: They are coming now.

[PHILOCOMASIUM *comes out, greatly distressed,* PALAESTRIO *comforting her.*]

PALAESTRIO: Try to stop crying now, there's a good girl.

PHILOCOMASIUM: How can I help crying? Leaving the place where I've been so ... happy ...

PALAESTRIO: Look, here is the man come from your mother and sister.

PHILOCOMASIUM: Yes ... I see him ...

PYRGOPOLYNICES: Palaestrio!

PALAESTRIO: Sir?

PYRGOPOLYNICES: Why don't you tell the men to bring all that baggage out?

[PALAESTRIO *goes to the door and pretends to give orders within, but keeps an eye on the proceedings outside.*]

PLEUSICLES: I'm glad to see you, Philocomasium.

PHILOCOMASIUM: I am glad to see you.

PLEUSICLES: Your mother and sister send their love to you.

PHILOCOMASIUM: I hope they are well.

PLEUSICLES: They want you to come along at once, while the wind's fair, so we can be off. They would have come with me, only your mother's eyes are bad.

PHILOCOMASIUM: I'll come ... hard as it is ... one must do one's duty ...

PLEUSICLES: I know; you're a good girl –

PYRGOPOLYNICES: Living with me has taught her much.

PHILOCOMASIUM: Indeed you could sharpen any girl's wits, sir ... Oh, how can I bear to part from such a wonderful man! ... Living with you gave me such ... courage! Now I shall be just an ordinary girl.

PYRGOPOLYNICES: There, there, don't cry.

PHILOCOMASIUM: I ... can't do anything else ... when I look at you.

PYRGOPOLYNICES: No, no; cheer up.

PHILOCOMASIUM: No one but I knows what I suffer.

PALAESTRIO: Indeed, Philocomasium, I can understand what a happy life you had here, under the influence of that fine presence, that noble and manly character. Even I, a slave, cannot look at him without weeping to think how soon we are to be parted.

PHILOCOMASIUM: Please ... may I ... embrace you once before I go?

PYRGOPOLYNICES: You may.

PHILOCOMASIUM: Oh, light of my eyes ... darling of my soul! [*She makes as if to embrace Pyrgopolynices, but swoons and is supported by* PALAESTRIO, *who passes her over to* PLEUSICLES.]

PALAESTRIO: Help! ... Support the lady, or she may do herself harm.

PYRGOPOLYNICES: What has come over her?

PALAESTRIO: The pain of parting from you has shocked the poor girl out of her senses.

PYRGOPOLYNICES: Run in and fetch some water.

PALAESTRIO: Water won't be necessary. Just let her rest. Don't go too near her, please, while she is coming to.

PYRGOPOLYNICES [*suspiciously*]: I don't see why they need have their heads so close together. Hey you, boatman, take your lips away from hers, confound you!

PLEUSICLES: I was trying to see if she was breathing.

PYRGOPOLYNICES: You should have used your ear.

PLEUSICLES: I'll drop her, if you prefer it.

PYRGOPOLYNICES: No, no; keep hold of her.

[PALAESTRIO, *to cause a diversion, begins to make his farewells to the household altar.*]

PALAESTRIO: This is the saddest moment of my life ...

PYRGOPOLYNICES [*calling into the house*]: Come along there, with all that baggage I've given her. [*Slaves bring out the baggage during the following.*]

PALAESTRIO: Once more I salute thee, God of our house, before I depart hence. And you, my comrades, fellow slaves of either sex, farewell and luck be with you; and speak, I pray you, well of me, though I be far away.

PYRGOPOLYNICES: Be a brave man, Palaestrio.

PALAESTRIO: I cannot help but weep … at leaving you …

PYRGOPOLYNICES: Don't take it so hardly.

PALAESTRIO: No one but I knows what I suffer.

PHILOCOMASIUM [recovering]: Where am I? What has happened? What is that …? Ah, the blessed light! …

PLEUSICLES: Do you feel better now?

PHILOCOMASIUM: Ah!! What man have I embraced? Ah, shame! Am I out of my mind?

PLEUSICLES: Have no fear … my darling.

PYRGOPOLYNICES: What is going on there?

PALAESTRIO: She'd just fainted, that's all. [Aside to Pleusicles] Look out, or we shall be giving the game away if we're not careful.

PYRGOPOLYNICES [partly hearing]: What's that you say?

PALAESTRIO: I mean, all this stuff being carried after us through the town. People might say nasty things about you.

PYRGOPOLYNICES: To hell with them. It's my stuff I'm giving away, not theirs. Be on your way, and the gods be good to you.

PALAESTRIO: It's you I was thinking of.

PYRGOPOLYNICES: I know, I know.

PALAESTRIO: Goodbye, then.

PYRGOPOLYNICES: Goodbye, and good luck.

PALAESTRIO [to the others]: Go on ahead, I'll follow you. I must have a last word with my master.

[PLEUSICLES and PHILOCOMASIUM depart, with their attendants.] You know, sir, you may not always have found me your most loyal slave; nevertheless I am deeply grateful to you for everything. In fact, if you had so wished it, I would have much preferred to be your slave than be beholden to anyone else for my freedom.

PYRGOPOLYNICES: Take it like a man.

PALAESTRIO: But oh, when I think of the new ways I shall have to get used to – how I shall have to learn ladylike manners, and forget the army life!

PYRGOPOLYNICES: Well, try to behave yourself.

PALAESTRIO: It will be difficult. I seem to have lost all taste for it.

PYRGOPOLYNICES: Now run along, and don't keep your friends waiting.

PALAESTRIO: This is goodbye, then.

PYRGOPOLYNICES: And good luck.

PALAESTRIO: Oh, and please be sure ... if I do succeed in becoming a free man – I'll send you word – please be sure you won't forget me.

PYRGOPOLYNICES: As if I could.

PALAESTRIO: Remember, from time to time, how well I have served you. That way, I think, in time, you will come to know who were your good servants and who were the bad ones.

PYRGOPOLYNICES: I do know; I have often had occasion to know it.

PALAESTRIO: Then if you knew it before, today you'll know it better than ever. I warrant you'll have cause to thank me for this day's work for many a day to come.

PYRGOPOLYNICES: Upon my word, I've a good mind to keep you.

PALAESTRIO: No, don't do that. People will say that you are not to be trusted, that you're a liar, that you go back on your word. I was the only loyal slave you ever had, they'll say. Really, sir, I'd advise you to keep me if I thought you could do so with credit; but no, it cannot be done; don't think of it.

PYRGOPOLYNICES: Well, you had better go.

PALAESTRIO: I'll face it ... come what may.

PYRGOPOLYNICES: Take care of yourself.

PALAESTRIO [*choking back his uncontrollable emotion*]: I'd better go ... [*He goes, hastily.*]

PYRGOPOLYNICES: Goodbye! ... I had always taken him to be the worst servant in my house, until this business. Now I see he is really devoted to me. Now I come to think of it, I was a fool to let him go ... Ah, well ... Now for my lady-love ... Wait, though; I think I hear someone coming out.

[*A young* SLAVE *appears in the doorway of Periplectomenus's house, speaking to those within.*]

SLAVE: I know what to do, you needn't tell me; I'll find him, anywhere on earth; I won't give up till I've got on his tracks ...

PYRGOPOLYNICES: This lad must be looking for me. I'll go and meet him.

SLAVE: Ah, the very man I'm looking for. Greetings to you, most gracious hero, most magnificently blessed, most exceptionally beloved of the two divinities.

PYRGOPOLYNICES: What two divinities?

SLAVE: Mars and Venus.

PYRGOPOLYNICES: Clever boy!

SLAVE: The lady begs you to enter, she wants you, she's looking for you, she's anxiously awaiting you. Come to the rescue of a lady in love. Won't you go in, sir? What are you waiting for?

PYRGOPOLYNICES: Yes, I'll go.

[*He goes in, and the sounds indicate that he is receiving an unexpectedly warm welcome.*]

SLAVE: There he goes; head first into the net. The trap's all ready for him. The old man is at his post, all set to tackle this self-fancying fornicator who thinks every woman falls in love with him at first sight, when really he's detested by man and woman alike. Hark at 'em! I'm going in to join the fray.

[*But the fray comes outside, led by* PERIPLECTOMENUS, *whose slaves drag Pyrgopolynices out of the house.*]

PERIPLECTOMENUS: Bring him along. If he won't come quietly, pick him up and throw him out. Toss him in the air, tear him limb from limb.

PYRGOPOLYNICES: Help! Mercy! Periplectomenus, I appeal to you.

PERIPLECTOMENUS: No use appealing to me ... Have you got that knife good and sharp, Cario?

CARIO [*a cook brandishing a knife*]: Ay, ay, sir, it's been thirsting long enough for a taste of blood from this bastard's belly. We'll soon have a string of baubles hanging round the little boy's neck.

PYRGOPOLYNICES: Help!! They're murdering me!

PERIPLECTOMENUS: Not yet; you speak too soon.

CARIO: Shall I get at him, sir?

PERIPLECTOMENUS: Not yet; he must be flogged first.

CARIO: Give it him hot, then.

[*Slaves prepare to operate.*]

PERIPLECTOMENUS: You dare to play fast and loose with another man's wife, do you, you shameless monster?

PYRGOPOLYNICES: She offered herself to me, I swear she did.

PERIPLECTOMENUS: He's lying. Beat him.

PYRGOPOLYNICES: No, wait! Let me explain.

PERIPLECTOMENUS [to slaves]: Get on with it.

PYRGOPOLYNICES: Please let me speak!

PERIPLECTOMENUS: Speak then.

PYRGOPOLYNICES: I was earnestly begged to go and see her.

PERIPLECTOMENUS: And you had no hesitation in going. Take that! [He starts the beating, and the slaves follow suit.]

PYRGOPOLYNICES: Oh!! Enough, enough!

CARIO: When does the carving begin?

PERIPLECTOMENUS: As soon as you like. Spread-eagle him, lay him out flat.

PYRGOPOLYNICES: Mercy, mercy! Hear me before he cuts!

PERIPLECTOMENUS: You may speak.

PYRGOPOLYNICES: It wasn't my fault. I thought she was unmarried. That is what her maid, her bawd, told me.

PERIPLECTOMENUS: Take an oath. Swear that you will do no harm to any person for what you have suffered, for this day's flogging, or for any flogging you may receive in the future, if we permit you, grandson of Venus, to depart from this place alive.

PYRGOPOLYNICES: I swear by Jupiter and Mars that I will do no harm to any man for this day's flogging, and I acknowledge that it is deserved, and that I shall have been let off lightly for my offence if I am allowed to go from this place with my faculties intact.

PERIPLECTOMENUS: And if you break that oath?

PYRGOPOLYNICES: May I be impotent for life.

CARIO: Let's give him another whacking, sir, and let him go.

PYRGOPOLYNICES: Heaven bless you, my man, for speaking up for me.

CARIO: It'll be a hundred drachmas, please.

PYRGOPOLYNICES: What for?

CARIO: For letting you go from here a whole man, grand-sonny of Venus. A hundred drachmas, or you don't get away, so don't think it.

PYRGOPOLYNICES: You shall be paid.

CARIO: Sensible fellow. You can say goodbye to your tunic, cloak, and sword; you won't be taking them with you. [He collects the perquisites.]

A SLAVE: Am I to give him another beating, or is it peace?

PYRGOPOLYNICES: I'm all in pieces with your beating. Spare me, for pity's sake.

PERIPLECTOMENUS: Let him go.

PYRGOPOLYNICES: I thank you.

PERIPLECTOMENUS: But if ever I catch you here again, it'll cost you all you've got.

PYRGOPOLYNICES: I have no more to say.

PERIPLECTOMENUS: Come along, Cario. [*He and his servants retire.*] [*As* PYRGOPOLYNICES *betakes himself painfully towards his house, he sees his slaves returning from the harbour,* SCELEDRUS *among them.*]

PYRGOPOLYNICES: Here are my men coming back ... Has Philocomasium gone yet? Tell me, has she gone?

SCELEDRUS: Ay, some time ago.

PYRGOPOLYNICES: Curse it!

SCELEDRUS: You may well say so, when you know what I know. That fellow with a patch over one eye ... he was no sailor.

PYRGOPOLYNICES: Who was he, then?

SCELEDRUS: Philocomasium's lover.

PYRGOPOLYNICES: How do you know that?

SCELEDRUS: It was obvious. They hadn't hardly got outside the city gate when they started hugging and kissing each other.

PYRGOPOLYNICES: Fool, fool that I am! Now I see what an ass they've made of me; and it was Palaestrio, the double-dyed villain, that lured me into the trap ...

Well, it was a fair catch, and justice has been done. Serve all lechers so, and lechery would grow less rife; the sinners would have more fear and mend their ways.

Get you in ... and [*to the audience*] now your thanks.

EXEUNT

PSEUDOLUS

INTRODUCTORY NOTE TO
PSEUDOLUS

THE briefest of prologues, prefixed to one of the longest of the
Plautine plays, may or may not be from Plautus's own hand; it is
apparent from some other instances that a prologue might be either
wholly or partly rewritten for a later revival of a play. In the present
case, at all events, it was obviously right to dispense with preamble –
and little will be added here. No preliminary explanations were
needed to introduce that hackneyed old plot: slave helps young man
to rescue girl from slavery and prostitution – this was one of the stock
stage situations which, it may be remembered, were spoken of with
disapproval in the Epilogue of *Captivi*.

But if Plautus found no lack of examples among his Greek pre-
decessors (and no one model can be identified), it is not difficult to
recognize his hand in the adaptation. He has paid scant attention to
the love intrigue, using it only as a starting point. *Pseudolus* is the title
of the play, and the wiliness of Pseudolus ('the liar') is its main subject
and centre of interest, seconded by the nastiness of the arch-pimp
Ballio.

The play is not faultlessly constructed; there are repetitions and
loose ends; but the effect of these is rather to enhance the air of
improvisation in the fast-moving train of events. Thus Charinus is
brought in as an accomplice, only to be discarded in favour of a
more suitable candidate; and Callipho is asked to 'stand by' but no
further use is made of him.

We have Cicero's word for it that this comedy was a product of the
author's old age, and one which gave him particular satisfaction.
And it so happens that there is confirmation of its date in the *didascalia*
(programme note) preserved in the Ambrosian MS; this records the
production of the play at the Megalesian Festival in the spring of
191 B.C., being about the sixty-third year of Plautus's life.

CHARACTERS

SIMO	*an Athenian gentleman*
CALIDORUS	*his son*
PSEUDOLUS	*his chief slave*
CALLIPHO	*a neighbour and friend of Simo*
CHARINUS	*a friend of Calidorus*
BALLIO	*a pimp*
PHOENICIUM (*mute*)	*a girl in the possession of Ballio and loved by Calidorus*
HARPAX	*an officer's orderly*
SIMIA	*a slave*
A COOK	*hired by Ballio*
A BOY	*slave of Ballio*

Other slaves in Ballio's house
Women in Ballio's house
Cook's assistants

*

The scene is at Athens, outside the houses of Ballio and Simo. The house of Callipho may also be visible.

PSEUDOLUS

PROLOGUE: If anyone wants to stand up and stretch his legs, now is the time to do it. The next item on the programme is a play by Plautus – and a long one.

*

[*Enter* CALIDORUS, *a young man in a state of deep depression, with* PSEUDOLUS, *his father's chief slave.*]

PSEUDOLUS: You're very silent, master. If I could learn from your silence what troubles and torments are torturing your soul, I'd be glad to save us both trouble – me the trouble of asking and you the trouble of replying. But as that is impossible, I must needs put a few questions to you. Can you tell me, master, why you've been going round half dead these last few days, and carrying that tablet with you everywhere, and soaking it with your tears, instead of finding someone to confide in? Come on, master, tell me. Let me into your secrets.

CALIDORUS: Oh Pseudolus, I am the most unhappy wretch alive.

PSEUDOLUS: Jupiter forbid it!

CALIDORUS: Jupiter has got nothing to do with it. I'm suffering under the tyranny of Venus, not Jupiter.

PSEUDOLUS: Won't you tell me all about it, then? I've always been your chief privy counsellor up to now.

CALIDORUS: You still are.

PSEUDOLUS: Then tell me what the trouble is. Money, service, or advice, all I have is at your disposal.

CALIDORUS: Look at this letter, then, and see for yourself what kind of pain and misery is wasting my life away.

PSEUDOLUS: I will. Give it here ... What – what in the world does this mean? [*Peering at the writing as if it was illegible.*]

CALIDORUS: Why?

PSEUDOLUS: All these letters – they seem to be playing at fathers and mothers – crawling all over each other.

CALIDORUS: Oh, if you're going to make a joke of it –

PSEUDOLUS: It would take a Sibyl to read this gibberish; no one else could make head or tail of it.

CALIDORUS: Why are you so unkind to those dear little letters, written on that dear little tablet by that dear little hand?

PSEUDOLUS: A chicken's hand, was it? Some chicken surely scratched these marks.

CALIDORUS: Oh, you are an idiot. Read the letter or give it back to me.

PSEUDOLUS: All right. I'll read it. Give me your attention.

CALIDORUS: I have no attention.

PSEUDOLUS: Then you must find some.

CALIDORUS: You read the letter and I'll say nothing. All my attention is in that tablet, not in my mind.

PSEUDOLUS [*looking at the letter*]: Oh Calidorus, I can see your sweetheart!

CALIDORUS: Where, for goodness sake?

PSEUDOLUS: Here, full length, in the wax, on this tablet.

CALIDORUS [*exasperated*]: May all the gods and goddesses –

PSEUDOLUS: – save me.

CALIDORUS: You made my heart spring up like grass in summer; up one moment and the next moment dead.

PSEUDOLUS: Well, keep quiet, while I read the letter.

CALIDORUS: Why *don't* you read it, then?

PSEUDOLUS [*reads, with difficulty*]: 'By this messenger of wax and wood and writing ... Phoenicium to her lover Calidorus ... with trembling heart ... with mind and soul distressed ... with tears ... sends her wishes for his health ... and please will you send help ...'

CALIDORUS: Alas, Pseudolus, I don't know where to turn for help to send her.

PSEUDOLUS: What kind of help?

CALIDORUS: Money ... silver.

PSEUDOLUS: You want to send her a gift of silver in exchange for a gift of wood? That's no way to do business.

CALIDORUS: Read on. Then you'll see how urgent it is for me to get some money from somewhere.

PSEUDOLUS: 'I have been sold, my darling ... by my master, to a foreigner, a Macedonian officer ... for two thousand drachmas. The man paid fifteen hundred before he left ... and we're only waiting for the other five hundred. The officer left a token here ... his image sealed in wax ... and when he sends a man back with the same seal, I am to go with him. He fixed a day for this ... next Dionysia.'

CALIDORUS: That's tomorrow. I'm doomed, unless you can find some help for me.

PSEUDOLUS: Let me finish the letter.

CALIDORUS: Yes, go on, and I can imagine I am talking to her. Read on – though it is a bitter-sweet potion you mix for me.

PSEUDOLUS: 'This is the end of all our happy hours ... our loving meetings ... our talks and games and jokes ... our kisses and blisses ... our lovers' close embraces ... soft lips that sweetly nibble ... breasts that quiver gently pressed ... and all love's mystic raptures ... all now shattered, scattered to the winds, all lost beyond recall ... if I can find no help in you nor you in me. I have told you all I know ... now I shall be waiting to learn how much you love me ... or how much you pretend to love me. Farewell.'

CALIDORUS: It's a terrible letter, Pseudolus.

PSEUDOLUS: Terrible.

CALIDORUS: Doesn't it make you weep?

PSEUDOLUS: No, I've got eyes like pumice stones; can't squeeze a drop out of them.

CALIDORUS: Why –

PSEUDOLUS: All our family are a dry-eyed lot.

CALIDORUS: Well, aren't you going to help me?

PSEUDOLUS: What can I do?

CALIDORUS: Ah me!

PSEUDOLUS: You can save your 'ah me's'. I can do that much.

CALIDORUS: I'm lost. I don't know where to borrow any money.

PSEUDOLUS: Ah me!

CALIDORUS: And I haven't a penny of my own.

PSEUDOLUS: Ah me!

CALIDORUS: And tomorrow that man will take the girl away.

PSEUDOLUS: Ah me!

CALIDORUS: Is that all you can do to help me?

PSEUDOLUS: It's all I've got, sir. I've got a pile of 'ah me's' put away in my money-box.

CALIDORUS: But I'm desperate. Can't you lend me a single drachma? I'll pay you back tomorrow.

PSEUDOLUS: By God, I couldn't raise a drachma, not even if I pawned my own body. But what do you want to do with a drachma?

CALIDORUS: Buy a rope.

PSEUDOLUS: What for?

CALIDORUS: To hang myself. I am resolved before night falls to take refuge in everlasting night.

PSEUDOLUS: Then who'll pay me back my drachma? Is that your idea, to go and hang yourself on purpose to do me out of a drachma if I lend you one?

CALIDORUS: I tell you I cannot live if she is taken from me and carried off.

PSEUDOLUS: There's nothing to cry about, you silly cuckoo. You'll live.

CALIDORUS: Nothing to cry about – when I can't raise a drachma, not know where in the world to turn for a piece of silver?

PSEUDOLUS: Well, it's silver tears you'll have to weep, as I understand it from this letter. You might as well try to catch rain in a sieve, for all the good the tears you're shedding now can do you. But cheer up; I'll never desert a master in love. Somewhere or other, before the day's out, by hook or crook – or by this hand – I think I can find you some pecuniary assistance. Where it's coming from I can't exactly say at the moment; but it will come, that's all I know; I know by the twitch of this eyebrow.

CALIDORUS: Heaven send you'll be as good as your word.

PSEUDOLUS: Lord love you, you know what I can do when I wave my magic wand, what a dust I can stir up when I set about it.

CALIDORUS: All my hope of life rests on you.

PSEUDOLUS: Suppose I promise to get your girl back for you today or give you two thousand drachmas – how will that do?

CALIDORUS: It'll do very well, if you can do it.

PSEUDOLUS: Ask me for two thousand, then – in proper form, so that there'll be no doubt what I'm promising. Go on, ask me, please; I'm dying to promise it.

CALIDORUS: Will you give me two thousand drachmas today?

PSEUDOLUS: I will. Now don't say another word. One thing I warn you, though – so don't say I didn't tell you – if all else fails, I shall have to touch your father for it.

CALIDORUS: Heaven bless you and keep you mine for ever! But . . . as a dutiful son . . . I feel bound to say – why not try my mother too?

PSEUDOLUS: Leave it all to me, and you can sleep sound, on whichever eye you like.

CALIDORUS: Whichever eye? Don't you mean *ear*?

PSEUDOLUS: I like to vary the common expressions. [*He proclaims to the audience*] Now let all take notice – and let none say he has not received notice – all adults here present, all citizens of this city, all friends and acquaintances of mine, are hereby warned and advised, this day . . . to be on their guard . . . against me . . . and not to trust a word I say.

CALIDORUS: Sh! Be quiet, for goodness sake!

PSEUDOLUS: What's up?

CALIDORUS [*indicating Ballio's house*]: Ballio's door rattled.

PSEUDOLUS: I'd like to hear his shins rattle.

CALIDORUS: And here comes the old sinner himself.
[*They withdraw to a corner.*]
[BALLIO *storms out of his house, brandishing a whip and rounding up a miscellaneous gang of slaves.*]

BALLIO: Come along there, out here, the lot of you – idle rascals, scurvy scoundrels, not worth your keep! . . . Look at 'em; not one of them has any idea of how to behave; if I didn't keep them up to the mark with *this*, I should never get a day's work out of them. Asses – more like asses than any men I ever saw – with hides tanned till they can't feel it any more. Beating them hurts you more than it does them; just wasters of whip-leather, that's what they are. They've only one rule of life: watch your chance to steal, rob, plunder, loot, eat and drink, and do a bunk. That's all they think they're here for. You might as well leave wolves in charge of sheep as let these chaps look after your house. And yet they don't seem such bad chaps to look at; it's their work that's rotten. Now then, pay attention all; and, mark my words, if you don't pay attention, if you can't wipe that sleep out of your eyes and wake up those weary carcases, I'll draw such pretty patterns on your ribs with these whipcords as you never saw on any Campanian painted fabrics or Egyptian carpets with zoological embroideries. I gave you your orders yesterday, didn't I, and gave each man his place? Yes, I did; but you lazy louts are blessed with so much intelligence that you can't remember your duties without a sharp reminder. That's the sort you are. You're that obstinate, me and my friend here [*the whip*] can't make any impression on you … Look at 'em – I ask you – they don't give a damn; thinking of something else all the time … Pay attention to me, will you, and listen to what I'm telling you – generation of deadbeats! I'll show you which is the tougher, your skins or my rawhide … How's that, then? Did that hurt? That's what a slave gets for not paying attention to his master …

In line, everybody! Line up here, facing me – and *pay attention*!… That man with the water-pot, go and draw water and get the cook's copper filled. You with the axe, you're appointed chief of the chopping department.

SLAVE: This axe is blunt, sir.

BALLIO: I don't care if it is. You all are – worn down with flogging; that's no reason why I shouldn't get some work out of you, is it? … You, get the house cleaned up. Well, what are you waiting for? Inside, at the double! … You can be bedmaker … You, polish the silver and lay the tables. And mind, I want to find everything ready when I come back from town, everything swept, washed, polished, tidied, bright and shining. It's my birthday today and I'd like you all to help me celebrate it … You, boy, get some ham, bacon, sweetbread, and sow's udders into the stewpot. Do you understand? I want to entertain some important gentlemen in tiptop style, so that they'll think I'm well off … Inside, all of you, and get busy; I don't want any delay when the cook arrives. I'm going to market, to see what sort of a bargain I can strike with the fishmonger.

[*All the slaves have now been sent about their business, except one boy who carries a purse.*]

Lead on, boy; and I'll keep an eye on that purse to see that nobody picks it.

Oh, wait a minute, though. I nearly forgot; I've some more orders for the household. [*He goes back to the house door.*] Girls! Where are you? Come out here and listen to me.

[*Several of his women parade in front of the house, among them* PHOENICIUM, *the beloved of Calidorus.*]

Now then, my pretties, all *you* have to do is to enjoy your little selves in comfort, ease and luxury, and make yourselves the most desirable companions for the highest gentry in the town. I'm going to put you to the test today. I'm going to find out which of you is only interested in her own freedom, or her stomach, or in lining her own purse, or just going to sleep. I shall have to decide which I'll choose to make a free woman of, and which to put back on the market. I want to see your lovers bringing me a whole pile of presents today. I want supplies for a year brought to this house this day, or else tomorrow you'll be out on the streets. As you are aware, today is my birthday. So where are they? Where are the lads for whom you are supposed to supply the light of love, the joy of life, the sweet sips of honeysuckle lips, the pressed caress . . .? Where are they? I want to see them in massed battalions outside this door, with their hands full of presents for me. Why do you suppose I provide you with clothes and ornaments and everything you could possibly need? And what return have you shown me for it so far? Nothing but dead loss. Drink is the only thing you miserable creatures are interested in; your stomachs are filled to bursting, while I go dry.

Now, the best thing I can do is to address you personally, one by one; then nobody can say she hasn't been given explicit instructions. Attention, all! . . . Number one, Hedylium – you're the favourite in the corn market; all your clients have got stocks of grain as high as mountains in their warehouses; make it your business to see that supplies come this way – a year's supply of grain for me and my household; I want to be a corn-king so rich that folks will call me King Jason instead of Pimp Ballio.

CALIDORUS [*aside to Pseudolus*]: Listen to the old crook. Did you ever see such a high-handed tyrant?

PSEUDOLUS: A low-minded scoundrel, I should call him. But don't say anything. Watch him.

BALLIO: Who's next? Aeschrodora – your clients are the butchers, and they're as bad as us pimps for making a dishonest living by bad faith – here are your instructions: get me three meat-frames loaded with fat heavy carcases before the day's out, or ... like Dirce in the story, tied to a bull by the sons of Jupiter ... I'll have you pegged up, not to a bull, but to a butcher's meat-frame.

CALIDORUS: His language makes my blood boil.

PSEUDOLUS: I don't know how the young men of Athens can tolerate his existence. Where are they? What's become of all his youthful and able-bodied customers? Why don't they join together to rid the city of this pest? ... But of course, that's the sort of silly thing I would say ... as if they'd dare to do anything to someone to whom they're enslaved by their lust, which won't allow them to lift a finger against him.

CALIDORUS: Oh do shut up.

PSEUDOLUS: What's the matter with you?

CALIDORUS: You're a nuisance; I can't hear what he's saying if you keep on interrupting.

PSEUDOLUS: I won't say another word.

CALIDORUS: Well, *don't* say another word, instead of *saying* you're not going to say another –

BALLIO: Now you, Xystilis; can I have your attention, please? Your friends are the oilmen, with gallons of the stuff in store. So I want bags and bottles of it delivered here without delay, or ... tomorrow I'll have you bottled up in a bag and delivered to the shop down the road; where they'll give you a bed all right, not to sleep on, but to lie on till you're fagged out with ... if you follow the drift of my remarks. Do you hear, you serpent? With all those friends of yours simply swimming in oil, have you done anything yet to win a drop of it with which to beautify the pretty heads of any of your fellow prisoners? Or to make my salad dressing a tiny bit more tasty? Oh yes, I know, you don't care so much for oil; you go for the wine. All I can say is, you mark my words, and obey my instructions, or by Hercules I'll settle the score with you on the nail. Next! Phoenicium ... ah yes, the gentlemen's pet, who's always on the point of bringing me the price of her freedom

– always got a bargain to make, but not so clever at making it good. Well, just you see that my larder is stocked with everything your rich friends can provide – or tomorrow, my Phoenician pet, your back will be striped with Phoenician colours and you'll be on the market too.

[*While he is hustling them back into the house,* CALIDORUS *and* PSEUDOLUS *are still watching unseen.*]

CALIDORUS: There, Pseudolus – do you hear what the villain says?

PSEUDOLUS: I hear him, master. I'm giving the matter my full attention.

CALIDORUS: I must stop him putting my girl on the streets. What do you think I ought to send him?

PSEUDOLUS: Keep calm; don't worry. I'll do the worrying for both of us. He's an old friend of mine, and I'm one of his; we know each other well. I'll send him a birthday present – a nice fat packet of trouble.

CALIDORUS: What good will that do?

PSEUDOLUS: You mind your own business.

CALIDORUS: But –

PSEUDOLUS: But, but, but!

CALIDORUS: Oh, this is torture!

PSEUDOLUS: Bear it like a man.

CALIDORUS: I can't.

PSEUDOLUS: You'll have to try.

CALIDORUS: How can I possibly help feeling as I do?

PSEUDOLUS: You don't want to consider your feelings in time of trouble. Think about something helpful.

CALIDORUS: That's absurd. A lover must behave like a fool or there's no fun in it.

PSEUDOLUS: Oh, give over!

CALIDORUS: Pseudolus dear, let me make a fool of myself; let me go my own way –

PSEUDOLUS: Go where you like; I'm going myself –

CALIDORUS: No, wait! Wait, and I'll do anything you like.

PSEUDOLUS: That's better.

[BALLIO *shuts his house door and returns to the boy.*]

BALLIO: I must be off, time's flying. Lead on, boy.

CALIDORUS: He's going, he's going! Call him back!

PSEUDOLUS: Keep calm; all in good time.

CALIDORUS: But he'll be gone.

BALLIO: Get a move on, boy; we haven't got all day.

PSEUDOLUS [*calling to Ballio, but still from a distant or concealed place*]: Coo-ee! Happy birthday to you! Happy birthday to you! You! Birthday boy! Come and talk to us. Spare us a moment, can't you? Hey! Someone wants to talk to you.

[BALLIO *has paused, probably recognizing the voice but refusing to look.*]

BALLIO: What's that? Some fellow wasting my time when I'm busy?

PSEUDOLUS: An old friend.

BALLIO: An old friend is a dead friend. Present friends are what I need.

PSEUDOLUS: You're being very offensive.

BALLIO: You're being a damned nuisance.

CALIDORUS: Stop him, Pseudolus. Go after him.

PSEUDOLUS: We'll head him off this way. [*They intercept Ballio.*]

BALLIO: Jupiter destroy you, whoever you are.

PSEUDOLUS: I want to speak to you.

BALLIO: I don't want to speak to you – either of you. Come round this way, boy.

PSEUDOLUS: Can't you let me speak to you?

BALLIO: I can, but I don't want to.

PSEUDOLUS: Not even if it is in your own interest?

BALLIO: Can't you let me go on my way, damn it?

PSEUDOLUS: Now, now, not so fast.

BALLIO: Take your hands off me.

CALIDORUS: Listen, please, Ballio.

BALLIO: If you've only words to spend, I'm not listening.

CALIDORUS: I have always paid you when I could.

BALLIO: I'm not asking for what you *have* paid.

CALIDORUS: And I'll pay you again when I have the money.

BALLIO: When you have the money, you can have the goods.

CALIDORUS: Oh dear, then all the money and gifts I've brought you were just wasted.

BALLIO: You're wasting your breath now, you young fool, offering me words with no assets to back them.

PSEUDOLUS: Do you know who you're talking to?

BALLIO: I used to know him; who he is now, he alone knows. Step along, boy ... [*He again reaches the far end of the stage.*]

PSEUDOLUS [*in a more ingratiating tone*]: Ballio – do you think an attractive proposition could persuade you to give us a moment of your attention?

BALLIO [*stopping*]: Ah, now that's different. I'll listen to an attractive proposition. If I were in the middle of making an offering to Jove Almighty, standing there with the giblets ready in my hand – if someone came up with an attractive proposition, I'd postpone the ceremony rather than miss a good chance. You can't afford to be disrespectful to profit, when all's said and done.

PSEUDOLUS [*to Calidorus*]: He doesn't give a damn for all the holy gods.

BALLIO: Yes, I'll have a word with him ... [*He comes back to Pseudolus*] Good morning to you, worst slave in the town.

PSEUDOLUS: May the gods give you all that I and my friend could wish for you – or if you want it in other words, may they bless and help you nevermore.

BALLIO [*pleasantly*]: And how is my friend Calidorus?

CALIDORUS: Sick of love and poverty.

BALLIO: I'd be sorry for you – only I can't feed my family on sympathy.

PSEUDOLUS: We know your feelings all right; you needn't tell us. Do you know what *we* want?

BALLIO: I can guess; you want to see me ruined.

PSEUDOLUS: Well, partly that; but what we want you for now – if you will kindly listen a minute –

BALLIO: I'm listening. But I'm busy, so come to the point as quickly as possible.

PSEUDOLUS: My master is extremely sorry he has not been able to pay you, as he promised you, and on the day he promised to pay you, the two thousand drachmas for his girl's freedom.

BALLIO: I dare say he is; it's easier to be sorry than to be sore. He's sorry he hasn't paid the money; I'm sore at not getting it.

PSEUDOLUS: But he will pay it; he'll find it. Just give him a few more days. What he's afraid of is that you will sell her to spite him.

BALLIO: He could have paid me long ago if he had wanted to.

CALIDORUS: How could I, if I hadn't got the money?

BALLIO: You'd have found some way, if you'd been really in love – borrowed it from a friend, gone to a money-lender and offered him his bit of interest, or robbed your father.

PSEUDOLUS: Rob his father? You scoundrel. I'm sorry for anyone who expects good advice from you.

BALLIO: It's not a ponce's job to give good advice.

CALIDORUS: I couldn't possibly rob my father – the old man is far too clever for that. And if I could, my duty would forbid it.

BALLIO: All right, all right. Then you'll have to take your duty to bed with you instead of Phoenicium. You seem to think more of duty than of love. But everybody isn't your father; haven't you a friend whom you could ask for a loan?

CALIDORUS: Loan! There's no such word nowadays.

PSEUDOLUS: Lord bless you, no. No one's such a fool as to lend any money these days – ever since certain nameless gentlemen made their fortunes and closed their banks, after collecting their own debts and making sure that nobody else got his money back.

CALIDORUS: No, I haven't a hope. I can't raise a penny anywhere. All I can do is die – die of love and die of destitution.

BALLIO: You could buy oil under the counter and sell it in the open. You'd make twenty thousand in no time that way, I reckon.

CALIDORUS: But damn it, I'm under age – don't you know the law? – no one would dare give me credit.

BALLIO: Yes, I know the law; and I don't dare give you credit, much as I'd like to.

PSEUDOLUS: I bet you would. Aren't you satisfied with what you've got out of him already?

BALLIO: He's no true lover who isn't ready to keep on giving. He must pay, pay, and pay again. When he's got nothing left, he must stop loving.

CALIDORUS: Haven't you any pity at all?

BALLIO: Not when you come empty-handed. Your words don't ring on my counter. All the same, I'd be glad to see you alive and well.

PSEUDOLUS: What do you think he is, dead and buried?

BALLIO: He's dead as far as I'm concerned if he comes to me with that kind of story. A lover might as well be dead as come whining to a man of my profession. Come to me any day you like, my boy, with a solid silver proposition; when you come wailing about having no money – you're only asking your stepmother for pity.

PSEUDOLUS: I didn't know you'd ever married his father!

BALLIO: God forbid!

PSEUDOLUS: Look here, Ballio; just do us a favour, can't you? On my word of honour, if you're afraid to trust him. Give me three days and I'll produce the money for you from somewhere on land or sea.

BALLIO: You expect me to trust you?

PSEUDOLUS: Why not?

BALLIO: Why not? God almighty! I'd as soon trust you as tie up a stray dog with a string of sheep's guts.

CALIDORUS: And after all I've done for you, is this how you show your gratitude?

BALLIO: So what do you want me to do – eh? What do you want me to do now?

CALIDORUS: Just wait for five or six days before selling the girl and making her lover die of despair.

BALLIO: Cheer up, sonny. I'll wait six months if you like.

CALIDORUS [astounded]: You will? Oh you glorious man!

BALLIO: I can give you some even better news too.

CALIDORUS: What's that?

BALLIO: Your girl is not for sale any more.

CALIDORUS: She isn't?

BALLIO: I promise you she isn't.

CALIDORUS: Pseudolus! This man is Jupiter Almighty! I must give him a sacrifice! Go and find offerings, victims, butchers! He is Jupiter for me, more mighty than Jupiter!

BALLIO: I don't want any victims, thanks. Just a few lamb cutlets will do me.

CALIDORUS: Lambs, Pseudolus! Hurry up, do you hear what Jupiter orders?

PSEUDOLUS: I'll be as quick as I can; but I shall have to run as far as the city gate and farther.

CALIDORUS: Why must you go there?

PSEUDOLUS: To find a couple of throat-slitters, chain-swingers; and

at the same time I'll rustle up a few bundles of birch rods, so we'll
have enough and to spare to give your Jupiter a grand ovation.

BALLIO: You go to hell.

PSEUDOLUS: That's where the Prince of Pimps is going, all right.

BALLIO: It'd suit you fine to have me dead, wouldn't it?

PSEUDOLUS: Would it?

BALLIO: It would, by God; as long as I live, you'll never come to
any good. On the other hand, you'd be sorry to see me dead.

PSEUDOLUS: Would I?

BALLIO: Because when I'm dead, you'll be the wickedest man in
Athens.

CALIDORUS: But tell me, for goodness sake, are you serious? You're
not selling my girl now?

BALLIO: I assure you I'm not. She's sold already.

CALIDORUS: How can she be sold?

BALLIO: How? Just as she stands, no clothing included, but with
all her bodily organs complete.

CALIDORUS: So you've sold my beloved!

BALLIO: That's right, for two thousand drachmas.

CALIDORUS: Two thousand!

BALLIO: Or four times five hundred, whichever you like; to a
Macedonian officer; and he has paid me fifteen hundred on account.

CALIDORUS: I can't believe it!

BALLIO: Oh yes, she's been turned into good money now.

CALIDORUS: How could you dare!

BALLIO: She was mine to do as I liked with.

CALIDORUS: Pseudolus, a sword! Bring me a sword!

PSEUDOLUS: What do you want a sword for?

CALIDORUS: To end his life, and mine.

PSEUDOLUS: End yours if you like; his will soon end in starvation.

CALIDORUS [*to Ballio*]: Didn't you swear to me, you most shameless
perjurer in all the world; didn't you swear you'd never sell her to
anyone but me?

BALLIO: That's right; I did.

CALIDORUS: In express and formal terms.

BALLIO: All properly sewn up.

CALIDORUS: And you've broken your oath, you scoundrel.

BALLIO: But I've filled my purse. So I'm a scoundrel, and I've got

money to spend; you're an honest man, of an honest family, and
you haven't a penny to bless yourself with.

CALIDORUS: Pseudolus, just stand on the other side of him, will you,
and call him all the names you can think of.

PSEUDOLUS: With pleasure. With as much pleasure as I'd run to
court to claim my freedom.

CALIDORUS: Smother him with curses.

PSEUDOLUS: I'll tongue-twist you ... you ... you dirty man!

BALLIO: Granted.

CALIDORUS: You ... wicked man!

BALLIO: Correct.

PSEUDOLUS: You scourgeable scoundrel!

BALLIO: Undoubtedly.

CALIDORUS: Grave-robber!

BALLIO: Certainly.

PSEUDOLUS: Gallows-meat!

BALLIO: That's a good one.

CALIDORUS: Who'd deceive his best friend.

BALLIO: That's my trade.

PSEUDOLUS: Assassin!

BALLIO [to Calidorus]: Now your turn.

CALIDORUS: Blasphemer!

BALLIO: Oh, sure.

PSEUDOLUS: False swearer.

BALLIO: Think of something new.

CALIDORUS: Law-smasher!

BALLIO: Well done.

CALIDORUS: Corruptor of youth.

BALLIO: Precisely.

CALIDORUS: Thief!

BALLIO: Boo!

PSEUDOLUS: Escaped convict.

BALLIO: Bah!

CALIDORUS: Public nuisance.

BALLIO: Evidently.

PSEUDOLUS: Cheat.

CALIDORUS: Scum.

PSEUDOLUS: Pimp.

CALIDORUS: Ordure.

BALLIO: Ha, ha! What a charming pair of songsters.

CALIDORUS: I know you beat your parents.

BALLIO: Oh, I did – and killed them, to save their keep. Nothing wrong in that, was there?

PSEUDOLUS: We're pouring water in a sieve – sheer waste of time.

BALLIO: Is there anything more you wish to say, gentlemen?

CALIDORUS: Is there nothing you're ashamed of?

BALLIO: I'd be ashamed of having to confess myself a suitor with nothing to offer – as hollow as an empty nutshell. However, although you've called me all those dirty names, I can tell you this: if I don't get that five hundred the Macedonian owes me – today is his last chance, according to our agreement – if he doesn't pay up, I shall do what I consider my duty.

CALIDORUS: What will that be?

BALLIO [slyly confidential]: You bring me the money, my boy, and his deal is off. That's what I consider my duty. I'd be delighted to discuss it further with you, but I'm busy just now ... if you'll excuse me ... [going]. Only remember – without the money it'll be no use your coming to me with cries for mercy. That's my last word; you'd better go and think it over.

CALIDORUS: No, wait a minute.

BALLIO: Sorry, I've a lot of things on my mind. [He goes.]

PSEUDOLUS: You'll have a lot more presently ... I've got him, sir; I've got him, if gods and men don't let me down. I'll bone and fillet him like a cook splitting a lamprey. See here, Calidorus, I shall want your assistance.

CALIDORUS: At your service, sir.

PSEUDOLUS: We've got to besiege and capture the position before the day's out. For this purpose we shall need a sharp, intelligent, careful, and crafty man – one who will carry out his instructions to the letter, and not go to sleep at his post.

CALIDORUS: What are you going to do? Do tell me.

PSEUDOLUS: I'll tell you when the time comes. No point in going over it twice – plays are long enough as it is.

CALIDORUS: You can count on my assistance, anyway.

PSEUDOLUS: Hurry up, then, and get your friend here as soon as possible.

CALIDORUS: I have plenty of friends, but precious few whom I could call reliable.

PSEUDOLUS: Well I know it. So you've got two things to do; make a short list out of the many, and then pick the one man you can count on.

CALIDORUS: I think I can find somebody for you ...

PSEUDOLUS: Off you go, then. Don't waste your own time talking.
  [CALIDORUS goes.]
That leaves me, on my own. Now what are you going to do, eh, Pseudolus? You've entertained your young master with a feast of fine talk. And what does it amount to now? As for having a ghost of a definite plan, let alone money – no, I don't know what I'm going to do. No, Pseudolus, you haven't a clue, which end to start weaving or where to finish off. Well, after all, when a poet sits down to write, he has to start by looking for something which doesn't exist on this earth, and somehow or other he finds it; he makes a fiction look very much like a fact. That's what I'll do; I'll be a poet; I'll invent two thousand drachmas, which at present don't exist anywhere on earth. As a matter of fact, I had promised to find it for him some time ago, and I meant to train my sights on the old man; but he got wind of me somehow ... Hullo, here he comes ... my master Simo and his neighbour Callipho. I must cut short this oration. Here he comes ... Now I've got to dig two thousand out of this old coffin to give to the young master. I'll keep out of the way and hear what they're talking about.
  [He withdraws to a corner. SIMO and CALLIPHO appear.]

SIMO: If the Athenians were looking for a dictator among their most notable prodigals and libertines, I reckon my son would be their first choice. He's the talk of the town; everybody knows he wants to buy his girl out and hasn't got the money for it. People keep telling me this, but of course I had my suspicions long ago. I nosed him, but I wasn't going to let on.

PSEUDOLUS: Oh, he nosed him, did he? So it looks as if my scheme is sunk already; nothing doing. My plan to go foraging for supplies – cash supplies – is frustrated; road completely blocked. He had his suspicions; so there'll be no booty to be picked up.

CALLIPHO: If I had my way, I'd hang all tale-tellers and all who listen to them; I'd string 'em up, the tellers by their tongues and the listeners by their ears. All those tales you hear about your son wanting to wheedle money out of you, to further his love affair, may very well turn out to be lies. And even if they are true, what of it? Has he done anything surprising – as things go nowadays? Is it anything new for a young man to be in love and want to buy his girl's freedom?

PSEUDOLUS: That's a sensible old gentleman.

SIMO: It may not be new, but I object to his doing it.

CALLIPHO: You can object till you're blue in the face. As if you hadn't been the same when you were a young man! A father must have a clear conscience if he expects his son to be as good a man as he was, or better. As for you, your sins and extravagances were numerous enough to be distributed round the whole population, one per man. Why should you be surprised if your son takes after his father?

PSEUDOLUS: Zeus! How rare is a man of proper feeling! That's the sort of father a son ought to have.

SIMO: Somebody spoke. [Seeing Pseudolus] Oh, so it's my slave Pseudolus. This is the rascal who is corrupting my son; he's the tempter and tutor; I'd like to get him on the rack.

CALLIPHO: It'll do you no good to make a show of temper. The best thing would be to approach him peaceably and ask him whether the tales you hear are true or not. In a tight place, gentleness is half the battle.

SIMO: I'll take your advice.

[The old gentlemen move towards Pseudolus.]

PSEUDOLUS: Look out, Pseudolus, they're coming. Get a good speech ready for the old man. [He greets them.] Greetings to my master first, as is right and proper . . . and to his neighbour a share of what is left over.

SIMO: Good day to you, Pseudolus. What are you doing out here?

PSEUDOLUS: Just . . . standing here . . . as you see.

SIMO: Standing there . . . and in a very princely pose, don't you think, Callipho?

CALLIPHO: Oh indeed, I can see he knows how to stand up for himself.

PSEUDOLUS: An honest servant, I presume, with a blameless record, has a right to stand up for himself, especially in his master's presence?

CALLIPHO: There is a certain matter, which we know of, mistily as it were, which we have heard about, and about which we would like to ask you a few questions.

SIMO: You be careful, Callipho; he'll talk your head off till you feel as if you're arguing with Socrates instead of Pseudolus.

PSEUDOLUS: I am quite aware, sir, that you have long had a very low opinion of me. I realize that you place little confidence in my loyalty; nevertheless, insist as you may on my being good for nothing, I am determined to prove myself good for something.

SIMO: Then kindly throw open your auricular temples, so that my words may find their desired destination.

PSEUDOLUS: Pray do not let my displeasure prevent you from speaking with perfect frankness.

SIMO: Displeasure, eh? Can a slave be displeased with his master?

PSEUDOLUS: You find that surprising?

SIMO [with heavy irony]: From the way you talk, by Hercules, I can see that I shall have to beware of your wrath. You evidently have it in mind to give me a drubbing, of a different kind from those that I give you. What do you think, Callipho?

CALLIPHO: Well, I must say I think he has a right to resent it if you show you have no confidence in him.

SIMO: Let him resent it as much as he likes. I'll take care he doesn't do me any harm. [To Pseudolus] Now then, kindly answer my questions.

PSEUDOLUS: Ask what you will. For all that is within my knowledge, consider me your oracle.

SIMO: I'll hold you to that promise. Listen then. Do you know anything about my son being in love with a singing girl?

PSEUDOLUS [oracularly]: Ay, verily.

SIMO: And that he wants to free her?

PSEUDOLUS: Ay, again verily.

SIMO: And do you know anything about two thousand drachmas which you are planning to get out of me by some crafty and underhand trick?

PSEUDOLUS: Me? Get money out of you?

SIMO: Exactly – money for you to give to my son, for him to pay for his girl's freedom. Is that true or not?

PSEUDOLUS: Ay, verily.

CALLIPHO: So he confesses it.

SIMO: What did I tell you, Callipho?

CALLIPHO: I know.

SIMO [to Pseudolus]: Why didn't you tell me, when you first discovered how things were? Why was it kept from me? Why wasn't I informed?

PSEUDOLUS: If you want to know, it was because I refused to be a father to the nasty practice of denouncing one's master to one's other master.

SIMO [to Callipho]: You'd have him packed off to the mills for this, wouldn't you?

CALLIPHO: Really, Simo, has he done anything wrong?

SIMO: Of course he has; the most grievous wrong.

PSEUDOLUS [to Callipho]: Don't trouble yourself, sir. I know what I'm about. If I am in the wrong, it's my own doing. [To Simo] I'd like to tell you, sir, if you please, why I kept you in ignorance of your son's affair. I knew it was the mill for me if I did otherwise.

SIMO: And didn't you know it would be the mill for you if you said nothing?

PSEUDOLUS: Yes, I knew that too.

SIMO: Then why not tell me?

PSEUDOLUS: It was a choice between a present evil and a more distant one – immediate punishment or a few days' grace.

SIMO: I see. So now what do you propose to do? Nobody is going to get any money out of me, I can tell you, now I'm on the alert. I'll have a proclamation made forbidding any loan to be made to you.

PSEUDOLUS: Don't you worry, sir; I promise I won't go begging to anyone else, as long as you're alive. You'll give it me all right; you're the one I'll get it from.

SIMO: You think you'll get it from me?

PSEUDOLUS: I'm sure of it.

SIMO: Gods! May I lose an eye if I give you anything.

PSEUDOLUS: You'll give it me. I'm only telling you, so that you can be on your guard.

CALLIPHO: Well, all I can say is, if you do get it out of him, you'll have performed a most remarkable feat.

PSEUDOLUS: I shall perform it.

SIMO: What if you don't succeed?

PSEUDOLUS: Flog me. But what if I do succeed?

SIMO: If you do succeed ... by Jove, I'll give you impunity for life, and that's a promise.

PSEUDOLUS: Don't forget it.

SIMO: Do you imagine I can't take care of myself, after I've been forewarned?

PSEUDOLUS: Well I am warning you; take care. That's my advice; take care. Take care. Before the end of this day, you'll be giving me money with those very hands.

CALLIPHO: Ye gods! The man's a living marvel – if he can be as good as his word.

PSEUDOLUS: I shall. Take me for your slave if I don't.

SIMO: That's a very generous offer. You're no longer mine, at all events.

PSEUDOLUS: Would you like me to tell you something else even more exciting?

CALLIPHO: I would indeed. I could listen to you all day.

SIMO: Oh yes, do; I've no objection to your talking.

PSEUDOLUS: Before I engage on the ... contest I've mentioned, I'm going to try my skill in another contest; and a famous and memorable contest it will be.

SIMO: What sort of a contest?

PSEUDOLUS: You'll see. I'm going to wage war on a neighbour of yours, the pimp Ballio; I'm going to employ some artful diplomacy and cunning tactics, in order to remove neatly from his grasp the singing girl who has inspired a fatal passion in your son's heart.

SIMO: What – ?

PSEUDOLUS: And I expect to have two victories to my credit by this evening.

SIMO: Ah well, if you can do all you promise, you'll be a greater man than King Agathocles. On the other hand, if you don't, you will agree I am entitled to commit you to the treadmill?

PSEUDOLUS: Absolutely; not for a day only, but for all eternity.

But the point is this: if I succeed in my first object, will you then give me some money to give to Ballio – as a kind of generous gesture on your part?

CALLIPHO: That's a very fair request, Simo. Say you will.

SIMO: I'm not so sure. Do you know what occurs to me? How do we know the villains haven't come to an understanding and cooked up this ingenious plot to get money out of me?

PSEUDOLUS: You think I'd dare to do such a mean trick? I'd be the most audacious rogue alive! But seriously, sir – if we have hatched up anything between us or come to any understanding or conspired together in any way on the subject ... you can scribble me over from head to foot with birch rods for pens, like writing words in a book.

SIMO: Very well; announce the contest as soon as you please.

PSEUDOLUS [to Callipho]: I'd like you, sir, if you will, to put yourself at my disposal for today, and cancel all your other engagements.

CALLIPHO: I'm afraid I made arrangements yesterday to go to the country today.

PSEUDOLUS: Couldn't you change your plan of campaign?

CALLIPHO: All right, I will. I'll stay on your account. I wouldn't miss that contest of yours for anything. And if I find he refuses to give you the money as agreed, I'll give it you myself rather than have your scheme fall down.

SIMO [grumpily]: I shan't default.

PSEUDOLUS: Of course you won't. .... [Aside] If you do, you'll never hear the last of it ... Come on, then, let's have you two out of the way and leave me room to do my stuff.

CALLIPHO: Right-o; you're the boss.

PSEUDOLUS [apart to Callipho]: Don't forget I want you to be on hand at your house.

CALLIPHO: I'll be there. [He goes into his house.]

SIMO: I'm going to town. I shan't be long. [He goes.]

PSEUDOLUS: Come back as soon as you like ... [To the audience] I imagine ... that you good people imagine ... that I have no intention of doing what I've just said I'm going to do ... that I'm only making these rash promises for the purpose of keeping you amused as long as the play lasts. Well, you're wrong. I shall keep my word. And I can tell you another thing ... another thing I can promise you for certain is that I haven't the slightest idea *how* I'm going to do it . . . all I know is that it will be done. What's an actor for, if he is not to bring some new kind of surprise on to the stage? If he can't do that much, he'd much better make way for someone who can. And now, if you'll excuse me, I'd like to leave the stage for a few minutes, in order to make a mental mobilization of my forces of ingeniosity. I'll be back soon . . . shan't keep you long. In the meantime our musician will entertain you. [*He introduces the flute-player, and exit.*]

*

[*After the interlude,* PSEUDOLUS *reappears, in high spirits.*]
PSEUDOLUS: Glory be to Jupiter! Everything's lovely, everything's going fine! No more doubts, no more fears; I've got it all safe in here [*slapping his chest.*] Only a fool would entrust an important enterprise to a faint heart. The way things go is the way you make them go; give your mind to a job and you can do it. And I've got all my forces lined up in my mind, arts and stratagems two and three deep; [*orating grandiloquently*] wheresoever we may grapple with the adversary – and I say this, my friends, in the confidence inspired by the valour of my forebears, by my own determination and my unscrupulous villainy – victory is certain, deception will defeat and despoil the enemy. This enemy, our common enemy, my enemy and yours, this Ballio, will be scienti-fically and ballistically destroyed. Watch me. I intend to besiege and capture the position this very day. Here [*indicating Ballio's house*] is where I shall make the first attack. Having captured this ground and made the way here clear for my allies, I shall proceed with my troops to assault this ancient fortress [*the house of Simo*], where I expect to load myself and my confederates with more booty than we can carry, and let my enemies know that I was born to scourge them with rout and terror. For I am born of noble stock, and it behoves me to do such deeds of note, whose fame shall long live after me . . . [*He breaks off abruptly.*] But hold! Whom do I see? Do my eyes discern a stranger? A stranger with a sword? What can he be doing here, I wonder? I must conceal myself and spy on his movements. [*He conceals himself.*]

[*The newcomer is* HARPAX, *the emissary of the Macedonian officer;
he is a smart and intelligent soldier.*]

HARPAX: Somewhere about here, I should think, must be the place
I was told to find. Yes, this seems to agree with the captain's
directions. Seventh house from the gate, he said, and I was to give
the pimp who lives there this money and the token. I wish I could
find someone to tell me for certain which is this Ballio's house.

PSEUDOLUS: Sh! Not a word! This is the man I want, or I'm no
friend of gods or men. I shall have to change my tactics now; this
alters the situation. This'll have to be dealt with first and all my
previous plans shelved. Just watch me deliver a *coup de grâce* to this
military emissary.

HARPAX: I'll knock at this door and fetch somebody out.

PSEUDOLUS [*accosting him*]: Wait a minute, whoever you are. I shall
be obliged if you will refrain from knocking at that door. I've
come out here on purpose to protect the interests of that door.

HARPAX: Are you Ballio?

PSEUDOLUS: Not exactly; I'm his sub-ballio.

HARPAX: What does that mean?

PSEUDOLUS: I'm the getter-in and giver-out; supply officer.

HARPAX: Kind of head butler, then?

PSEUDOLUS: No, I'm the man who gives orders to the head butler.

HARPAX: Slave or free?

PSEUDOLUS: Slave – up to now.

HARPAX: I should think so; and always will be, by the look of you.

PSEUDOLUS: You might take a look at yourself, before insulting
other people.

HARPAX [*aside*]: He's up to no good, I'll be bound.

PSEUDOLUS [*aside*]: The gods are on my side! This man will be the
anvil on which I'll forge a lot of forgeries today.

HARPAX: I wonder what he's talking to himself about?

PSEUDOLUS: Listen to me, laddie.

HARPAX: Pardon?

PSEUDOLUS: Is it or is it not a fact that you've been sent here by a
Macedonian captain? Are you not the servant of a man who bought
a girl from us here, who paid my master, her employer, fifteen
hundred for her, and still owes five hundred?

HARPAX: That's right, I am. But where in the world have you met

me before? You've never seen me or spoken to me, have you?
I'm sure I've never set eyes on you – never been to Athens before in
my life.

PSEUDOLUS: I just thought you looked as if you had come from him.
It's some time since he went away; and today, according to the
agreement, was the last day for paying over the money; and it
hasn't come yet, so –

HARPAX: And now it has come.

PSEUDOLUS: You've brought it?

HARPAX: I have.

PSEUDOLUS: Come on, then; why don't you give it me?

HARPAX: Give it to you?

PSEUDOLUS: Of course. I look after all my master's business and
accounts. I receive all money for him, make all payments and
settle all debts.

HARPAX: No, thank you. I'm not trusting you with any petty cash,
not even if you're treasurer to God Almighty.

PSEUDOLUS: You might as well. We can get the whole business tied
up in a jiffy.

HARPAX: I'd rather keep it tied up in my purse.

PSEUDOLUS: Blast you, who are you to cast aspersions on my
probity? As if I wasn't trusted to handle six hundred times that
amount every day, on my own responsibility.

HARPAX: Because others like to trust you, that's no reason why I
should trust you.

PSEUDOLUS: You might as well say straight out that I intend to rob
you.

HARPAX: Yes, you might as well say that; and I might as well suspect
that you will. What is your name?

PSEUDOLUS [aside]: Ballio has a slave called Syrus – that'll do ...
My name is Syrus.

HARPAX: Syrus?

PSEUDOLUS: That's right.

HARPAX: Well, we're only wasting time talking. If your master is
at home, why don't you call him out, so that I can do the business
I was sent to do?

PSEUDOLUS: If he were at home, I would call him out, Mister whatever your name is. But if you'd like to give me the money, the

241

business will be settled just as quickly as if you gave it to him, or quicker.

HARPAX: Yes, but don't you understand? My master sent me here to *pay* this money, not to *lose* it. And I can see very well that you're getting into a fever at not being allowed to get your claws into it. I'm not paying a penny to anyone but Ballio in person.

PSEUDOLUS: Well, he's busy just now – got a court case on.

HARPAX: Good luck to him. All right, then, I'll come back when I think he's likely to be at home. You can have this letter to give him; it bears the seal agreed between my master and yours in the matter of this girl.

PSEUDOLUS: Yes, I know about that. He said the girl was to be handed over to the person who would bring the money together with a seal showing his own likeness. He left a copy of it here with us.

HARPAX: You know it all.

PSEUDOLUS: Why shouldn't I know it all?

HARPAX: Then just give him that sealed letter.

PSEUDOLUS: I will. By the way, what is your name?

HARPAX: Harpax.

PSEUDOLUS: Then run away, Harpax; I don't like the look of you. I'll see you don't get into this house; we don't want any of your *harpacity* here.

HARPAX: I'm noted for snatching my victims alive off the field of battle; that's how I got my name.

PSEUDOLUS: More likely snatching brass pots from other people's houses!

HARPAX: You're quite wrong. But ... do you know what I'd like you to do for me, Syrus?

PSEUDOLUS: I shall know when you tell me.

HARPAX: I'm staying at a tavern outside the gate, third house down, kept by an old dame called Chrysis – a fat old barrel with a limp.

PSEUDOLUS: So what can I do for you?

HARPAX: Just send word to me there when your master comes in.

PSEUDOLUS: I'll do that with pleasure.

HARPAX: I'm pretty tired after my journey and I want to freshen up.

PSEUDOLUS: That's a good idea; very sensible of you. But mind you're there when I send for you.

HARPAX: I'll be there. I'm going to have a bit of lunch and then all I shall want is some sleep.

PSEUDOLUS: I'm sure you will.

HARPAX: That's all, then?

PSEUDOLUS: That's all; have a good sleep.

HARPAX: Right-o then. [*He goes.*]

PSEUDOLUS: And get them to give you plenty of blankets! It'll do you good to sweat it out! ...

Oh the blessed gods! That man's coming has saved the day. He found me wandering and brought me back on to the right road at his own expense, bless him. Fortune herself could not have made a more fortunate appearance than his fortunate arrival with this letter. Here I've been presented with a cornucopia containing all my heart's desire; everything is wrapped up in here – all the schemes and tricks and dodges I could need, the money, and my loving master's loving mistress! Now I can crow and puff my chest out! ... Of course I had it all worked out before – how I was going to set about getting the girl out of the pimp's hands, I had everything prepared and provided, just as I wanted it to be; I'd thought of everything and planned it all out ... But you know how it is ... and always will be. The best laid plans of a hundred skilled men can be knocked sideways by one single goddess, the Lady Luck. It's a fact; it's only being on good terms with Dame Fortune that makes a man successful and gives him the reputation of being a clever fellow; and we, as soon as we hear of someone striking it lucky, we admire his shrewdness, and laugh at the folly of the poor devil who's having a run of bad luck. For that matter, we're all fools though we don't know it, for running so hard after this or that, as if we could possibly tell for ourselves what's good for us and what isn't. We lose the certainties while seeking for uncertainties; and so we go on, in toil and trouble, until death creeps up on us ... But enough of this philosophizing. I do run on, don't I? ... By the gods, that little fib was worth its weight in gold ... saying I was Ballio's slave ... it just came to me on the spur of the moment. Now with this letter I can hoodwink three people, my master, the pimp, and the chap who brought it. [*Looking down the street*] And whoopee! here's another stroke of luck. Here comes young Calidorus, and he's got someone with him.

[CALIDORUS *arrives with his friend* CHARINUS; PSEUDOLUS *stands aside.*]

CALIDORUS: Now I have told you all the facts, pleasant and unpleasant. You know all about my love, my misery, and my need.

CHARINUS: Yes, I've got it all clear. All I want to know is, what you want me to do.

CALIDORUS: It was Pseudolus who wanted me to find him a useful and sympathetic friend.

CHARINUS: You have carried out your instructions admirably. You have found a friend and sympathizer. But this Pseudolus? He's new to me.

CALIDORUS: Oh, he's a living marvel. He's my chargé d'affaires. He has undertaken to bring off the scheme I told you of.

PSEUDOLUS [*aside*]: I must address the gentlemen in my best manner.

CALIDORUS: Did I hear a voice?

PSEUDOLUS: Hail to Pseudolus's lord and master – with thee, O king, ay with thee I crave a word, that I may bring thee joy, thrice three times triple triumph truly won by threefold stratagem from foemen three, by guile, by cunning and deceit; the which I here present to thee within this tiny tablet signed and sealed.

CALIDORUS: This is the very man.

CHARINUS: A tragic villain to the life!

PSEUDOLUS: Approach, advance, come forth, stretch out thy hand, to grasp thy fortune.

CALIDORUS: As Hope or Victory shall I greet thee, Pseudolus?

PSEUDOLUS: As both.

CHARINUS: Welcome, both. But *do* tell us what has happened.

PSEUDOLUS [*not much impressed with the look of Charinus*]: There's no cause for alarm.

CALIDORUS: This is the man I've found for you.

PSEUDOLUS: You *found* him, did you?

CALIDORUS: I mean I brought him here.

PSEUDOLUS: What's his name?

CALIDORUS: Charinus.

PSEUDOLUS [*with ironical courtesy*]: Charmed to meet him, I'm sure. [*He has obviously decided that this young man will be of little use to him.*]

CHARINUS [*peeved by his reception*]: If there is anything I can do for you, why don't you say so straight out?

PSEUDOLUS: You are very kind. Thank you very much, Charinus. But I don't think we ought to trouble you.

CHARINUS: Trouble? It won't be any trouble, I assure you.

PSEUDOLUS: Wait a minute, then. [*He produces the letter.*]

CALIDORUS: What have you got there?

PSEUDOLUS: This is the letter, and token, which I have intercepted.

CALIDORUS: Token? What token?

PSEUDOLUS: The one from the Macedonian officer, which has just been brought here. His servant arrived here with it, bringing five hundred drachmas also, and was to take your girl away with him – but I pulled the wool over his eyes.

CALIDORUS: How did you do that?

PSEUDOLUS: Well, look, this play is being acted for the benefit of the audience; they know what happened because they saw it happen. I'll tell you about it some other time.

CALIDORUS: All right; what do we do next?

PSEUDOLUS: You're going to have your girl free and in your arms today.

CALIDORUS: I am, really?

PSEUDOLUS: Yes, you, your very self – provided nothing happens to me; and provided you can find me a *man* in less than no time.

CHARINUS: What sort of a man?

PSEUDOLUS: A bad man; a wily man, an experienced man; one who, having grasped the essentials of a job, can carry it through by his own intelligence and initiative; and who is not too well known round here.

CHARINUS: Any objection to his being a slave?

PSEUDOLUS: I should much prefer a slave.

CHARINUS: I think I can provide the very man for you, an experienced rascal whom my father has just sent over from Carystus; he has never been outside the house since he arrived, that was yesterday, and this is the first time he has been in Athens.

PSEUDOLUS [*with a new respect*]: My friend, you're invaluable. I shall also require five hundred drachmas – a loan, of course, which I shall repay before the end of the day; his [*Calidorus's*] father owes me that much.

CHARINUS: You needn't look any further for that. I can let you have it.

PSEUDOLUS: You're a benefactor, sir. And I shall want a soldier's cloak and sword and hat.

CHARINUS: I can get you those.

PSEUDOLUS: Blessed gods! This Charinus is a charitable institution! Now this slave of yours from Carystus – is he a foxy sort of fellow?

CHARINUS: Goaty, by the smell of his armpits.

PSEUDOLUS: We'll have to give him a long-sleeved tunic. Sharp, is he?

CHARINUS: As an acid-drop.

PSEUDOLUS: And suppose we wanted him to serve up the sweet stuff, can he produce that too?

CHARINUS: Easily. Spiced wine, raisin wine, fruit cordial, honey cup, sweet drinks of all kinds – they say he once set up as a one-man refreshment bar!

PSEUDOLUS: Well done! Jolly good, Charinus! You can beat me at my own line of patter. By the way, what name does this chap go by?

CHARINUS: Simia.

PSEUDOLUS: Can he do a quick turnabout in a tight corner?

CHARINUS: He can spin like a top.

PSEUDOLUS: Proper twister, eh?

CHARINUS: He's been properly twisted for his crimes often enough.

PSEUDOLUS: What would he do if he were caught in the act?

CHARINUS: Slip out like an eel.

PSEUDOLUS: He's a man we can rely on, then?

CHARINUS: Reliable as an act of parliament.

PSEUDOLUS: From your account of him, he must be a model of all the virtues.

CHARINUS: Just wait till you meet him. As soon as he sets eyes on you, he'll tell you exactly what you want him to do. What do you want him to do?

PSEUDOLUS: I'll tell you. When I've got him suitably dressed up, I want him to play the part of that soldier's servant. He'll bring this token to Ballio with the five hundred drachmas, and get the girl from him. That's the long and the short of it. I shall have coached him, of course, in all the details and how he's to go about it.

CALIDORUS: Come on, then, let's get on with it.

PSEUDOLUS: You bring the fellow to me as soon as you can, properly dressed and equipped, at Aeschinus's bank. Look sharp.

CALIDORUS: We'll be there before you.

PSEUDOLUS: Get a move on, then. [*The young men go off.*] That sets my mind completely at rest; any doubts or uncertainties I had before are quite cleared away; it's all plain sailing now. The bird is on my left, the auspices plainly propitious, and I am ready to lead my ranked battalions forward to the field; now I know beyond doubt that I can destroy my adversaries ... And the next thing to do is to go to the forum and cram this Simia with all the necessary instructions, so that he can do his bit of sleight-of-hand like an expert, with no bungling. And then, by Jupiter, we'll take by storm this citadel of pimpery! [*He goes off to the town.*]

*

[*A slave* BOY, *of very unprepossessing appearance, creeps out of Ballio's house.*]

BOY: To make a boy a slave in a pimp's house – and on top of that, to make him an ugly boy – I should think that's the most cruel and miserable thing the gods could do to him. That's the sort of slave I am here; all the troubles great and small are piled on my shoulders. I can't find anyone to take any interest in me; nobody loves me; so naturally I don't bother to make myself presentable. And now today it's the boss's birthday, so he's been threatening us all, from the oldest to the youngest, that anyone who hasn't given him a present will die tomorrow with terrible tortures. So what can a poor boy like me do? I'm damned if I know what I can do. I'd do what the other boys do if I could but I can't. And if I can't find the money for a present for the boss today, tomorrow I shall have to swallow a dose of fuller's mixture. That'll be a sad fate for poor little me. It's not a very pleasant prospect, but I dare say I can grin and bear it. I could grin and bear anything, however unpleasant, if someone were to make it worth my while! But now I must shut my mouth; here's the boss coming back from town, and a cook with him.

[BALLIO *returns from his marketing, bringing with him a hired*

COOK *and one or more underlings carrying provisions and the cook's implements. The 'ugly boy' makes himself scarce, or perhaps waits to help with the provisions.*]

BALLIO: Cooks' Market they call that place – of all silly names; more like a Thieves' Kitchen, I should say. If I'd pledged my life to find a worse scoundrel of a cook than this one I've got here, I couldn't have done it. I couldn't have found a more garrulous, glib-tongued, stupid, and useless specimen. I don't know why Pluto hasn't carried him off to hell before now, unless it's so that there can be someone left here fit to cook dinners for dead bodies. There's no one better qualified to please those customers.

COOK: If that is what you think of me, why did you hire me?

BALLIO: Sheer necessity. There was nobody else. If you call yourself a cook, how comes it you were the only one still waiting to be engaged?

COOK [*ever smiling, obsequious, and professionally ingratiating*]: I will tell you why, sir. If I appear to be a bad cook, it is by no fault of my own, but because of other people's meanness.

BALLIO: How do you make that out?

COOK: It is like this: when the gentlemen come to hire a cook, none of them is looking for the best and most expensive; they only want the cheapest. That is why I am sitting there alone in the market. One drachma is all those poor creatures want to pay; I must have nothing less than two drachmas or I am not getting on my feet. Mine is not the sort of cooking you will get from ordinary cooks, who will give you big platefuls of farm produce, carefully spiced with condiments, treating your guests like cattle, filling them up with greenstuff and using more greenstuff to give it a flavouring. They will give you coriander, fennel, garlic, parsley, with heaps of cabbage, sorrel, beet, spinach; all smothered in silphium, pounds and pounds of it, and grated mustard – horrible stuff, which stings the eyes out of the boys who have to grate it, before they've finished. That kind of cook – it's not seasonings they use but screaming screech-owls that peck the living insides out of your guests. It is no wonder people have such short lives in these parts, when they stuff their bellies with that kind of fodder; disgusting to speak of, let alone eat. Men here eat plants which animals will not touch.

BALLIO: So what do you use? If you find fault with that kind of cooking, what's yours like? Cooking fit for the gods, eh? Able to prolong a man's life?

COOK: Why, yes, indeed it is, sir; I would be so bold to say it. A man who eats of my cooking will live for two hundred years. When I spice a dish with a bit of ciciliander [*he is now inventing imaginary herbs*] or cipoliander or macarosis or secatopsis, she immediately hots herself up in no time. Those of course are the seasonings for sea creatures; for the terrestrial meat I use chicimandrium, halitosis, or cataracticum.

BALLIO: May Jupiter and all the gods blast you to blazes with your fancy condiments and your lying tongue!

COOK: But I have not yet finished.

BALLIO: Then finish, and be damned to you.

COOK: When I have all my dishes nice and hot, I take off the covers, and *pouf* – the odour flies hot-handed to heaven.

BALLIO: A hot-handed odour?

COOK: No, I mistake – I meant to say hot-footed.

BALLIO: And what if nobody employs you – what happens to Jupiter's supper then?

COOK: He goes to bed with no supper.

BALLIO: And you can go to the devil. Do you think I'm going to pay you two drachmas for that sort of nonsense?

COOK: My cooking is very expensive, I know. But I promise you I give value for money to any gentleman who hires me to cook for him.

BALLIO: To rob him, you mean.

COOK [*still smiling*]: Ah well ... you do not expect to find a cook anywhere who has not got claws like a bird of prey?

BALLIO: Do you expect to be allowed to cook anywhere without having your claws safely tied up? [*To his slave*] Here you, boy – you, the one that belongs to me – get inside quick, and have everything that we possess cleared out of the way; and then keep your eyes fixed on this man's eyes; wherever he looks, you look that way too; wherever he goes, go with him; whenever he puts out his hand, get yours ready too; if he picks up something of his own, let him; if it's something of ours, get hold of the other end of it. When he moves, you move; when he stands still, you stand

near him; when he squats, you squat. Yes, and every one of these
underlings of his shall have a man told off to watch him.

COOK: I assure you, sir, you do not have to worry.

BALLIO: I don't have to worry, don't I, when I give you the run of
my house?

COOK: Wait till you see what my *bouillon* will do for you. Like
Medea cooked up old Pelias and with her possets and potions
made his old bones like young again – that is what I shall do for
you.

BALLIO: Eh? Are you a poisoner too?

COOK: Ah no – a life preserver.

BALLIO: Indeed? How much would you charge to teach me your
recipe for that?

COOK: For what?

BALLIO: For preserving myself from your pilfering.

COOK: Two drachmas, if you trust me; if not, nothing less than a
hundred. But tell me, sir, who is it you are giving this dinner for
today? Friends, or enemies?

BALLIO: Friends, of course; what do you think?

COOK: Why not ask your enemies instead? I shall be serving your
guests such a delicious feast, so sweetly and delicately seasoned, the
first taste of it will give them such a ravenous appetite that they will
be biting off their fingers.

BALLIO: Then for God's sake, before you serve a single guest, take
a taste of it yourself, and give your lads some, and bite off your
own thieving fingers.

COOK: I think perhaps you do not believe all I am saying.

BALLIO: Oh, shut your cackle; you make me tired. That is my house.
Get inside and cook the dinner ... *toute suite*.

COOK'S SLAVE [*perkily*]: You can sit down to table right now,
mister, and call the guests in; dinner's as good as cooked, and
spoiling.

[*The Cook's party enter the house.*]

BALLIO: That's a cheeky young brat too; a proper crafty cook's
dish-licker. Damn it, I don't know on which side to be on my guard
first – with thieves in my own house and bandits next door. I must
tell you, I just met my next door neighbour, Calidorus's father, in
town, and he warns me most emphatically to beware of his slave

Pseudolus and not trust him an inch. He's got some plot, it seems, to get that girl away from me this very day – has given his solemn promise to Simo that he'll remove Phoenicium from my house by some trick or other. I shall go and give notice to all my people that none of them is to trust Pseudolus for a single minute. [*He goes in.*]

*

[PSEUDOLUS *now returns from the town. As he comes in he is talking to* SIMIA *whom he presumes to be following but who is actually lagging behind and not yet visible.*]

PSEUDOLUS: If ever the everlasting gods wanted to help a man, they must certainly want to help me and Calidorus to live and the pimp to die, otherwise they wouldn't have produced such a brilliant brainy chap as you to be my assistant . . . But where has he got to? Am I off my nut, talking to myself like this? . . . By God, I believe he's made a monkey of me. It's a poor look-out if one rogue can't keep an eye on another better than that! By golly, if he has done a bunk that's the end of me, and of my chance of bringing off this job today . . . Ah, no, here he comes . . . and a walking whipping-post he is too. Look how he swaggers along . . .

[SIMIA *arrives, a slick and self-confident youth, dressed in a military rig.*]
Well, I've been looking for you everywhere; I was beginning to be afraid you'd been clever enough to hop it.

SIMIA: It wouldn't have been the first time, I can tell you.

PSEUDOLUS: Where have you been?

SIMIA: Where I wanted to go.

PSEUDOLUS: Well, I know that.

SIMIA: Then if you know, why ask?

PSEUDOLUS: What I want to do is to give you some advice.

SIMIA: Don't trouble; I could give you some.

PSEUDOLUS: You seem to be adopting a somewhat haughty tone with me, my lad.

SIMIA: I have to, don't I, if I'm supposed to be a bold army man?

PSEUDOLUS: All right, but I want to get on with this job we're doing.

SIMIA: Well, I am getting on with it, aren't I?

PSEUDOLUS: Quick march, then.

SIMIA: I'd rather take it slowly myself.

PSEUDOLUS: But now's our best chance; I want you to get in first, while the other chap's asleep.

SIMIA: Oh, take it easy, man, there's no hurry. By God, I hope that other chap turns up too, what's his name, the officer's servant. I'll make a better Harpax than he is, you see if I don't. You don't have to worry, chum. I'll have everything nicely worked out for you. I'll have some tricky patter ready for this foreign soldier man, that'll scare the life out of him and make him admit that he's not himself but I am!

PSEUDOLUS: How can you do that?

SIMIA: Oh for God's sake! You kill me with your everlasting questions.

PSEUDOLUS [appeasingly]: All right, all right, there's a good chap.

SIMIA: You needn't try to teach me my business; I'll show you I can give you points at faking and fiddling.

PSEUDOLUS: Then Jupiter be with you, for my sake.

SIMIA: For my sake too. How do I look? Is this kit all right?

PSEUDOLUS: It's perfect.

SIMIA: Good.

PSEUDOLUS: All I ask is that the good gods give you all you could wish for; I won't say all you deserve – that would be nothing, or less. [Aside] I'm sure I've never seen a more accomplished villain than this one.

SIMIA: Were you referring to me?

PSEUDOLUS: No, nothing. [Fussing him again] Oh what won't I give you, what won't I do for you, if you'll really take this job seriously and make a success of it!

SIMIA: Can't you stop jawing at me? It makes a chap forget all he remembers, to be constantly reminded not to forget what he knows he knows quite well. I've got it all; it's all in here; I've got my tactics all worked out.

PSEUDOLUS: That's a good boy.

SIMIA: We're neither of us good boys.

PSEUDOLUS: But you never know; you might make some slip.

SIMIA: Shut up, can't you!

PSEUDOLUS: On my solemn oath, as the gods love me –

SIMIA: As they won't, if they hear any more of your lies.

PSEUDOLUS: – I swear, Simia, you're such a crafty fellow I love you, I respect you, I look up to you.

SIMIA: You can't give me that pap; I know too well how to dish it out to others.

PSEUDOLUS: You'll see, my boy, you'll see what a wonderful treat I shall have in store for you – *if* you make a success of this.

SIMIA [*sick of this repetition*]: Oh ... no! ...

PSEUDOLUS: There'll be wonderful food, wonderful wine, perfumes, delicious dishes, and delicious drinks to go with them; and a wonderful girl all to yourself, to kiss and kiss –

SIMIA: You're too kind.

PSEUDOLUS: Oh, you'll thank me ever so much more than that – if you succeed.

SIMIA: And if I don't succeed, the executioner can treat me to a capital reception. Now come on, show me which is this pimp's front door.

PSEUDOLUS: The third from here.

SIMIA: Look out! Keep quiet; the den's mouth is opening.

PSEUDOLUS: The den must be feeling sick.

SIMIA: Eh?

PSEUDOLUS: It's going to throw him up whole.

[BALLIO *has appeared in his open door, coming out hesitantly, while keeping an eye on the operations within.*]

SIMIA: Is that him?

PSEUDOLUS: That's him.

SIMIA: He doesn't look up to much. D'ye see how he walks, sideways like a crab, instead of frontways?

BALLIO: Perhaps that man is not so dishonest after all, as cooks go. He hasn't pocketed anything so far, except a cup and a spoon.

PSEUDOLUS [*to Simia*]: Now's your chance, laddie.

SIMIA: This is it.

PSEUDOLUS: Watch your step ... carefully now ... I'll stay here in ambush.

[SIMIA *comes forward and assumes the air of a stranger finding his way.*]

SIMIA: I'm sure I've counted right. He told me to take the sixth turning after the city gate; and this one here is the sixth turning all right. But what did he say was the number of the house? Blest if I can remember.

BALLIO: Who's that chap in uniform? Where has he come from, I wonder, and who's he looking for? I don't seem to know him. Looks like a foreigner.

SIMIA: Ah, there's somebody who may be able to solve my problem for me.

BALLIO: He's coming my way. I wonder what part of the world he comes from.

SIMIA [*hailing Ballio from a distance*]: Hey! . . . You there! Billy-goat-beard . . . tell me something, will you?

BALLIO: Can't you give me good day first?

SIMIA: Sorry; I've nothing good to give away.

BALLIO: Then you don't get anything either.

PSEUDOLUS: That's a good start.

SIMIA: Do you know anyone who lives in this alley? . . . I'm talking to you.

BALLIO: I know one . . . myself.

SIMIA: You're lucky. As men go, there's not one in ten can say he knows himself.

PSEUDOLUS: I like that. He's using his wits like a philosopher.

SIMIA: The man I'm looking for is a lawless, shameless, faithless, godless sinner.

BALLIO [*aside*]: Must be me. I answer to all those epithets. If he'd only mention my name . . . What's his name, then?

SIMIA: Ballio, a pimp.

BALLIO: What did I tell you? . . . Right, lad, I'm the man you want.

SIMIA: You are Ballio?

BALLIO: No doubt about it.

SIMIA [*fingering Ballio's clothes*]: From your clothes, I'd take you for a burglar.

BALLIO: And if you met me in the dark, you'd keep your hands off my clothes.

SIMIA: Well . . . my master wishes me to convey to you his cordial greetings, and I have a letter for you which he has told me to give you.

BALLIO: What's your master's name?

    [SIMIA *is at a loss.*]

PSEUDOLUS: That's torn it. He's in a mess now; he doesn't know the name; we're sunk.

BALLIO: Come on, tell me who that letter comes from.

SIMIA: You'd better look at the seal first; then you can tell me the man's name; so that I'll know you're really Ballio.

BALLIO: Give it here, then.

SIMIA [*handing over the letter*]: There you are. Tell me if you know that seal.

BALLIO: Oho, yes, that's Polymachaeroplagides – living image of him. Yes, I know him. See, young fellow, Polymachaeroplagides is the name.

SIMIA: That's right – Polymachaeroplagides. Now you've come out with the name, I know I did right to give you the letter, don't I?

BALLIO: And what is he doing now?

SIMIA: Oh, just what you'd expect a brave and gallant soldier to be doing. But if you'd have a look at that letter right away – that's all you need to do – and take the money, then I can take the girl, and that's it. I've got to be at Sicyon today or lose my head to-morrow; my master is like that – very strict with his orders.

BALLIO: You needn't tell me; I know him.

SIMIA: Well, hurry up and read the letter.

BALLIO: That's what I am doing – if you'll shut your trap. 'From Captain Polymachaeroplagides to Pimp Ballio, this letter, sealed with the likeness heretofore agreed –'

SIMIA: That's the seal on the letter, see?

BALLIO: I can see it; and I recognize it. But does he usually start his letters without a salutation of any kind?

SIMIA: Oh yes, that's the army way, Ballio. When a soldier wants to salute his friends he does it with his hand; likewise with his hand he damns his enemies. But go on, and see what it says there.

BALLIO: Then shut up, and listen. 'The bearer of this letter is my orderly, Harpax' – that's you?

SIMIA: That's me – in nature as in name.

BALLIO: '– from whom please receive the money, and allow the woman to return with him. Such compliments as it is fitting to offer in writing to an esteemed friend I should have been happy to offer to your good self had I esteemed you a fit person to receive them.'

SIMIA: What about it, then?

BALLIO: When I get the money, you can have the woman.

SIMIA: What are we waiting for, then? [*He hands over the money.*]

BALLIO: Come inside.

SIMIA: Ta, I will. [*They go into the house.*]

PSEUDOLUS: He's a wily rascal, that Simia, if ever I saw one. He puts the wind up me; I'm scared he'll take it into his head to use his wiliness against me as he has against Ballio. With one victory behind him, he may turn his offensive against me, if he sees a chance to try anything on. I should be sorry if he did, by Jove, because I like the fellow. So now I've got three things to be in a panic about: one, lest my assistant should desert me and go over to the enemy; two, lest my master should come back from town too soon and catch the bandits with the catch in their hands; and three, lest the real Harpax turn up here before my Harpax can get away with the girl ... Oh damn it all, they're taking a long time to come out. My heart is flitting ... it's all packed up and ready to leave me ... if he hasn't got the girl ... [*At last the door opens.*] Victory! Victory – the vigilant warders are outwitted!

[SIMIA *comes out with* PHOENICIUM.]

SIMIA: Now don't cry, love. You don't understand what's going on; but you soon will, I promise you, when you see who you're going to have dinner with. I'm not taking you to that tooth-gnashing Macedonian – that's what you're crying about, isn't it? I'm taking you to somebody you very much want to belong to. You'll see; it won't be long now before you'll have your Calidorus in your arms.

PSEUDOLUS: What kept you hanging about in there so long? My heart was knocked out of shape with banging at my ribs.

SIMIA: Hold your tongue, scum. Is this a time for asking questions, while we're still in the enemy's lines? Rapid retreat is the order now.

PSEUDOLUS: You're right, by God – though you're a wrong 'un. Forward march! For victory and the cup of triumph! [*They march off.*]

[BALLIO *comes out of his house.*]

BALLIO: So that's that. It's a relief to see that fellow safe off and the woman with him. Ha, ha! Now let that damned rascal Pseudolus

come and try his tricks to take her away from me! Upon my living
soul, I'd rather swear a thousand oaths and damn myself with perjury than let him make a monkey of me. By God, I'll have the
laugh on him when I see him. But I dare say he's on the treadmill
by now, where he ought to be. I'd like to see Simo here too, and
let him share the joke with me.

[SIMO *arrives*.]

SIMO [*to himself*]: I wonder how my Ulysses is getting on, and
whether he has succeeded in stealing the goddess from the Bal-
lioneum.

BALLIO: Congratulations, Simo. Come, give me the hand of a
lucky man.

SIMO: Why, what –

BALLIO: It's all over.

SIMO: What's all over?

BALLIO: You have nothing more to fear.

SIMO: You mean – ? Has Pseudolus been to see you?

BALLIO: No.

SIMO: Then what are you so joyful about?

BALLIO: That money's quite safe – the two thousand drachmas that
Pseudolus wagered he'd get out of you – it's safe and sound.

SIMO: Well, I hope it is, by Jove.

BALLIO: You can touch me for two thousand if he gets possession of
that girl today and hands her over to your son as he has undertaken
to do. Go on, ask me to promise it; please do; I'm longing to
promise it to you, to convince you that you're in the clear. I'll give
you a woman too, if you like.

SIMO: All right, on those terms I don't see that it can do me any
harm to clinch your bargain. You'll give me two thousand?

BALLIO: Two thousand I will give you.

SIMO [*aside*]: I look like doing pretty well out of this . . . But have
you ever met the fellow?

BALLIO: I have indeed – two of them.

SIMO: What did he say to you? What kind of tales did he spin?
Do tell me what he said.

BALLIO: The usual stage gags – and called me all the dirty names
that are given to pimps in comedies – schoolboy stuff. He said I was
a scoundrel, a criminal, a liar –

SIMO: He wasn't far wrong either.

BALLIO: I know; that's why I took it all in good part. You can't do a man any harm by reviling him, if he doesn't care a damn and doesn't try to deny what you say.

SIMO: But you were saying I had nothing more to fear from him. How is that? Explain, if you please.

BALLIO: Because whatever he does he will *not* be able to remove the girl from my house – not now. You remember my telling you that she had been sold to a Macedonian soldier?

SIMO: Yes, I remember.

BALLIO: Well, his orderly has just brought me a sum of money and a sealed letter, the token –

SIMO: What was that?

BALLIO: – the token, the sign agreed between me and the Macedonian. And the orderly has taken the girl away with him, not ten minutes ago.

SIMO: Is this true – on your honour?

BALLIO: If I had such a thing!

SIMO: Are you quite sure that our friend hasn't played one of his tricks on you?

BALLIO: I couldn't be mistaken; the letter and the likeness on the seal were perfectly genuine. Anyway, the man is out of the city with her by now and on his way to Sicyon.

SIMO: Splendid! Good work! Now for Pseudolus! Is there any reason why I shouldn't give him his ticket for Milltown? ... Hullo, who's this coming along – that man in a military cloak?

BALLIO: Hanged if I know; but we may as well see where he's making for and what he wants ...

[HARPAX *arrives.*]

HARPAX: He's a worthless slave who doesn't think his master's orders worth his attention. For that matter no man is worth anything who can't attend to his duty without being prodded. The sort of servants who think they are free men the moment they escape from their masters' sight, and spend all they've got on gay living and low company – it's a long time before they'll be anything but slaves. They have no good qualities at all, except persistence in their evil ways. They're not the sort I care to keep company with, or speak to at all; I've always kept clear of them. When I've been

258

given an order, even if my master is far away, he's present as far
as I am concerned. I go in fear of him, when he's not with me, so
that I can face him fearlessly when he is. So now I shall be about my
business. I've been waiting at the tavern for that Syrus, as he told
me to after I gave him the letter; he said he'd send for me as soon
as his master came home. But he hasn't turned up, nor sent word,
so I've come back on my own to see what's going on; I'm not
having him pulling a fast one on me . . .

The best thing I can do now is to knock at the door and get hold
of somebody. All I want is to make this pimp take the money
from me and let me have the girl. [*But he still hovers about, perhaps
not quite sure of the house.*]

BALLIO [*to Simo*]: I say.

SIMO: What?

BALLIO: He's mine.

SIMO: How do you mean, yours?

BALLIO: He's in my net. He's after the girl, and he's got the money.
Oho, wait till I get my teeth into him!

SIMO: You're going to gobble him up, eh?

BALLIO: That's right; while he's fresh, while he's hot, ready, and
ripe for eating. Good men are a dead loss to me; it's the wicked
ones I thrive on. Honest men may serve their country; only the
villains are any use to me.

SIMO: And the gods will use you as your villainy deserves.

HARPAX: Well, here goes. I'll knock and see if Ballio is at home.

BALLIO [*still to Simo*]: Venus is kind to me, anyway, sending me all
these money-wasters, loss-lovers, good-timers, eaters, drinkers,
and fornicators. Very different from your sort – who won't let
yourself have a good time and grudge it to those who do.

HARPAX [*at the door*]: Hey, anyone there?

BALLIO: You see, he's walking right into my hands.

HARPAX: Where are you all?

BALLIO: Hullo, young fellow. What do you want? [*Aside*] I'll make
a packet out of this chap; I know it; the omens are favourable.

HARPAX: Can someone open this door?

BALLIO: Now then, corporal, what are you after?

HARPAX: I'm looking for the owner of this house, the pimp Ballio.

BALLIO: Then you needn't look for him long, whoever you are.

HARPAX: Why not?

BALLIO: Because you're looking *at* him, in front of your nose.

HARPAX [*thinking he means Simo*]: Oh, is it you, sir?

SIMO [*indignant*]: Don't point at me, soldier, unless you want this crooked stick on your back; point at him, he's the pimp.

BALLIO [*referring to Simo*]: He's only a gentleman. [*To Simo*] But gentleman as you are, I've known the times you've been dunned for debt on the market and haven't known where to lay your hand on a shilling unless this pimp would lend it to you.

HARPAX: May I trouble you to speak to me for a moment?

BALLIO: With pleasure. What can I do for you?

HARPAX: I have money for you here.

BALLIO: And here's my hand ready to receive it.

HARPAX: Take it; five hundred drachmas good silver, counted and correct. I am instructed by my master Polymachaeroplagides to pay you this sum which he owes you, and to ask you to let me take the girl Phoenicium away with me.

BALLIO: Your master sent you, did he?

HARPAX: That's right.

BALLIO: An officer – ?

HARPAX: He is.

BALLIO: Macedonian?

HARPAX: That's right.

BALLIO: Polymachaeroplagides? He sent you to me?

HARPAX: That's quite correct.

BALLIO: To give me this money?

HARPAX: Yes. That is, if you are Ballio the pimp.

BALLIO: And I'm to let you have the girl?

HARPAX: That was the message.

BALLIO: Phoenicium? Was that the name he said?

HARPAX: You've not forgotten it, I see.

BALLIO: Just a minute. I'll be back. [*Turning away towards Simo.*]

HARPAX: Don't be long, then; I'm in a hurry. The day's going, look.

BALLIO: Yes, I see it is. I just want to consult my friend. You stay there, I'll be back in a minute. [*To Simo*] Now what about it, eh? How are we doing? I've caught him in the act now, haven't I, this fellow with his money?

SIMO: How do you mean?

BALLIO: Well, don't you see what's happening?

SIMO: I can't say I do.

BALLIO: Why, this man has been put up by your Pseudolus to impersonate the messenger from the Macedonian.

SIMO: And have you got the money from him?

BALLIO: You can see I have, can't you?

SIMO: Well, don't forget to give me half the loot; we ought to share it.

BALLIO: Ought we, indeed? That's what *you* think!

HARPAX: How much longer are you going to keep me waiting?

BALLIO: I'll be with you in a moment. [*To Simo*] What shall we do with him?

SIMO: Let's have some fun with this substitute spy, and see how long it takes him to realize he's being guyed.

BALLIO: Come with me. [*To Harpax*] Now, my lad. So you really are my friend's servant, are you?

HARPAX: Certainly I am.

BALLIO: How much did he pay for you?

HARPAX [*with proud dignity*]: It cost him his own valour and victory on the field of battle. I was a high officer myself in the place I came from.

BALLIO: Where was that? A prison perhaps – which he stormed?

HARPAX: If you're going to use insulting language, you'll hear the same from me.

BALLIO: How long did it take you to come from Sicyon?

HARPAX: A day and a half.

BALLIO: Quick work!

SIMO: Well, you can see he's a strong walker; look at those calves; you can tell he's got the right legs – for a pair of heavy chains.

BALLIO [*surveying him insolently*]: I suppose you slept in a nice bed when you were a boy, eh?

HARPAX: I suppose so.

BALLIO: And had a nice time in bed ... as lads do ... eh?

SIMO: Sure to have done.

HARPAX: What's the matter with you two? Are you crazy?

BALLIO: And I suppose you spent nights out with your officer on nightwatch, like good pals, his sword in your scabbard?

HARPAX: God damn you to hell.

BALLIO: Where you're going, all in good time.

HARPAX: Just send that girl out to me, please; or let me have the money back.

BALLIO [*catching the soldier's cloak as he turns*]: Wait a minute.

HARPAX: What for?

BALLIO: How much did it cost you to hire this cloak?

HARPAX: What do you mean?

SIMO: And that sword; how much is that worth?

HARPAX: These people need a dose of hellebore –

BALLIO [*grabbing at Harpax's hat*]: Hey! –

HARPAX: Get off!

BALLIO: What did its owner charge you for the loan of that hat?

HARPAX: Owner? What are you dreaming about? Everything I'm wearing is my own, bought and paid for out of my own purse.

BALLIO: The one you keep nearest your own belly, no doubt.

HARPAX [*aside*]: These old fools are well oiled; they need a good old rubbing down too.

BALLIO: No, but seriously, tell me; I want to know; what's in this for you? How much – or how little – did Pseudolus get you for?

HARPAX: Pseudolus? Who's he?

BALLIO: Your instructor – the one who put you up to this clever trick for getting the woman out of my house.

HARPAX: I don't know what Pseudolus you're talking about, or what clever trick. I've never met any such person.

BALLIO: Then you can take yourself off. There are no perquisites for impersonators here. Just tell your friend Pseudolus that what he's after has already gone, with another man, who was here before you, a man named Harpax.

HARPAX: Harpax! But I am Harpax!

BALLIO: So you say. [*To Simo*] He's a rogue, if ever I saw one.

HARPAX: Haven't I just given you the money? And a little while ago, when I first arrived, I gave one of your slaves the token, the sealed letter, here in front of this house.

BALLIO: You gave the letter to one of my slaves? Which slave?

HARPAX: His name was Syrus.

BALLIO [*shaken, but trying to stick to his own belief*]: Oh, no, that won't wash. The impostor is overplaying his part, and being a bit too clever. But by God, the impudence of that Pseudolus! The scoundrel had it all worked out – to give this chap exactly the sum the officer owed me, and send him to fetch the woman away!

HARPAX: I assure you my name is Harpax, and I am the servant of a Macedonian officer. I am not impersonating anyone or attempting to deceive anyone. As for that Pseudolus, I don't know any such person nor have I ever heard of him.

SIMO: At any rate, my dear pimp, it looks as if, short of a miracle, you are not going to see the woman again.

BALLIO: My God, that's what I'm beginning to be afraid of, the more I hear of this man's story. Syrus ... it gave me a nasty turn when he mentioned that name ... he gave the letter to Syrus, did he? ... I'll bet my boots that was Pseudolus. Hey you, what did he look like, this fellow you gave the letter to?

HARPAX: Ginger hair, fat belly, thick legs, dark skin, big head, sharp eyes, red face, and very large feet.

BALLIO: Large feet – that settles it! I'm a dead man! It's Pseudolus himself. I'm done for, Simo; I'm dying.

HARPAX: Not if I know it, you aren't; not before you give me back the whole two thousand drachmas.

SIMO: And another two thousand to me.

BALLIO: You're not going to dun me for the bet I made in fun?

SIMO: Villains deserve to lose both their bets and their booty.

BALLIO: At least you might let me have Pseudolus.

SIMO: Let you have Pseudolus? Why blame him? Didn't I tell you over and over again to beware of him?

BALLIO: He's ruined me.

SIMO: But only robbed me of a mere two thousand drachmas!

BALLIO: Well what am I going to do now?

HARPAX: You can give me that money back, then go and hang yourself.

BALLIO: To hell with you! ... All right, come along with me to the bank and I'll pay up.

HARPAX: I will.

SIMO: What about me?

BALLIO: I'll settle my foreign debts today; home business tomorrow.

Pseudolus got me sentenced to death today, when he put up that impostor to steal the woman from me. Come on, you. [*To the audience*] And don't expect to see me coming home by this street any more; in future I shall use the back way.

HARPAX: You could be in town by now, if you were as good a walker as you are a talker.

BALLIO: My birthday! From now on I shall call it my death-day. [*He and* HARPAX *depart.*]

SIMO: I got the better of him all right. And my man has got the better of his opponent too. Now what I'm going to do is to prepare a reception for Pseudolus – oh, no, not the kind of reception you have seen in many another comedy, a reception with whips and irons – no, I'm going into my house, and I'm going to bring out that two thousand drachmas which I promised to give him if he won. I shall bring it out and put it into his hands before he asks for it. For, by gad, he's the cleverest, craftiest, wickedest creature alive! The trick that took Troy, and all the wiles of Ulysses, are nothing to what Pseudolus can do! ... Yes, that's what I'll do; I'll go to my house, I'll fetch the money, and ... spring a surprise on Pseudolus! [*He goes in.*]

*

[*The day must be drawing to its close when* PSEUDOLUS *staggers home, after celebrating his triumph with his confederates.*]

PSEUDOLUS: Ups-a-daisy! ... Now then, feet, what are you thinking of? ... Can you stand up, or not? ... Or do you want someone to come and pick me up off the ground? By God, there'll be trouble if you let me fall down ... are you going to keep going, or aren't you? I can see I shall have to be angry with you before long. That's the worst of drink ... it goes for your feet first, like a crafty wrestler. Oh, by Pollux, I'm properly pickled, aren't I? ... But it was a wonderful party ... a reception fit for the gods ... wonderful food ... and all so friendly and jolly ... well, I mean to say, there's no need to beat about the bush ... after all, there's nothing else in life worth living for, is there? ... there's no pleasure, no beauty to compare with ... it makes a man feel at his most god-like, I reckon ...

When a lover . . . loves his lassie . . .
  Lips and tongues . . . together pressed . . .
Two in one . . . each with the other . . .
  Heart to heart . . . and breast to breast.

One pale hand . . . a cup of kindness
  Lifting to her bonny boy . . .
No hard words . . . no scowl of sadness . . .
  No one else to mar their joy.

Feasts of flowers . . . fragrant incense . . .
  Joy and beauty unconfined . . .
Fill the cup . . . and what comes after . . .
  What comes after . . .
                              never mind!

Oh yes, we had it good today, me and my young master . . . to
celebrate my glorious victory and the rout of my enemies. They're
still at it . . . lying there drinking . . . and loving, and . . . a girl
each . . . and one for me too . . . everybody enjoying themselves.
As soon as I could stand up, they asked me to dance! So I obliged
with a few capers . . . like this . . . pretty good, eh? . . . quite the
professional. Of course I've had lessons, Greek style and all that.
Anyway I put on a pretty tunic and in I came . . . like this. It was
a scream. Everybody applauded and shouted 'encore' to call me
back. So I started again . . . a bit different this time . . . like this.
All the time I was making up to my girl, hoping she'd let me . . .
and suddenly, doing one of my pirouettes, down I fell . . .
curtain! And made a mess of my nice tunic in scrambling to
my feet. They liked that best of all, seeing me fall down.
However, someone passed me a cup . . . and I drank it off;
then changed my dirty tunic for a clean one; and here I am,
for a breath of fresh air. Now, from young master to old master,
I'm on my way to remind the old 'un of our bargain. [*He
knocks at Simo's door.*] Hey there! Open up! Open up! Tell
Simo I'm here.

  [SIMO *comes out, carrying a large bag of money, which he is concealing, as far as possible, behind his back.*]

SIMO: That sounds like a notable villain shouting for me. Hullo! What's all this, then? What have we here?

PSEUDOLUS: Your humble servant Pseudolus ... crowned with flowers ... drowned with drink.

SIMO: Well, that's a nice way to behave, I must say. [*Aside*] Look at him ... not in the least ashamed in my presence, is he? I don't know whether to speak to him severely or kindly. I can't pitch into him now, with what I have here for him, unless I want to lose him altogether.

PSEUDOLUS: Greetings from a scoundrel ... to a gentleman –

SIMO: Bless you, Pseudolus –

PSEUDOLUS: Hup!

SIMO: Damn you, Pseudolus! Get away from me.

PSEUDOLUS: Who are you pushing?

SIMO: How dare you belch in my face, you drunken ruffian!

PSEUDOLUS: Put your arms around me, darling ... hold me gently lest I fall ... don't you see I'm soaked and sozzled? ...

SIMO: How dare you, Pseudolus, how dare you go wandering about like this in the daytime, dead drunk and with flowers on your head? What is the meaning of this?

PSEUDOLUS: It means ... I like it.

SIMO: You like it, do you? Stop breathing in my face.

PSEUDOLUS: I have a very sweet breath. Don't let it worry you, Simo.

SIMO: Rascal – you're capable, I've no doubt, of accounting for all the vintage of the Massic vineyards, four times over, in under an hour.

PSEUDOLUS: Better say a winter hour – a short one.

SIMO: You may well be right. Well, where have you come from? From what port is this well-laden vessel sailing?

PSEUDOLUS [*now more coherent*]: Your son and I have been carousing. Oh yes, Simo, we did it all right! We put it across old Ballio. I've kept my word, done all I promised.

SIMO: You're a rascal, Pseudolus.

PSEUDOLUS: Blame the wench, then. She's free now, and sitting by your son's side.

SIMO: I know all about it, and how you did it.

PSEUDOLUS: Well then? Aren't you going to give me some money?

SIMO: It is your right, I must admit. Take it, then.

PSEUDOLUS: So you're giving it me after all; and you declared you would never give it me. Come on, then; put it on my shoulder; and follow me where I'm going. [*He means to humiliate Simo by parading the booty, and his victim, through the streets.*]

SIMO: I am to put it on your shoulder?

PSEUDOLUS: Yes, please. I know you will.

SIMO: The rascal! What shall I do with him? Is he not only to have the money but make me a laughing-stock as well?

PSEUDOLUS: *Vae victis!*

SIMO: Give me your shoulder then.

PSEUDOLUS: Here it is.

SIMO [*still reluctant to hand over the money-bag*]: No, please! Oh, to think that it should come to this – me going down on my knees to you for mercy. Oh, whatever shall I do? [*Sobbing.*]

PSEUDOLUS: Stop that.

SIMO: But think how I suffer.

PSEUDOLUS: Think how I should be suffering if you weren't.

SIMO: Can you do it, my dear Pseudolus? Can you take all this money from your own master?

PSEUDOLUS: With the greatest of pleasure and satisfaction.

SIMO: Please, I beg you, couldn't you find it in your heart to let me off a little bit of this debt?

PSEUDOLUS: Now you're not calling me a greedy man, are you? You won't get a penny out of me that way. How much pity would you have had for my back, if I hadn't done this for you today?

SIMO: All right. But I'll get even with you, as sure as I live.

PSEUDOLUS: Threaten what you please; I can take it.

SIMO: Then take it! [*He puts the bag on Pseudolus's back and turns away.*]

PSEUDOLUS: Hey, come back!

SIMO: Why should I come back?

PSEUDOLUS: Just come back and you'll see. Come on, there's no catch in it.

SIMO [*coming back*]: Well?

PSEUDOLUS: You're coming with me ... to where the drink is flowing.

SIMO: I come drinking with you?

PSEUDOLUS: Orders is orders. Do as I tell you ... and maybe I'll give you half ... or maybe more ... of this.

SIMO: Lead on; take me where you will.

PSEUDOLUS: How now, Simo? Are you still angry with me, or with your son, for all this business?

SIMO: Indeed I am not.

PSEUDOLUS: Let's go, then. After you.

SIMO [*pausing*]: Shall we ... invite them all? [*Referring to the spectators.*]

PSEUDOLUS: My God, no! They never invite me anywhere; I'm not inviting them. But [*To the audience*] ... if you will please to show your kind appreciation of our company and our play ... we will invite you here again ... tomorrow.

EXEUNT

MORE ABOUT PENGUINS

Penguinews, which appears every month, contains details of all the new books issued by Penguins as they are published. From time to time it is supplemented by *Penguins in Print*, which is a complete list of all books published by Penguins which are in print. (There are well over three thousand of these.)

A specimen copy of *Penguinews* will be sent to you free on request, and you can become a subscriber for the price of the postage. For a year's issues (including the complete lists) please send 30p if you live in the United Kingdom, or 60p if you live elsewhere. Just write to Dept EP, Penguin Books Ltd, Harmondsworth, Middlesex, enclosing a cheque or postal order, and your name will be added to the mailing list.

Some other books published by Penguins are described on the following pages.

Note: *Penguinews* and *Penguins in Print* are not available in the U.S.A. or Canada.

Another collection of plays by Plautus

THE ROPE AND OTHER PLAYS

The plays of Plautus (*c.* 254–184 B.C.) are the earliest complete works of Latin literature we possess. Plautus adapted for the amusement of Roman audiences the Greek New Comedy of the fourth century. His wit is clever and satirical and his entertaining portrayal of slaves firmly set the style for the 'low' characters of Elizabethan comedy, of Molière, and many others. In this new translation E. F. Watling presents, in a form suitable for the modern stage, *The Ghost* (*Mostellaria*), *The Rope* (*Rudens*), possibly the best of the plays, *A Three-Dollar Day* (*Trinummus*), and *Amphitryo*, a cheerful story involving the gods.

THE PENGUIN CLASSICS

The Most Recent Volumes